Workers'
Expressions

SUNY Series in the Anthropology of Work
June C. Nash, Editor

Workers' Expressions

Beyond Accommodation and Resistance

John Calagione, Doris Francis, and Daniel Nugent
Editors

STATE UNIVERSITY OF NEW YORK PRESS

Portions of "Eating Out of One Big Pot: Silk Workers in Contemporary China,"
by Lisa Rofel, were previously published in "Hegemony and Productivity:
Workers in Post-Mao China," in *Marxism and the Chinese Experience: Issues
in Contemporary Socialism*, edited by Aris Dirlik and Maurice Meisner and are
reprinted here by permission of M. E. Sharpe, Inc., Armonk, New York, 10504.

Published by
State University of New York Press, Albany

©1992 State University of New York Press, Albany

For information, address State University of New York
Press, State University Plaza, Albany, N.Y., 12246

Production by E. Moore
Marketing by Theresa A. Swierzowski

Library of Congress Cataloging-in-Publication Data

Workers' expressions : beyond accommodation and resistance / John
    Calagione, Doris Francis, and Daniel Nugent, editors.
        p.   cm.—(SUNY series in the anthropology of work)
    Includes bibliographical references and index.
    ISBN 0-7914-0835-3.—ISBN 0-7914-0836-1 (pbk.)
    1. Work—Social aspects. 2. Leisure—Social aspects. 3. Popular
culture. 4. Economic anthropology. I. Calagione, John.
II. Francis, Doris. III. Nugent, Daniel. IV. Series.
HD4904.6.W67 1992
306.3'6—dc20   90–26178
                                                                CIP

10 9 8 7 6 5 4 3 2 1

Contents

Acknowledgments

We would like to thank Professor June Nash for the idea of producing a volume from these papers and for her continuing encouragement and support. We also want to thank Rosalie Robertson, our editor at SUNY Press, Maria Vesperi, and the Society for Humanistic Anthropology. Calagione and Nugent also acknowledge the support they received from Scott Stirton, Rana Segal, and Mr. Alan Waters in Chicago, as well as friends in New York City and Austin, Texas, while Francis extends her particular thanks to the Municipal Employees Union, Local 237.

JOHN CALAGIONE
DANIEL NUGENT

1

Workers' Expressions: Beyond Accommodation and Resistance on the Margins of Capitalism

The studies in this volume analyze the cultural, political, social, and day-to-day expressions of workers throughout the world in a range of contexts not commonly observed in the anthropology of work. The authors examine actions such as ritual, leisure, and popular entertainment, as well as relationships organized by age, ethnic, and gender distinctions which are present in sites of production, but often unrecognized by scholars working with a narrow notion of "economic" activity. Our aim is not to extend a polarity between culturalist and productionist positions, but we do wish to deepen appreciation for the range of cultural discourses that are engaged in working, to show that the labor process is itself a cultural process.[1]

One of our central concerns *is* to analyze and understand the organization and outcomes of the labor process and how they effect the way people are or are not mobilized to work. "The labor process" constitutes a social fact—frequently overlooked by many social scientists—of major importance in every cultural and historical situation. Our position is that this process cannot be understood without paying attention to the aesthetic and narrative forms that are embedded in and shape both quotidian activities and production. These studies open up a new space for an anthropology of work, a space beyond rigid dichotomies such as the contrast between work and leisure or between accommodation and resistance. The latter distinction, in particular, has oriented much recent research in political economic and cultural studies of subaltern groups and classes (see, e.g., Abu-Lughod 1990; Guha 1982a; Scott 1985).

Rather than provide synopses of the chapters which follow, our introduction simply discusses some of the issues that emerge from critically reflecting on what the "anthropology of work" might be expected to accomplish. While other chapters are mentioned in passing where relevant, this chapter is concerned above all with two issues. First, we discuss some of the absences in the literature on the anthropology of work, and new directions for research. Second we suggest a rethinking—not all that radically new—of the way work and labor are conceived by anthropologists that more closely follows the way workers themselves think about it. Throughout, we argue for looking at the rich material on leisure, popular entertainments, and ostensibly nonwork activities—certainly not connected to a restricted notion of "economic" action—to gain insight into the labor process.

WORK AND SOCIAL THEORY

Volumes edited recently by R. E. Pahl and H. Applebaum, among others, provide excellent introductions to the diversity of approaches to the study of work. We assume that readers of the present volume are familiar with this diversity, and understand how the proposition that "employment is simply one *form* of work" (Pahl 1988:11, emphasis added) allows for an examination of related practices and discourses. Having said that, it is surprising that researchers show remarkably little agreement on what the study of work and workers should involve beyond the study of employment. The routinely invoked but very problematic distinction between "tradition" and "modernity" has figured in much of this literature. The idea that a "coherent set of work values valid for the entire society" is appropriate for "nonmarket" societies (i.e., an holistic approach is possible) but not tenable in industrializing societies owing to the alleged "complexity" of the latter (Applebaum 1984:1) is the organizing feature of some of this research. "Work literature" thus becomes an analysis of occupational cultures or "work cultures" (see Applebaum 1984) and avoids addressing how the latter are embedded in specific cultural and historical formations. While this approach provides an appreciation of the diversity of working situations, it makes comparison difficult or impossible. We feel that this conundrum diminishes the possibility of providing a critical assessment of historical processes of differentiation between workers throughout the world.

The literature on work and the labor process is voluminous and in many ways co-extensive with modern social inquiry. In the decades immediately after World War II, the massive economic subjugation of what began to be called "the developing world" was realigned by new ideologies of development and change. During that period, a burgeoning literature on "modernization" and "development" shaped research into a grid which analyzed social relations, including those involved in work, in the light of instrumental rationality.[2] From the 1960s onward, a number of critical theories—dependency, underdevelopment, and world-systems— emerged. Among other things, these theories emphasized structural factors and the systemic features linking, integrating, and disintegrating work and labor in the First and Third Worlds, in the (capitalist) core and on its periphery.

The differences between a "development" approach and an "underdevelopment" approach are profound with respect to their theoretical emphases and fundamental with respect to the empirical research oriented by each. Nevertheless, they are not totally devoid of similarities. One characteristic they share is that both, to different degrees, make it difficult to carry out detailed studies of the ways working people labor in connection with everyday routine, public performance, religious representation, and gender and ethnic distinctions. Both the emphasis on instrumental rationality, and the reliance on structural explanations pose certain limitations. The tendency to naturalize the consolidation and extension in time and space either of "modernity" or of "the world capitalist system" devalues the position of cultural practices in the study of working and the labor process. Development theory and underdevelopment theory alike obscure from view the very practices according to which people work through situations and under conditions inimical to their perpetuation both as individuals and as members of social classes. Furthermore, they cannot provide adequate models for understanding people whose workplace is not entirely subsumed by the metaphor of the shop floor.

Anthropologists and other social scientists long relied upon unexamined and unstated ideas about the meaning of work to anchor their classifications of identity and class. In recent years, some researchers have interrogated these classifications. One collection edited by Sandra Wallman, *The Social Anthropology of Work* (1979), for example was an innovative attempt to map analytic intersections of cultural meanings associated with the category of work. In studies focusing on nonwestern societies, different authors considered the consequences of work in relation to culturally constructed categories of time, value, person, and technology. While the range of the essays was broad, offering different theoretical orientations and examining different cultural contexts, they mostly explored what Wallman identified as "two fundamental human issues":

> While preoccupations of work are directly concerned with the work of making a living, they are indirectly but equally concerned with the work of personal and social identity (Wallman 1979:vi).[3]

The present collection extends the explorations of Wallman et al. through the presentation of evidence about how categories of work and identity are reciprocally constituted. In exploring how the apprehension of personal and historical consciousness shapes the contexts of work, and how work itself shapes consciousness, we hope to challenge and transform one of the most tendentious and enduring analytic distinctions of modern social inquiry: that between action and knowledge.

Challenging that distinction poses a number of questions: How does one conceive of or separate practical activity and consciousness? More specifically, what are the implications of rethinking that exaggerated distinction for our understanding of how cultural discourses orient terms of domination, and of resistance to domination? Do the accounts of the labor process routinely produced by researchers adequately examine the cultural representation of work for members of particular societies? In short, what are the boundaries of or separations between work and nonwork and how do these distinctions help create historical representations and self-representations of subjects?

REPRESENTATIONS OF WORK

The papers in this collection address the lacunae in the textual representation of work by analyzing the interventions of popular culture and performances through which the labor process is redefined. They demonstrate how elements of popular culture enter into the labor process. Representations of working experiences generated by workers themselves may articulate forms of resistance—and sometimes accommodation—to domination and exploitation. The point of reference of those representations is not, however, invariably restricted to the labor process per se; it includes social relations more generally and, of particular importance, performance dimensions of work and of leisure. One proposition orienting all of these studies is that since separations between work and leisure and between instrumental and noninstrumental definitions of time are not coeval with subjectively experienced reality, they should not be maintained in analyses of social life.

The meaning of work has long been regarded as centrally important for the analysis of class formation. Yet providing only histories of inequalities and describing the formation of class ideologies in capitalist development runs the risk of reducing labor to merely an effect of a system of dominant economic forces. Once labor is imagined as thoroughly dominated by economic forces, analysts have trouble connecting it to everyday life. If it is so cut off, we must then ask: How can labor produce everyday life? How are the two related? As Bruce Brown (1972) reminded us, Freud and Marx, the two great theorizers of sublimated and masked determination, were both questioning precisely the connection between productive activity and everyday life.

In our view the domains of work, leisure, and popular culture, of productive activity and everyday life, will always overlap, which is to say that there is no fixity to the character of the relations between them. Senses of self, of performance, and of mastery are not equivalent to the practices explicitly labeled and understood as economic pursuits. The production of historical self-consciousness cannot be reduced to the production of economic value alone because even economic activity itself is continuously redefined, reordered, and rearticulated in cultural and situational terms.[4]

In positivist discourses, on the other hand, labor is singled out as the nexus of economy and class and privileged as the *dominant* representation of human agency; the variety of activities, practices and factors that comprise social (re)production remain unexplored and underexamined (by way of contrast, see Turner 1986). Our perspective is shaped by the idea, shared with many other critical thinkers, that social representations are not produced as a single signifier-signified relation (see, e.g., Timpanaro 1975:135–219; Palmer 1990 xi–47 for discussions of this issue). Precisely because the labor process signifies a range of meanings and relations between meanings, the examples of social representation and the labor process presented in the present volume are considerably more complex than positivist versions.

A recent discussion of multiple cultural significations of work /labor is found in J. and J. L. Comaroff's study of Tshidi peasant proletarians in South Africa. For the Tshidi " . . . the making of the social world past and present . . . " (Comaroff and Comaroff 1987:193) is encoded in their oppositional distinction between their own terms for "work" and Afrikaans' terms for (wage) labor:

> . . . in the Tshidi imagination work contrasts with labor as does self construction with self destruction; as time logged 'out there' with the creative process of production and reproduction 'at home' (*mo gae*); as the enduring value of cattle with the capricious flow of money (Comaroff and Comaroff 1987:192).

A more dated, but equally apposite, example of a popular cultural construction of economic activity and value, which at the same time demonstrates the mutual imbrication of work and construction of self, is found in Placido Chavez's introduction to his account of a peasant revolt in northern Mexico at the end of the nineteenth century:

> My father and my uncles were decidedly of the humble class, they never disposed of capital; their only capital, the greatest and most precious, was their work, their self-esteem and their honor, an honor without flaw or stigma, natural faculties which they conserved to the final days of their lives (Chavez 1964:6).[5]

These examples from the Tshidi of Botswana and the peasants of Chihuahua provide arguments for using a noneconomistic understanding of the labor process. Further, they point to a variety of activities that can be classified as socially (re)productive, in light of which both work and labor may have multiple significations. Intersections of work and everyday life are not simply confined to the rankings of occupations or careers in society. Understanding the meanings of work entails the position that it is at all points creative and—not merely productive—human activity.

Several points emerge from this discussion. Work means something different to those who do it and to those who analyze it. In studying work and workers we sometimes refer now to work, now to "labor," to signify creative activity on the one hand and economically productive activity on the other. It is convenient, for example, to consider productive activity as laboring, the exercise of labor power. But even when labor power is systematically alienated, productive activity is culturally constituted and not productive *only* of economic value.

The distinction between the terms work and labor is not without problems, but it is useful for organizing a general analysis of the multiple forms of power present both within and outside of the workplace. The distinction marks an arena of contestation. Workers and nonworkers fight over how the production process will be organized. Workers try to turn labor into work, while capitalists struggle to transform work into labor. This arena of contest provides the subject matter for this book.

THE LABOR PROCESS

The alternation of meaning attached to production as purposive economic activity (labor) and as a kind of social relationship (work) is not an *absolute* separation. Raymond Williams points out that there is an "interesting relation" between the terms:

> *Labour* and *toil* are still harder words than work, but manual workers were generalized as *labourers* from c13, and the supply of such work was generalized as *labour*. Work was then still available for a more general sense of activity (Williams 1983:335).

Analyzing cultural significations of work and labor as continuous with subjectivity and socially constituted identity *embeds* them within modalities of power and social abstraction.

Pursuing a direction of study first elaborated in Marx's *Paris Manuscripts* (1964 [1844]) and the *Grundrisse* (1973 [1857–8]) Arendt (1958), for example, examines the distinction between work and labor, present in all European languages, and how that distinction figures in the Western philosophical tradition. In her view, labor is performed in service to and at the command of others, while work leaves a product behind which outlasts its own activity and forms a durable addition to the human artifice (Arendt 1958:138). This valuation was at the heart of the emergence of the justifying logic of scientific-technical thought.

According to Arendt, contemporary analytic categories for identifying and understanding the labor process have been shaped by a logic that assumes the automated worlds of production and the freedom from necessity to labor, as a teleology of the good in human life. Arendt notes that such a project depends upon the continuous consumption of products as a substitute for the "artifice" of work. It enjoins the philosophical equation of happiness with " . . . perfect balance of life process of exhaustion and regeneration . . . " (Arendt 1958:134). Her more general epistemological point is that as social theorists, we have devalued our approach to the labor process because we fail to understand life and labor cycles as fundamentally creative and constitutive. We might add that this kind of ideologically motivated longing for "perfect balance," justified by the functionalism of 1960s sociology and continued by "organizational" theory, is precisely what underlies the carving up of consciousness and social reality into realms of "work and leisure." The labor process is about more than just labor, however, and as anthropologists we should try to open a space for problems of value and resistance to the dominant ideologies of capitalism to be reapprehended.[6]

In the field of labor studies, the problem of value and resistance has been most frequently engaged in traditions of Marxist scholarship. Since the publication of Braverman's *Labor and Monopoly Capital* in 1974, an entire school studying the labor process has arisen (e.g., Burawoy 1985; Edwards 1979; Cohen 1987; Sirianni 1981; Zimbalist 1979). Braverman's book was subtitled "The Degradation of Work in the Twentieth Century" and constituted nothing less than a theory of how managerial ideologies (particularly those of Taylor) fashioned an environment in which craft mastery and skill were systematically devalued. While Braverman's argument involved more than this, its implications and consequences were far reaching. The book spurred discussion of the importance, both locally and globally, of workplace skill and control in the continued expansion of capitalism. It also detailed the rise of managerial ideology and the way managerial domination figured in the formation of resistance to rationalized ideologies of productive and industrial intensification.

Sheila Cohen's critical discussion of the impact of Braverman's work finds that researchers have been seduced by his critique of deskilling and control of the labor process while ignoring the central point of his argument. She argues that Braverman's analysis really hinges on recovering Marx's "central dynamic of the relations of production, that is, exploitation and the generation of surplus value" (Cohen 1987:39). With such a point in mind, it is easy to see how focusing solely upon "control" diverts analysis from the complex and contradictory conditions of resistance and transformation that surround any working situation.[7]

Much of Braverman's argument was presaged by Gramsci's writing on "Americanism and Fordism" in his prison notebooks (see Gramsci, *Selections from the Prison Notebooks* 1971:279–318). Gramsci was concerned about the implications of rationalized work disciplines for working class ("subaltern") subjects and members of the new classes of the dominant order (Gramsci: ibid.). Gramsci's interest was piqued by the convergence of managerial ideologies with the historical sense of purpose and individual human agency which he saw as a necessary component of an emergent hegemonic class. The growth and extension of such ideologies, particularly in the United States, was identified as a new ground for production of unequal social relations, in which even the physical, sexual, and imaginative being of those who worked was continually subject to the ordering of information about production and interwoven with the fabric of social experience (Gramsci 1971:300–305).

Gramsci's expansive notion of discipline, instead of control, provides insights into the ordering of subjectivity not only in connection with the production process but also within everyday life. This requires a recognition of the power dimension involved in just "getting by." As Lila Abu-Lughod writes:

> work on resistance influenced by Bourdieu and Gramsci recognizes and theorizes the importance of ideological practice in power and resistance and works to undermine distinctions between symbolic and instrumental, behavioral and ideological, and cultural, social and political processes (Abu-Lughod 1990:41).

A key concern of this volume, in other words, is understanding the establishment of forms of hegemony under capitalism, and analyzing how those forms are challenged and contested (if not always successfully). In engaging the latter set of issues, researchers need to look beyond the shop floor, and beyond the misidentification of the "informal sector" as only a product of, rather than a response to, the expansion of capitalism. Instead we must reengage the cultural forms through which labor, nonwork (and not just the heroic refusal to work), pleasure, desire, and performance are organized by working people. Much historical and ethnographic research on work has been conducted without these concerns in mind. The result has been the generation of a fundamentally impoverished understanding of the labor process, of work and nonwork, of subjects' apprehension of social possibilities, of resistance to domination, and of when and why resistance does or does not occur.

A focus upon cultural meanings of work, pleasure, gender, and representation can enrich the Marxist debate about what constitutes ("objective") material conditions. In such a light the analysis of modes of production and the labor process assumes a radically different character. Eric Wolf made an important intervention in this debate in his study of the self-reproduction of societies in nonwestern regional and historical perspectives (*Europe and the People Without History* 1982). That book succeeds at presenting culturally framed analyses of the labor process while providing an account of the importance of noncapitalist modes of production in the ongoing formation of capitalism on a world scale. Yet as Asad has noted, the global perspective entailed in Wolf's project necessarily calls for more studies attuned to modalities of inequality and power (Asad 1987:606).

The papers included in this volume analyze some manifestations of the social relations of power and work, of production and reproduction, of action and meaning. We think that they fall under the purview of " . . . the story of transformations that have reshaped those conditions which are not of people's choosing but within which they must make their history" (Asad 1987:607; cf. Marx 1963 [1852]:15). For some time research carried out in the anthropology of work has provided rich material for studying precisely the modalities of inequality and power which are manifest equally at the center and on the margins of capitalism (see Nash and Fernandez-Kelley 1983). But this positive outcome of the research has been neglected or overlooked since much of the "anthropology of work" has uncritically constructed workers as "objects" for study akin to what an earlier anthropology did to "primitives." As what should be now familiar modalities of exploitation and development penetrate into more societies, a critical anthropology of work needs to be sensitive to ideological mystifications of the meanings of work and productivity (see Ong 1987).

In another context, commenting on the valorization of heterogeneity in our increasingly routinized metropolis, Jean Franco described how:

> The Third World becomes the place of the unconscious, the rich source of fantasy and legend recycled by the intelligentsia, for which heterogeneity is no longer a ghostly, dragging chain but material that can be loosened from any territorial context and juxtaposed in ways that provide a constant frisson of pleasure. The intelligentsia no longer speaks for the masses but productively transposes mythic material (Franco 1988:505).

Rather than transpose mythic (or mundane) material, the thrust of these essays is simply to look around the corner, to the margins of capitalism, where millions labor, and some still manage to work. By examining the creative determination and social complexity of work and labor, we achieve an understanding of the reciprocal narrative constitution of work and identity, and the way performances and audiences contribute to that process.

2

Working in Time:
Music and Power on the Job
in New York City

Throwing rockstone upon a dumper truck
Throwing rockstone upon a dumper truck
Men standing over I and I and we are not wild
Forcing jack hammers through the concrete wall
That's the only way a dread can make a bread
Satta dread satta you time soon come
            Black Uhuru from the album "Red"

In the hot summer of 1981, young Jamaican construction workers in New York City listened to this lyric by the group Black Uhuru, biding their time until their work was once more their own.[1] The title, "Rockstone," refers to the construction task for which these workers, recent immigrants, were in greatest demand: building demolition and debris removal. Demolition is, of course, the first step toward renovation, and anyone who lives in or visits a large urban center in the northeast United States can appreciate how great the demand for this labor has been during the past decade.

Our cities have been remade by huge "post-modern" sky-scrapers and developments surrounded by industrial areas reconfigured into luxury loft housing. I encountered the Jamaican workers in such an area of Manhattan, where newly transformed lofts recently inhabited by artists who had rented them from relocating manufacturers, were aggressively marketed to affluent artists and others anxious to appear like them. In a penetrating examination of this phenomenon in this section of Manhattan, Sharon Zukin chronicles how:

> the real significance of loft living lies on a deeper level than that of the market—indeed on the level of an underlying terrain that represents a space, a symbol and a site under contention by major social forces (Zukin 1989:174).

Zukin's project details the role and uses of artists in defining this terrain, and illustrates how urban planners, speculators and manufacturers use the legitimate needs of artists for urban space to forge an accumulation strategy which she calls the artistic mode of production. In turn, this mode of production sustains a logic of urban transformation and growth used by dominant classes in many contemporary cities. In this paper, I suggest this process of urban transformation is also constituted on an everyday basis by engaging multiple cultural discourses of working people in New York City.

As the means and end of production, renovated luxury lofts represent the polarizations of power between those concentrated in a center of global finance, communications, and art industries and those workers who are peripheralized to the margins of the city, the so-called "outer boroughs." Zukin points out that plans to concentrate workers in the outer boroughs (a term I have never heard used outside Manhattan) date back to the earliest part of this century (Zukin 1989:40), but conform to the ethnic and racial residential patterns of workers in the late nineteenth century as well (ibid.:5). Thus contemporary dialectics of New York City's center and periphery are interwoven with much older global mobilizations of migrant labor. The histories and contributions of those who are often thought "incidental" to the artistic mode of production are necessary for recovering the multiplicity of urban voices, meanings and spaces.

The very male-centered construction world of residential renovation is, as far as I know, an underexamined phenomenon of the reshaping, indeed the redefining, of the urban landscape. The renovation industry is a terrain of migrant exploitation in the United States that remains hidden behind the more publicized manipulation of agricultural workers. Recent immigration "amnesty" laws comprise part of a state labor policy that reaches also into the workplace situation of Caribbean migrants in northern cities. However, rather than engage directly with how this policy shapes the workplace, in this paper I am more interested in the workplace itself. Beginning an analysis of work by looking at policy objec- tives, risks reducing the workplace to that which policy aims to control. Instead, this paper discusses how Jamaican and other West Indian workers used recorded music to link subjective and collec- tive aspects of the experiences of labor migration with urban con- struction and renovation work.

PART I

The renovated or "gentrified" city is often seen as the perfect symbol which joins a new sensibility about form and space with the experiences of diversity and multiculturalism (Harvey 1989). But often the multicultural aspect of constructing the post-modern city is left behind once the packing district has become the gallery district. Instead, (and ironically, after renovation) the manufac- turing and warehouse neighborhoods that provided initial, point- of-entry employment for succeeding series of immigrant work- ers are permanently transformed. The profusion of languages and working traditions that formerly broke out on the street when shifts changed, is silenced.

The process of transforming sections or neighborhoods in cit- ies is a complex one. While many analysts are willing to provide a "reading" of new appearances and their cultural/economic import, few accounts pay attention to the hidden producers and builders of the transformed urban space—the people who actually lift, pour, hammer, and plaster. Instead, in a logic that has become numb- ingly familiar to city residents and readers of the Sunday paper, urban renovation is analyzed and proclaimed by the champi- ons and critics of "progress," design, real estate speculation and "development."[2]

From an ethnographic point of view, we have produced cri- tiques and analyses of development and "modernization" for many parts of the world once considered outside the metropolitan cen- ters of learning and industry. We have been sensitive to the de- struction and manipulation of distant others by planners and modernizers who carry out programs for purely "economic" rea- sons. Yet, we rarely turn these analyses upon our own cities to con- nect them with the presence of those laboring, preindustrialized "others" who have been compelled to migrate to "developed" met- ropolitan centers. Hence, at the risk of becoming one more critic of what *exactly* marks post-modern reality, I suggest that much of the emphasis on the polarizations of contemporary, multicultural cities in fact points to historical continuity with class determinations of systems of exploitation and (the extraction of surplus) value. In a particular metropolitan distortion of symbolic capital, the mere presence of exploited and marginally employed others has become necessary for the imagination of difference. This distinction is, in turn, critical for figuring the urban "self" (see Harvey 1989).

In this paper, I draw upon my participation and experience in the renovation of four large warehouses on the lower west side of Manhattan's riverfront. The entire renovation lasted from late 1979 until late 1982. This area is now mostly residential, although as recently as twenty years ago, there was a heterogeneous, multi-languaged work force that filled jobs in meat-packing, warehousing, printing, transportation (railway and shipping), marine supply, longshoring and other dockworking. The mostly male workforce incorporated recent migrants to the city, and offered cheap river-front accommodation and proximity to the large working class shopping districts of 14th Street and the Lower East Side. Today, only some remnants of a once huge meat-packing industry still survive.

During the late 1970s and early 1980s, while I lived and worked in this area, many recent immigrants from the Caribbean, Latin America and Eastern Europe who would formerly have found employment here as dockworkers, meatpackers, and so forth, instead joined in as members of construction crews that transformed both landscape and economy. This process of regentrifying and re-"class"ifying the area continues today. Now that the men have finished building new spaces, mostly immigrant women work in them as low paid members of a new international service economy. As domestics, child care workers, building maintenance and restaurant personnel, they cater to the needs of a predominantly white upper class that spurred this development in the first place.[3]

Essentially then, the recent immigrants who would once have walked the streets looking for employment on any basis (day, casual, or full-time labor), found that buildings marked on the outside as warehouses, printers, and packing plants, could provide employment only to those willing to engage in construction renovation—that is, the deconstruction of a permanent site of labor possibility—either by joining the local crew already in place, or bringing on a crew of others who were willing to work. In New York City, as in many other cities, residential construction is dominated by nonunionized crews. Typically, work is done by small general contractors and/or subcontractors who hire a few experienced workers who are willing to practice several trades (carpentry and masonry, plastering and painting, etc.). The balance of the crew generally consists of laborers under the direction of the tradesmen.

My information was gathered over the course of twenty months of participatory research during the years 1979–1982 with Jamaicans who are employed in the building construction trades in New York City. During this time, a Jamaican contractor employed me as a carpenter and building layout man. His crew was in turn employed by an architect, a real estate developer, and a number of private clients. The latter owned residential apartments and lofts; the work usually involved structural, but included all phases of, renovation from rough to finish. My own exposure to a variety of ongoing renovations provided an accurate picture of the tenuous and erratic employment patterns which many of these workers described to me and which appeared to them as a continuation of their working histories.

When the contractor was hired as foreman for a real estate developer, his entire crew was employed for a year at Riverwest, a project involving the joining together, conversion and total renovation of four former warehouse buildings into expensive co-op apartments. Riverwest greatly affected many of these workers; for most it was their longest period of sustained employment in the United States. As a layout man, I could trace the significance of the experience in a unique way because my duties were to interpret blueprints, and set final measurements while circulating among different teams of masons, tenders, laborers, and carpenters. My translating of blueprints into marks on the floors and walls where windows and doors and stairways were cut from the thick brick of the seven story warehouses was also an occasion for discussing how work in general should be organized and thought about.

The Jamaican workers were not the only recent immigrants employed by the developers. During the twelve months of extensive structural alteration of the buildings, immigrants from the Dominican Republic, Greece, Italy, Mexico, Poland, and various countries of Central and South America, were represented. During peak construction, the job attracted approximately one hundred workers of various trades, but most were general laborers. Some stayed only briefly, disgusted by the dangerous work and low wages. Most of the twenty-seven Jamaican and other English speaking West Indian workers felt that they were secure in this job, since the foreman guarded their positions and relied upon them for difficult and skilled tasks.

Many of us noticed that the developers wanted to create an intense rivalry between different workers. The progress of the building provided an arena for displaying the general situation of recent male migrants to the city, each called upon to show how his physical performance embodied the capabilities and essence of what management believed was his "group." The possibility of unemployment was constantly below the surface, yet I was always impressed by the ability of the Jamaican workers to evade domination by this essentializing ideology of competition. Particularly for migrants from the Caribbean, conventional, economic "push-pull" or "reserve army" (Ross and Trachte 1983) theories do not address the complexity of cultural links between African peoples in different parts of the new world. Prevailing paradigms for studying migration have privileged questions that obscure what "work" signifies in the context of a whole life (history) and mask the relation of work to knowledge, power, and recollection.[4] For Caribbean and Latin American workers the values extracted from steady employment in the cities of the United States reach beyond the neighborhood or workplace into status and position in "home" communities, (c.f. papers by Alonso and Nugent in this volume). The possibilities of return, and historically entwined continuities of dependence and transformation through the impact of remittances to home islands, pervade United States working experiences and color future histories that may have been put on hold, but were hardly abandoned. In this context, migratory workers are not well-served by arbitrary theoretical separations which subdivide life into work and leisure situations or pre and post immigrant work experience.

In asking about Jamaican definitions of work I found that informants in New York felt that there *were* real continuities between their prior experiences of "farm work" and "scuffling"[5]— even though specifying them was often a matter of describing the emotional terrain of being a young male worker within the informal economies of Kingston, Jamaica and Brooklyn. Jamaican music's images of hardship and camaraderie parallel workplace metaphors for migrant labor such as "breaking new field," "scuffling," "slavery," "going foreign" and "breaking rockstone." These expressions are more than a popular style or a series of repeated lyric structures. Black Uhuru's assurances (quoted in beginning of the paper) that we are "not wild" and that "your time soon come" are evidence of persistent attempts to resist being belittled (or "downpressed") in the process of work. They also indicate an awareness of the centality of work in the historical constitution of social identity for African Jamaicans, and the conviction that there are other outcomes (possibilities) in which they are the actors and controllers (Alleyne 1989).

My theoretical position for understanding migratory workers is that their historical experiences should not be reduced to a simple continuum or a set of discontinuities which stretches from the rural to urban, from peasant to metropolitan ethnic. This position runs contrary to populist expectations that the actions of workers from different countries within the United States can be comfortably summarized as the historical collision of ethnic identities or the surging forth of a more essential ("primordial") identity that buttresses workers against the totalizing rule and impersonal values of material production. This perspective is dominant in recent social histories of New York City (see Bender 1988). It is even employed as a general premise about working class cultural identity by Gutman (1977) following Geertz's definition of "primordial identity." Yet ethnic/migrant identities are themselves constituted by and subject to complex social relations of urban experiences and the historical processes of migration within the sending societies.

Recognizing this complexity compels a finer focus on the ways in which workers define and represent their situations as part of their ongoing personal histories that are part of, but not confined to, working in New York City. They create the culture of the city in many ways. Indeed my co-workers often pointed out that New York is the largest Caribbean city in the world. The multiple entertainment, clothing, speaking, and cultural styles of Spanish, English, and French speaking immigrants are constantly recast with a New York flavor, woven into the fabric of everyday life and consumed as elements of authentic New York experience by natives and visitors alike. The fact that their contributions are not well recognized can partially be attributed to longtime colonial status within the U.S. economy, but the complexity of their experience remains to be written. In the context of recording some of that history I feel that it is equally important to show how the city itself is a presence within the cultural processes that emerge on the job.

Thomas Bender calls for an appreciation of the contested and contradictory nature of public culture in order to establish an urban history that goes beyond liberal pluralism and recognizes the voices and presence of the unrepresented (Bender 1988:264). Created in this process are actors' subjective and collective understandings and spatializings of social relations upon a contested terrain:

The "public" in all these permutations represents an arena where different interests, commitments, and values collide and resolve themselves into a reciprocal multivoiced, perhaps even carnivalesque civic sense that is shared as a *relation*, not as a sameness or consensus.

If the modern city and its distinctive experience are defined by the simultaneity of multiple meanings and actions in public, then public life is a constitutive arena where these meanings and interests are brought into contact sometimes as conversation, sometimes as confrontation (ibid).

Bender's sensitivity to the relational and constitutive nature of urban culture, points us toward an appreciation of how multiple cultural discourses intersect and continuously create "the city." Relations of domination and subordination are constant components of this process, but they too are lodged within particular histories and situations. Insofar as the contemporary carnivalesque incorporates the discourses of non-dominant others within the city, it functions to invert everyday working routines.

PART II

"Rockstone" is just one of hundreds of popular Jamaican tunes. In a recent analysis of Caribbean musical styles in Britain, D. Hebdige (1987) points out that embedded in popular Jamaican music is the plea to "give me back me language and me culture." The Jamaican workers at Riverwest felt this need acutely. Besides apparent reconstructions of past identity in lyrics, the "ridims" or drum patterns themselves are encodings of African rhythmic patterns that have persisted throughout the cultures of the Caribbean, sometimes unchanged, other times surfacing only to be reworked for new purposes (Bilby 1985, Alleyne 1989).

However, Jamaican immigrants are also eager to encounter all kinds of North American ("yankee") music, for both its musical style and the emotional attitudes displayed in lyrics. Hebdige has shown how the lyrics of reconstructed African identity played a part in the politics of popular music and culture in Britain during the 1980s (Hebdige 1987). My own experience shows that Jamaican workers seek to fuse such reconstructed identity with contemporary experiences by also employing the representational means and musical/lyrical traditions of others.

Having said this about Jamaican identity, it is worth noting the most frequently played song on the job in the summer of 1981 was Freddy Fender's "Before the Next Teardrop Falls." The first and most popular verse was:

> If he brings you happiness
> Then I wish you all the best
> It's your happiness that matters most of all
> But if he ever breaks your heart
> If the teardrops ever start
> I'll be there before the next teardrop falls.[6]

Why did the Jamaican workers choose this song to depict their concerns? The answer isn't an easy one, but it raises some possibilities which Hebdige's analysis doesn't address. First, the "country-western" style of Freddie Fender is one kind of yankee music which virtually all Jamaican men have encountered before emigration. They like and claim to prefer it over American pop and rock styles, including rhythm and blues, because of the "beautiful and true stories it tells." Although they were enthusiastic about many African American soul standards, they often preferred Jamaican "dub" versions to the originals.[7] Freddy Fender frequently records by alternating English and Spanish verses. The fact that North American materials had been reworked in the cultural discourse of others was obviously appealing to the Jamaican workers. Indeed, as reggae music had become a continuing domain for exploring the expanding global African heritage and values, they were acutely aware of the artificed and syncretic nature of racial and ethnic identities, particularly New World ones. The discussion and literal playing out of these perceptions was made concrete in Freddy Fender's brilliant alternation of the major linguistic codes of Caribbean migrants. This was, in effect, a way of addressing management's tactics of using these differences to prevent solidarity among workers about issues such as seniority/security, low wages and dangerous working conditions.

As the job expanded, new workers were not Jamaican or even English speaking West Indians.[8] The work force slowly shifted to 50% Spanish speaking and the significance of Freddy Fender became even more pronounced. Some Jamaicans, cognizant that they had worked on the jobsite too long to expect any more raises or rewards from the developers, became angry that their work was not valued and that others charging lower wages were being hired. The contradiction between workers and management became one of appreciating and rewarding progress. The work done by the Jamaican crews was obviously "valuable" since the changes in the building were dramatic. As windows appeared and the work schedules were met, it became apparent to the Jamaican workers that they were not compensated very well for their labors. They felt that if they were to stay on, they deserved higher wages. Management felt that their demands were in effect *too* high for work they could obtain by paying $5.00 per hour for laborers who were not necessarily Jamaican.

This state of affairs caused a great deal of friction all around and, accordingly, as a kind of peace offering, one of the Jamaicans brought a tape of Freddy Fender, and cranked up the volume whenever a Spanish-speaking crew approached.

The Jamaican workers *did* like the song though and often used the refrain "The next teardrop" as an opening gambit for discussing ("reasonin") about life in general, and about the fact that they would soon be replaced by "Puerto Ricans" and hence would shed the next teardrop about this job. These "reasonin" sessions angered management because they changed the *pace* of the workday, while injecting a context of comment between (what were supposed to be) disparate groups. All groups of workers were surprised by this anger, since they understood the use of music on the job as a statement about the conditions that management had created. As far as workers were concerned, management was mistaken in reading or hearing a consensus to slow down the workday with frivolous music. On the contrary, workers felt that the music defused a volatile situation. Playing music created a public discourse that simultaneously recognized difference and allowed the possibility of further action together. The workers were surprised because they hadn't recognized the extent to which they had countered hegemonic discourse about subjective and cultural expression.

The Puerto Ricans appreciated the Jamaicans' peace efforts; they, after all, were not offended by Freddy Fender. However, they preferred rap and American pop music, and would good naturedly try to change tapes or radio stations.

Puerto Ricans were not the only Spanish speakers on the job. The Mexican workers were faintly amused but told me that this song was predictable since it was one of a few widely popular hits sung in Spanish that was played. They thought Freddy Fender was a poor imitator of the genuine North American country and Western style. I should add that these Mexican workers told me repeatedly that the reason they had come north at all was to hear and buy great rock and roll. While they eschewed Freddy Fender, they could accept Jamaicans like the greatest of Rastafarian singers, Bob Marley, as genuine rockers.

Workers from the Dominican Republic were somewhat less appreciative of this song and curious that the Jamaicans found it worthy of play and comment. They preferred Trinidadian soca music, pointing out that the beat was more danceable than reggae and much more like their own. Soca was well-liked by all West Indians (despite Hebdige's misgivings about its apolitical message [Hebdige 1987:157]), as it often served as a kind of universal dance music at parties and ballroom dances sponsored by neighborhood and voluntary associations. The young Jamaicans greeted these responses positively, feeling at least that their "meditations" about music on the job successfully created dialogue.

The manifestation of a profusion of musical tastes prompted by Jamaican attempts to make a statement about the unequal and unfair power dimensions of the job ties in to the use of popular music in contemporary Jamaican history. As Alleyne points out the profusion of musical styles in the past thirty years has accompanied political and religious movements for independence and spiritual renewal (Alleyne 1989:150).

Reggae and rasta lyrics seek both to educate, and to focus discourse about everyday life in terms of a set of historical givens. What are they? These givens include slavery, and the continuation of economic oppression, the continuing exploitation of African people outside of Africa and the need for self-respect and love for one's fellow human beings in the face of Babylon (the world of Euro-American exploitation and exile outside of Africa). Although none of the men I worked with identified themselves as *true* Rastafarians (none, for example, recognized Haile Selassie as a deity), Rasta thought was considered an expression of *authentic* Jamaican identity. The insights offered by Rasta thought were considered guideposts for negotiating a Jamaican place within the city. But the question which many of the Jamaican workers face is *how* Babylon could be contended with and perhaps subverted from within.

The strategic deployment of "ridims" in the workplace included playing recorded music, repeating favorite lyrics, or singing bits of call and response patterns. These activities articulated a more generalized attempt by the Jamaican workers to subtly control the pacing of the day's tasks, and to insert workers from different localities (in Jamaica) into the flow of the crew's work. Infusing the New York job with music is again analogous to the use of worksongs, a practice that was present in early accounts of Jamaican slave labor and which continues in some areas today. Lewin lists some of these contexts:

There are worksongs for digging, sugar boiling, picking cotton, planting corn, peas and yam, timber cutting, rice beating, house cleaning, house hauling, women's work, fishing, and loading bananas onto boats . . . (Lewin 1974:128–9, quoted in Alleyne 1989:115)

A rich tradition of co-operative and reciprocal labor arrangements, day work, task work, partnerships, and exchanges has been found in Jamaica (M. G. Smith 1956). And while these are predominantly rural pursuits, a great deal of "casual" specialization in skilled trades on estates and in large towns also occurs (ibid.; R. T. Smith 1956; Mintz 1974). The perpetuation of reciprocal exchanges was modified in New York, when men would switch roles of specialist-helper (i.e., "controller") to prevent management from specifying their exact duties and obligations. This rotation disguised how much skilled work any one man was capable of and forced management to rely upon two, three, and four man teams, with each man assuring management that *he* was the one capable of craftsmanship, but that all were needed for the job.

In New York, as in Jamaica, wage workers and small craftsmen were liable to initiate disputes with employers over differences concerning the proper organization of tasks. Criteria of dispute could be age generational, as in who was the senior craftsman and who the helper, arguments over "fair" amounts of time spent on tasks and when to begin and end preparation and job set ups, how to handle meals, breaks, and the responsibility for providing food, in short, all variations upon the pacing and structure of the working day.

This careful attention to the "day" as a unit of work which should be particularly subject to workers' intentions was also evident in New York. Workers often preferred to reach an agreement among themselves about the amount of work which should be accomplished during the day. At the same time they resented any changes in these arrangements, and expected full "cooperation" from management, especially by way of providing sufficient apprentices, helpers, and materials toward the end of completing these tasks. They resisted changing locations and tasks during the day, and insisted that they could only do good work if they completed the tasks they had started, preferably with the same helpers and masons. Jamaican masons especially wanted to consult with other teams of masons to arrange the flow of bricks, mortar, and steel lintels (from laborers to tenders). They based their criteria for deciding who had priority upon how much work each team of masons could do. While people recognized that some worked faster than others, since the tenders and helpers were shared by all, the net effect was, of course, to even out the pace. This pacing also subverted any competitive comparison of teams that had been set up by the foremen or management.

I have described how for the Jamaican workers, music on the job and music in general, conjoins both subjective and collective class-based experiences. Those experiences are about the struggle to form a kind of cultural strategy to survive migration. Work regimes, work disciplines, are often defined by "whites" who control both local plantation economies and economies here in the United States. Thus for Jamaicans, "race" is often experienced as an effect in a vertical dimension of relations between management and workers. However in this context the Jamaicans recognized class affiliation across "races" as a kind of bond. They also understood very much and wanted to emphasize how music (reggae and dub) encoded an African cultural perspective that Jamaicans particularly had developed to transcend the historical inequities and indignities of laboring for others.

Freddy Fender and his creolization of yankee music was the vehicle to conjoin general, situational (class based) concerns with particular Jamaican ones. His music was an olive branch and kind of propadeutic for signaling certain possibilities of alliance and resistance in the midst of that struggle to maintain their position on the job vis-a-vis Spanish speaking workers who were being used to replace them.

There is another, more inchoate perspective on time that was pervasively woven into this workplace. The building itself was both the locus and product of work. The completion of the product held consequences for the ongoing practice of work in the city and of what presence (and employment) in the city could mean. This ever-changing spatial object invited speculation among the workers about its ultimate fate and importance in the surrounding landscape.

The internal structure of the luxury-style condominiums signified a whole range of tastes, references, necessities, and desires which are the accouterments of an affluent urban elite. These living spaces, for example, concretize different class separations between work and home. The carefully artificed leisure of the urban upper class home concentrates on designing elaborate spaces for bathing and sleeping. Whirlpool bathtubs and soundproofed bedrooms are fully wired for music and electronic play. The "work spaces" within these homes are constructed as extensions of these comforts, offices which are not merely for production but conspicuously about the personal tastes of the owner.

The production of this space creates only a negation for the *future* participation by immigrant workers once it is complete. They cannot live there according to the segregated racial and class prerequisites of this new residential area. Neither does the actual construction *firm* hold a future, since these workers were made to understand in various and subtle ways that they were only means to securing the transformation of "raw space" into profitable and exclusive real estate. Once the building was completed, there would be no firm, and no hiring until another building was "developed" and they were needed once again.

PART III

We should recognize the intensity of Jamaicans' concern with work as a question about what proportion it "should" play in the life cycle. For the Jamaicans (as well as any interpreter) it is important not simply to define the world of work as the world of exploitation. Instead one should take the opportunity to "meditate" upon how that world is created and lived. In their case, the use of music is considered an essential framework for meditation upon one's lived world. Based upon such an analysis, I suggest that Jamaican cultural representations about work should be understood as dialogically fashioned rather than epiphenomena of class and status structures, or emblematic of extraction of surplus value. In societies which are directly created out of the legacy of European colonial expansion, there is no question that notions of competence and skill are not limited to the actual scene of the workplace, but are historically "charged." Occupation and skill, as criteria of status, were both fused with a racial/class hierarchy as early as the seventeenth century Jamaican sugar plantation, and thus still function as a dominant metaphor for the total society (R. T. Smith 1982). While the economic significance of plantations has waned, the explanatory power of its powerful connotations remain pertinent to images of race, class, and personal power. I suggest that we can look to the workplace in New York City as one area upon which the grounds of the old hierarchy were, and are, continually questioned, renegotiated and disposed.

In this paper, I have suggested that bringing music onto the job shows that concepts of both time and the "workplace" play a central role in the life of Jamaican migrant construction workers. However, "place" in the context of their own interpretation of themselves and their history has a densely packed meaning. As Ken Pryce points out for West Indian immigrants in the United Kingdom, distinctions about *kinds* of work frequently form the basis for assertions about personal identity and capacity. This point is valid even if Pryce's *overall* method of distinguishing "orientations" within a "West Indian community" in Great Britain does not explore/question *how* social distinctions and class formation are interrelated.

The Jamaican workers I knew had a keen sense of their role as international migrant workers. Several had already worked in either the United Kingdom or Canada. Others had grandparents who had worked in Cuba, and virtually all of them knew about the role played by West Indian workers in the building of the Panama Canal, as cane-cutters all over the Caribbean and southern United States, and as crewmen on merchant ships and tankers throughout the world.

This knowledge, added to their often-stated determination to distinguish themselves from native-born Afro-Americans, infused their creation of a "space" within the routine of the entire building renovation. Desire to distinguish themselves as a collectivity from Black Americans was not an act of hostility, but one of good-natured rivalry. This may sound like a circuitous formulation of a straight-forward case of "ethnic" differentiation, but the latter term has become so politically charged in New York that it is useless as an analytical category. I want to emphasize instead that the sense of multiple and shifting sets of subject positions within work crews and between all workers versus management intensified as the building renovation progressed.

Another way of putting this formulation is in negative terms. Often anthropologists or sociologists have asked whether I was analyzing the "survivals" and "construction/formation" of something called Jamaican or West Indian ethnicity; or perhaps I was analyzing the development of the "new" post-1965 immigration law working class. My experience however, convinces me that neither of these formulations is entirely appropriate because they are premised on an assumption that immigrants are constrained by the interests of the "little community" within the city. Such assumptions do not sufficiently recognize that the symbolic forms of urban popular culture indicate what Stuart Hall has called "the double movement of containment and resistance" (Hall 1981:282). Hence, in international immigrant culture, "New York City" as space and symbol is as important as the "little community" that one is perforce enmeshed in.

I think that the demarcation of workplace (through the use of music) indicates a narrative situating of the "new world" (and new space) of the jobsite in terms which are larger than the job itself, terms that are part of the entire situation of migration (enforced migration, slavery) but not reducible to it. (For a similar point see Nugent in this volume.) The Jamaican workers perceive that residential renovation jobs in New York City involve issues about the economic and social relationships and determinations between members of an urban workforce. Rather than simply and *boldly* stating that "we are the best workers, we deserve these jobs more than you, and so on.," and thereby falling prey to the constituting logic of their employers and the commonsense mythology of North American immigration, they choose to recast their own situations as unique ones, ones that they and their people survived through time.

These workers still live outside of Manhattan, mostly in Brooklyn, Bronx or Queens where there are large West Indian neighborhoods and business districts. Most of the men I worked with (especially younger ones) lived in more than one location. This is partially an effect of immigration laws which require sponsorship or kinship for obtaining a visa. During the late 1970s and early 1980s, the demand for domestic, health, and home care jobs in the New York area was filled largely by women from the Caribbean and Latin America. Often this meant that men were sponsored for visas by female kin or affines who they had not seen in many years. They explained their need to change households so as to keep a certain sense of proportion and control over their personal fates. The frequency of changing living accommodations was much lower for men who were married. The existence of an all West Indian crew was a source of genuine pride for them. The contractor, employing many of the same men, did well for several years expanding his interests into a taxi and livery company in Flatbush (Brooklyn) before going out of business. Such small businesses never require a large number of permanent workers, and by 1985, those who I worked with had gone on to other contractors or had set themselves up as independent subcontractors, charging a day rate for themselves and an occasional helper. Although everyone does not work together often, they continue to exchange telephone numbers, personal news, and job referrals. I have not seen some of these men for several years, and I know that others have not had an easy time in the competitive renovation labor market. Although they find this disheartening, they remain certain that the capacity to practice their crafts is a form of cultural expression not reducible to a single work discipline. Despite many drawbacks, the large scale renovation is remembered as a time when the job seemed to run the way it should, because workers framed possibilities for change in what they viewed as cultural terms.

The guiding precepts of urban speculation and renovation, progress and development, build themselves on discarded labor and bodies while producing images of subalterns competing for the limited riches of the global city. Yet I found that the Jamaican workers refused to be overwhelmed by the rankings of "cultural" and personal power and capacities that are attached to those images. By changing time in the workplace, they reconfigured those terms from exploitative attributions by the others into terms of empowerment for themselves.

3

Popular Musical Culture in
Rural Chihuahua:
Accommodation or Resistance?

INTRODUCTION

The following remarks on popular musical culture in rural Chihauhua are based on research carried out from June of 1983 until October of 1985 and again during the summers of 1986 and 1989 in Namiquipa, Chihuahua, Mexico.[1] Namiquipa is the center of a rural municipality approximately two hundred miles from the United States border on the eastern slope of the Sierra Madre Occidental. For the past two centuries, the town of Namiquipa has been the site of a community not of indigenous peoples, but of Indian-fighters. From 1778 until 1821 it was the headquarters of a *compañia volante*, a "flying company" of presidial soldiers serving the Spanish Crown. From the 1830s until the 1880s Namiquipans joined other settlers to fight Apache bands contesting control of the area. In the decades preceeding the Revolution of 1910 Namiquipa became the site of agrarian and political resistance, and during the

1910–1920 period the municipality was an important center of *villismo*, the armed, popular movement of the North that destroyed the pre-revolutionary state but in the end failed to establish an alternative, popular regime throughout the country. For example, Namiquipa was the base from which General Francisco Villa set out in March of 1916 with five hundred men to invade the United States (see Katz 1978, Calzadiaz 1979, Alonso 1988c). Namiquipans succeeded in exacting some dramatic concessions from the state in the post-revolutionary period. In 1926, for example, they secured recognition of the *pueblo's* collective rights to a quarter of a million acres of land.[2]

This *pueblo*, then, had a violent tradition, and a long and contradictory relationship to the Mexican nation-state. The region provides an interesting context in which to investigate, among other things, community-state relations from the colonial period to the present, the process of state formation, the consequences of state-implemented agrarian reform in the twentieth century and the fate of the peasantry in northern Mexico. Using ethnographic and archival materials it is also possible to examine local histories in a global context, the contradictory agrarian ideology of Namiquipans and aspects of their popular culture considered in relation to Mexico and the United States.

This paper is concerned with the latter issue but approaches it through an examination of somewhat unassuming popular entertainments in the 1980s, rather than through a dry and dusty account of agrarian history or a "heroic" account of a "revolutionary" pueblo. An interpretation of Chihuahuan popular culture in relation to Mexico and the United States is advanced by exploring the attitudes of Namiquipans towards North Americans as expressed through musical forms that have currency within the community. To the extent it is about *work*, this essay is about the work (including my own) of musicians. But this particular kind of work—perhaps more accurately described as leisure or nonlaboring activity—related to collective performance by musicians and audience alike and the ways specific modalities of expression within it are articulated, is not the primary subject of the essay so much as the more general social context in which the meanings so generated are produced. The focus, then, is on popular entertainments among Mexicans who inhabit a countryside as strongly linked to the United States as to the center of Mexico. Their musical expressions and productions are embedded in, and constitutive of, a regional culture, bearing echoes from both sides of the border even as they mark out a political and ideological space that transcends the border, or subverts it.

The analysis examines expressive events and the people involved in them in the expanded context of community-state relations. How (and to what extent) may dances in northern Mexico (and musical performances generally) be explained in terms of the relationship between the inhabitants of this region and the Mexican national state? Another question is: what was the character of my intervention, as a North American ethnographer/part-time musician, into these popular cultural forms, and what consequences, if any, did that intervention have upon them?

POPULAR CULTURE IN A REGIONAL CONTEXT

The night before I left Chicago for Chihuahua in 1983, I spent several hours in a bar with some older, experienced anthropologists. The conversation came around to what I might actually do while "in the field." My only clear memory of the evening's conversation was that much of it dealt with what kinds of notebooks to use: three ring binders? spiral notebooks? clipboards? At the time, the furthest thing from my mind was that I might wind up as I did a year later, standing before a microphone in front of five hundred farmers, ranchers, and agricultural laborers yelling out at the top of my lungs "AWOPBOPALUBOPBAWOPBAMBOOM".[3]

My fieldwork took place during a violent period, both within the *pueblo* of Namiquipa and for the Mexican people as a whole. Chihuahuans were experiencing the onset and deepening of what Mexicans call "the Crisis," and witnessing or participating in a variety of local, regional, and national-level agrarian and political struggles.[4] Within the municipality of Namiquipa there occurred agrarian and political violence associated with land-invasions and electoral conflicts. That was coincident in time with debates in the United States over the implementation of a new Immigration Reform and Control Act.[5]

My pre-fieldwork expectations included finding (1) a determined, revolutionary, anti-capitalist agrarian ideology still alive in rural Chihuahua, and (2) a vigorous and generalized anti-gringo, anti-imperialist sentiment on the part of Namiquipans (the town, after all, had been occupied by five thousand U.S. Army troops during the Spring of 1916). I did not expect to be received with warmth and openness *because* I came from the United States, and even less did I anticipate spending a great deal of time learning the latest radio hit from *Los Tigres del Norte*, or teaching a group of Mexican musicians the English language versions of songs they had long played and sung in Spanish such as "Nadine," "Jailhouse Rock," or "Bony Moronie." But I was wrong. Namiquipans loved things and people North American. This was particularly evident in their taste in music—the music they would listen to on the radio or casette decks, and the music they liked and listened to at dances held in the community and surrounding towns and villages. I discovered this while travelling throughout Chihuahua as a working musician. I played a few dances with a Namiquipan dance band in 1983, and then between the Spring of 1984 and early 1985 we performed together in Chihuahua on more than forty occasions. In the Autumn of 1985 I played with the same band in several venues on this side of the border between Las Cruces, New Mexico and El Paso, Texas, and in 1989 we reunited in Namiquipa.

In order to arrive at a discussion of Chihuahuan popular musical culture, the work involved in its production, and how it exemplifies a type of activity that goes beyond accommodation or resistance, some remarks are required specifying how the concept of "popular culture" is being used and describing the region in terms of a few salient characteristics. Key to the argument is an examination of popular musical culture in an expanded framework that includes not only expressive forms—the folkloric productions or artefacts that are of such enduring interest to ethnographers—and the impositions of an externally generated or controlled "mass culture," but also the specific regional political and historical context in which music is produced, reproduced, and transformed. What does popular "culture" mean in the context of such an examination?

There is something equally unsatifactory about both orthodox and structural Marxist formulations of culture as a (semi-) autonomous level within the social formation determined "in the last instance" by the economic "base" (cf. Cohen 1978; Althusser 1971), and North American cultural anthropological formulations according to which culture may only be interpreted, but not explained (Geertz 1973), or is a system of symbols and meanings determinant of social action (Schneider 1980), or constitutes "the" symbolic code of human society (Sahlins 1976). What is understressed by both these general approaches, is the *power dimension* linking culture to the context of production of meanings. While a recognition of the power dimension may be implicit in both anthropologically "culturalist" and "marxist" approaches, anthropologists would do well to pay closer attention to some work in the field of "cultural studies," for example, by Stuart Hall, Nestor Garcia Canclini, and the late Raymond Williams.

The concept of popular culture is currently the subject of debate within cultural studies both in Europe and in Latin America (see García Canclini 1988). It is used in three main senses: (1) To refer to the "expressive culture" (music, art, narrative, ritual, theater) of the *campesinado* as well as the urban underclass and working class. On the whole, scholarship based on this sense of popular culture (highly influenced by an earlier tradition of studies of "folklore") fails to relate issues of meaning to questions of power (cf. García Canclini 1987 for an exemplary exception); (2) To refer to "mass culture," the culture produced by modern media of communication and disseminated downward. Work done from this perspective has tended to view popular culture as only an expression of cultural domination (see Swingewood 1979 for a scathing critique); and (3) To designate the symbols and meanings which are embedded in the day-to-day practices of subordinated groups.

I am using popular culture in this third sense, in which:

> what is essential to the definition of popular culture is the relations which define 'popular culture' in a continuing tension (relationship, influence and antagonism) to the dominant culture (Hall 1981:235).

Such a notion of popular culture does not *exclude* the analysis of either expressive forms or mass culure. However, this definition *includes* some meaningful practices that are excluded by both other senses of the term and postulates a different set of linkages between the production of meaning and relations of power. In particular, it supposes that investigation does *not* have to focus on privileged types of manifestly political social action (e.g., revolt, rebellion) in order to discern the power dimension. Neither does it represent popular culture as simply the antithesis or a miniature, local level version of dominant or official culture. According to this view, popular culture and dominant culture are neither wholly autonomous from each other nor wholly determined by one another. Indeed, the relationships between the two are constantly shifting and are part of the everyday struggle for power (Hall 1981). This notion of how popular culture is constructed in shifting fields of power allows us to examine popular music, for example, and discern in it people's struggles to reshape historical and political contexts through the deployment of expressive forms.

The remarks that follow concerning specific features of popular musical culture in Chihuahua may only be apposite in describing one region of Mexico, the northern frontier, long characterized by its distinctive socioeconomic development. Historically, the degree of the frontier's integration into the nation-state has been relatively less than that of other regions of Mexico. Northern regionalism is predicated on what Barry Carr (1973) characterized as the North's "peculiar" sociohistorical experience "shaped above all by [a] distinct mode of frontier conquest" resuling in "the development of structures of social reproduction specific to" the region (Alonso 1988c:205). There was more than a century of violent conflict between colonists and Apache Indians, persisting until 1886.

> During the decades of violence between colonists and indigenes, the defense of a regional territory fomented . . . a regional imagination of community [Anderson 1983]. Moreover, especially after Independence [but even before], . . . provincial rather than . . . central government[s] played the key role in the organizaton and regulation of frontier warfare [Alonso 1988a:35–91]. The Center's 'abandonment' of the North to 'the incursions of the savages' [as nineteenth century documents describe events] fostered a resentment of the national government among northern colonists . . . such as the peasants of Namiquipa, who bore the brunt of warfare against indigenes. In addition, conditions of frontier warfare resulted in the emergence of a distinct ethnic identity in the North. An invented tradition of origins affirmed (and continues to stress) the "whiteness" of the *norteños* in contradistinction to the "brown-ness" of the *"chilangos"* (a contemptuous term used by Northerners for Mexicans from the Center and South). This [homology of contrasts—between white/brown and *norteño*/*chilango*—constantly invoked in day-to-day life in Chihuahua], . . . is but one index of [the] regional sense of identity and community. . . .
>
> Concurrently, the degree of United States penetration and influence has been strongest on the frontier/border, historically a space across which people 'from both sides' have constantly moved. The perpetual 'pilgrimages' from one side to the other have led to the 'imagining' of this region as a distinct sociocultural zone [that] has more in common with the United States than with the rest of Mexico. . . . [An] identification with 'Americanness' . . . is mobilized by *norteños* to articulate their resentment of the mode of incorporation of the

frontier/border into the [Mexican] nation-state and to affirm their regional distinctiveness (Alonso 1988c:205–6).

One extreme, racist, and vulgarly violent slogan overheard in Chihuahua City was *has patria, mata a un chilango* ("Be patriotic, kill a *chilango"*).

WORKS AND THINGS

While *norteño* antipathy toward the Center of Mexico is fairly straightforwardly expressed through the idioms of an antithetical historical memory (Alonso 1988b, Nugent 1985) and a sense of ethnic difference (Alonso 1988a), the way Chihuahuans regard work in the United States and the things that can be taken back to Mexico from the United States is also illustrative as a highly mediated and indirect example of rural Chihuahuan's attitudes toward Mexican national culture. Namiquipans, and Chihuahuans or *norteños* generally, frequently identify more closely with "The Other Side" (i.e., the United States) than with the Center of Mexico, and routinely incorporate elements of North American culture into their own quotidian routines. This incorporation extends particularly to manufactured goods which originate in the United States, among other things, to the "cultural products" of the United States.

One example is the Namiquipan friend (a *joto*, who was very self-conscious about his dress and public appearence) who proudly wore a sweater that was a raggedy thing riddled with holes. As he pointed out, no matter how bad the sweater appeared objectively, it was particularly valuable since it, like Bruce Springsteen, was born in the U.S.A. Another example is the widely repeated *dicho* or saying in regard to manufactured items, *Hecho en Mexico es mal hecho* ("Made is Mexico is badly made"). When shopping for manufactured items, whether an ignition coil for a pick-up truck, tools, or denim pants, U.S.-made articles were preferred and valued over Mexican-made articles regardless of cost differentials or the difficulty of clearly determing the relative quality of things. Perhaps less surprising, then, is the northern Mexicans' familiarity with, admiration for and appropriation of cultural products, such as songs and music, which are produced in the United States.

However, Namiquipans' affection and respect for *things* from the other side does not extend to a love of the way those things are produced. The "benefits" of so-called advanced, industrial capitalism are abundantly evident to people who live in agricultural communities near the frontier.[6] But so too are they aware of the "costs," which they and North American workers must bear as a result of the organization of the labor process in the United States. Their evaluation of the organization of the labor process in the United States as particularly inimical to their own way of life is in part a function of the locally perceived contrast between the way work in Mexico and work in the United States are experienced and conceived.

The locally valorised ideal in Namiquipa is for men to be independent producers on land they own or control, and on which they direct the production process engaged in by themselves and unwaged family labor. This activity includes producing grains for the state-controlled monopoly, but production of cash crops such as fruit, or cattle, is thought to provide a greater guarantee of independence and autonomy from the state for the household. By way of contrast Namiquipans have a highly developed critique of the wage system and a disdain—based on more than a century of experience—regarding the pace of work and the organization of production in the fields, mines, construction sites, workshops and restaurants of the United States (cf. Alonso in this volume: Nugent 1988a:221, 240).

Nevertheless, temporary wage labor by men in the United States is tolerated as a means by which to guarantee the possibility of their reproduction as independent producers within the community. Freely selling their labor power outside the community, even as it involves entering into relationships of subordination and subjection to exploitative regimes of power, enables men to return to the *pueblo* with valuable commodities. While these commodities, such as pick-up trucks, tractor parts, washing machines, clothing, money, and so forth, often figure as centrally important instruments of social and domestic production, their value within the community is also partly a function of their provenance, that is, the United States. Furthermore, Namiquipan men[7] return from the United States with what they call "a capital," which may be used to supplement or consolidate their position as farmers, ranchers, or simply as neighbors (*vecinos*), as members of the community. One appealing feature of this labor is its nonpermanent character, and another is that the humiliations it entails are experienced outside the pueblo, that is, outside of the purview of the community vis-à-vis which men's reputations are established.

This raises the issue of power and value, where Namiquipans see power and value to be located, and how they see it to be engendered. One critical point to underline is that the efficient and rational exploitation of their bodies and their selves under a capitalist labor regime is conceived as occurring in its most profound form in the alien and alienating context of the United States. In other words, the efficiency and brutality of the labor regime is (mis-) construed as having more to do with the fact that it is well-established in the United States rather than having its basis in capitalism and capitalist relations of production. For even as they are engaged in selling their labor power in the United States to secure "a capital" with which to improve their fields, herds, and orchards in Mexico, they are not particularly sensitive to the manner in which a *capitalist* market for their independently produced goods in Mexico—whether grains, cattle, or fruit—subjects them to exploitative relationships. These latter relationships—to agents of the Mexican state's Rural Bank and the grain-purchasing monopoly CONASUPO, to cattle buyers, or to merchants and fruit packers— are formulated by Namiquipans in terms that are more personal than structural.[8]

Another critical point is that the investment of commodities and cultural forms with both power and value by different groups of people in Chihuahua varies depending on how members of the different groups define their own relationship to the Center of Mexico. For example, school teachers and party officials in Namiquipa, as well as intellectuals and bureaucrats from Chihuahua City (i.e., groups directly linked to national[ist] networks of power), often criticize the United States, particularly United States "cultural penetration" in Mexico. In doing so they refer to the manner in which United States cinema, music, television, and fashions have supplanted "Mexican" national traditions and forms of expression.

However among the popular classes living in the countryside, including the most evidently politically radicalized (e.g., agrarian and communist activists), the issue of United States cultural imperialism only infrequently came up in discussion as a problem. When it did, peasants criticized those by and large elite Mexicans who publicly disparaged the Other Side and the things which the popular classes appropriated from the United States, when in point of fact it is precisely the elites who are best situated to immerse themselves in north of the border indulgences. Victor Benoit, a Haitian community-activist, made a related point in early 1987; "It's not all black & white. . . U.S. music is tremendously influential in Cuba, yet Cuba remains a socialist country" (quoted in Chamberlain 1987:21). Toward the United States and its culural products such as music, the attitudes expressed by the people with whom I lived and worked in Namiquipa were invariably positive and favourable, and the fact that I was a *gringo* proved to be more of an asset than a hindrance, both to doing fieldwork in the contryside of Chihuahua and to working with the band.

PLAYING IN THE BAND (WORKING IN THE FIELD)

After a few months living in Namiquipa, I moved with Ana Alonso, who was also doing research in the town, into some storage rooms attached to the house of a young family. The household head was a musician who had played with other local musicians in a dance band in Namiquipa and in Arizona for approximately a decade. I play the guitar and by the following spring I had joined their group full time. We played steadily for the rest of the next year with jobs at least once a week, and sometimes several times a week. Our earnings were split evenly five ways. I was able to supplement my research grant, and the other musicians were able to earn five to ten times the official daily minimum wage from each night of playing for which we were paid. However, they were unable to support their families solely from their earnings as musicians, though that is what they aspired to do.[9]

The other members of the band were all peasants, or sons of peasants with no land of their own to work. For them the possibility of working as musicians was an alternative to tilling the soil. They were all in their late twenties, and while they had been playing together for more than a decade, their work as musicians had always been carried out in conjunction with other jobs such as cultivating the land, wage-labor in the United States, carpentery, brick-laying, plastering, and so forth. While I was with the band (and doing ethnography by day), the other members worked as carpenters or, seasonally, as day-laborers in a fruit-packing warehouse.[10]

The name of the group, *Fase Cinco*, was supposed to sound like a gringo name and was intended to signify the "Five Faces", with *Fase* standing for its acoustic cognate in English, and not, as I had originally thought, signifying Phase. The other guitarist in the band had emblazoned the side and front of his van with the name of the group, advertising the fact that they played "Country miusic" [sic]. Other bands that played in Namiquipa had at least one singer who would take a stab at "Wasted Days and Wasted Nights" (Baldemar Huerta/Freddy Fender 1959) in English.[11] After I joined the band, Fase Cinco had a member who could perform more than one song in English in the course of an evening, and the people of the towns we played in appeared to enjoy that. If my singing was terrible, my English pronunciation was unassailably correct, even though a certain obnoxious Utah twang crept into my voice each time I stood before the microphone and opened my mouth.

Our work involved playing dance music for northern Mexican peasants. The audiences ranged in age from children and teenagers to people in their sixties and seventies. They sometimes included wealthy cattle ranchers and fruit-growers, but primarily consisted of farmers, agricultural laborers, and peasants.

We did not play in the *pueblo* of Namiquipa every week, frequently relying on bookings in neighboring *pueblos.* The biggest town we played in was Chihuahua City, the furthest away was El Bufalo, in southern Chihuahua, almost in Durango. Routinely we would perform in barns, warehouses, and dancehalls, or in civic buildings located in the middle of rural villages and towns, such as the school or the meeting hall of the *ejido.* Occassionally we would set up outside in the central plaza of a town.

The music was played on drums and electrically amplified instruments (bass, guitars, and organ), and we sang through a public-address system. While this is somewhat different from the characteristic line-up of *musica norteña* bands, much of our repetoire—particularly the *corridos,* the *rancheras,* and the polkas—was indistinguishable from the songs performed by *musica norteña* bands. The *corridos* and *rancheras* are basically "story songs" similar in structure, and indeed in content, to much North American "folk" music; the life and action of people of the countryside, or the adventures and misadventures of migrant workers, or tales of unrequited love or lost honor, are sung about over repeating verses. The polkas were usually instrumentals played just this side of rhythmic control to which people would dance vigorously in a large undulating circle.

In addition we would play *cumbias, sambas,* and *baladas.* The *cumbia* is a dance beat which has its origins on the Caribbean coast of South America while the *samba* is from Brazil. The ballads served as an opportunity for people to engage in slow-dancing. Like many other bands in the region, we played *La Bamba* at every dance, long before the Hollywood movie was produced, and included one of the slightly risqué verses which Los Lobos left out of their recent radio hit. But finally, we also played country and western songs, blues, and a sort of Tex-Mex rock and roll. While as a rule I would sing the country, blues, and rock songs in English, some of those songs such as "San Antonio Rose," "Deep in the Heart of Texas," or "Jailhouse Rock" had long been parts of the local dance scene. The songs, the sounds, and the rhythms, indeed the very manner in which the music was presented as a combination of northern Mexican and United States styles, resonated with the life experiences of both performers and audiences.

LINES OF INQUIRY

Public dances in the Chihuahuan countryside are social and cultural events during which political and social relationships, sentiments, and notions of self-identity are articulated. Their analysis affords an interesting perspective from which to examine how the relationships between work (particularly the work of musicians), identity and inequality are articulated in public performances and how, at a more general level, the implication of indices of domination/subordination such as class, ethnicity, gender, and regionalistic lines of division, are manifest in the dances considered as collective performances. Such a line of argument can be corroborated by first outlining the contexts of the dances, three of which are immediately recognizable: (1) *rites de passage;* (2) national/patriotic holidays; and (3) fund-raisers.

Primary and secondary school graduations, baptisms, *quinceañeras,* and weddings were often the occassions for dances. Weddings in smaller towns are events in which virtually the entire community participates. *Quinceañeras* are fifteenth birthday parties for young women comparable to "coming out" parties, or "debutante balls." Wealthier families host these events, modelled on weddings and basically held to mark the transition from adolescence to adulthood and to announce the sexual availability of the young woman. These *rites de passage* (for school children, babies, fifteen year old girls, newly formed married couples) are the focus of attention for the entire community. A series of ritual performances—sometimes secular, sometimes sacred—are concluded with a collective celebration, the dance. Another set of occasions for dances were national or local holidays, such as May 5th, Independence Day (16 September), the anniversary of the Revolution (20 November), or the patron saint day of a *pueblo* (e.g., 19 October in Namiquipa). Third, dances were frequently held as fund-raisers by civic organizations such as The Society of Parents of School Children, the Women's Church Organization, the *ejido* (the administrative apparatus through which use of the community's land is organized), official organizations such as Desarrollo Integral Familiar (DIF) linked to the Partido Revoluctonario Institucional (PRI) which is regarded as identical to the national state, and so on. The fund-raisers occur in paticular locales on dates fixed through arrangement with municipal authorities.

Most of the dances took place on Sunday nights, began at nine o'clock, and lasted until two or three in the morning. Fundraisers and national holidays sometimes, but not invariably, occurred simultaneously, and in addition to providing (i.e., paying for) a band, sponsoring organizations would secure permission from the local government to sell beer and to charge a fee for reserved tables in the dance halls. During weddings and *quinceañeras*, by way of contrast, the sponsoring family was expected to provide all the food and liquor consumed during the event.

The dances we played at in Chihuahua suggest several types of analysis, depending on whether they are considered as ritual, social or political events. For example, it is quite evident that, at times, they serve as mechanisms for the redistribution of social and economic values (Sahlins 1972). This is clear both in the case of what are manifestly the culminations of *rites de passage*, as well as the fund-raisers and entertainments. Wedding and *quinceañera* dances have already been mentioned in this connection, but a word is in order regarding how the fund-raisers figure doubly in the redistribution of social and particularly economic values.

First, money is raised by charging admission to the dances, selling beer, and so on, and profits from the event are earmarked for one or another collective use such as painting a school house, repairing the roof of a public building, or purchasing a water pump to provide potable water in a community. However, one invariable outcome of the fund-raisers is that a portion of the funds raised the day of the dance "dissappears." This occasions complaint and alarm only when the theft is outrageously apparent or so great that the events wind up in the red. It is thought to be a foregone conclusion that some of the popularly-generated funds disappear; where they disappear to describes one circuit of redistribution among several.

The dances also serve as occasions for the demarcation of different kinds of power and the spaces in which such power is exercised. The clearest example of this is provided by the circumstance that large public dances of whatever type may only occur with the authorization of Municipal (and sometimes State-level) authorities. In other words, the political power of the state is exercised on communities through a specific organization of permissible "entertainment."

In one *pueblo* near Namiquipa there had been an agrarian war in the early 1980s. Dances were banned by the state government at the request of the less well-armed faction in the town, whose members argued that dances were events in which there was so much drinking and carrying on that they could provide the spark for a renewal of the shooting. Several "illegal" dances were nevertheless organized in this pueblo during the moratorium,[12] which was finally lifted on November 20, 1984. During this latter event which had the blessings of the state, members of both factions showed up. But while only one faction or the other had sponsored dances during the moratorium, elments of the opposed faction had also participated in those illegal dances. The popular concession to the state to dictate the timing and organization of dances could be regarded as a (collective) action of accomodation; "unauthorized" dances—with the good rockin' times and occasional mayhem and violence which ensue—would correspondingly figure as rituals of renewal or rebellion (Gluckman 1963).

State approval, however, is not the only way in which spaces of power are established during the dances. There also exist forms through which families, or domestic units for the production and reproduction of socialized individuals, participate in the shaping of community life. This form of participation is achieved through the movement of a "domestic" event such as a wedding into the "collective" sphere of action, where individual families appropriate a public space and invite the participation of nonfamily members to the end of situating domestic reproduction and ritual in the context of public action.

Further, an analysis of the dances in terms of power and spaces of power could be carried out in terms of analytical units besides the state and the family. One could examine the forms through which women identify their own power vis-à-vis men during the dances, or through which subaltern groups and classes "express themselves" in their own communities thereby deriving a reflexive self-understanding through the display and elaboration of media of self-identity. Yet another alternative would be to look at the dances, and the performances by musicians and dancers alike, as manifestations of collectively effervescent *communitas* or as "play" (Turner 1967; Huizinga 1949; Geertz 1973).

Employing yet another approach, the dances and the music could be made to appear exotic through the lens of a fine-grained formal and textual analysis. But that would put us on the ground of futilely searching for "authentic," autocthonous forms of expression in northern Mexican music. The very (anti-historical) postulation of popular musical culture as authentic, "traditional,"and so on draws the analysis away from any consideration of the economic, political and ideological bases for the complexity of the dances considered as events.

The ideas of "taste" and (aesthetic) "appropriateness" *are* arguably legitimate objects of ethnographic inquiry and comparison, and my experiences and perceptions as a musician provided the basis for a rare look at the constitution and formation of taste and (musical) appropriatness, or of "authentic musical tradition." But the forces of political and ideological domination—manifest in those very aesthetically-constituted "events" which invite a similarly aesthetically-informed style of analysis—at the same time resonate with political and economic forces and relations, consideration of which moves us far beyond "the little community," beyond the question of *what* "tradition" or "authenticity" are, to the question of how tradition and authenticity are formed in particular contexts in relation to particular states, geographies, regional histories, and other "extra-aesthetic" factors. To underline this point of the argument, we must return to the issue of how popular culture is defined.

Writing about the 1956 revolution in Hungary, Cornelius Castoriadis cites the emergence of "positive truths created by the people themselves . . . [,] positive because they were embodied in actions and organizations designed not only for the struggle *against* exploitation and oppression . . . but also as new forms for the organization of collective life on the basis of new principles" (Castoriadis 1976:8). This builds in a particularly radical way on what Raymond Williams pointed out as the three general categories or aspects involved in a definition of culture—"the ideal," "the documentary," and "the social" (Williams 1961:41). If culture is regarded as a set of values composing a timeless order (the ideal), a body of intellectual and imaginative work (the documentary), and a particular way of life, expressive of meanings and values (the social), then by emphasizing that meanings and imaginative work are *produced* or created by people, the ideal aspect of culture is reapprehended as itself an outcome or result, the "timeless" quality of which is thereby thrown into question. That intellectual and imaginative work generate social values is an historical phenomenon not restricted to the drawing rooms of polite society or the board rooms of the "culture industries"; such work also takes place in connection with struggles against exploitation and oppression. But even more important is that such work *also* takes place in the more prosaic contexts of day-to-day life, leisure, and entertainment. My contention is that we regard popular musical culture in these terms.

I am suggesting that we consider these dances and the music in terms of the relationship of the geographic and cultural region in which they are produced to the United States and the Mexican nation-states. Were we to situate the examination of these events in terms of the functioning and interrelationship of formal elements the characteristics of which somehow have to do with an authentic tradition, that would ignore an important feature of the dances, even at the level of graphic description. For the striking characteristic of the *content* of the dances and the music produced during them is the degree to which they are inflected and shot-through with decidedly non-Mexican and non-*norteño* elements. In other words, audiences as soon dance to Little Richard songs based on Mr. Penniman's adolescent experiences washing dishes in a Greyhound Bus Station (Shaw 1978:189–190) as to *corridos* about the experiences of migrant workers crossing the border from Mexico to the United States. And they applaud at the end of a song by Credence Clearwater Revival—the lyrics of which few people in the audience can understand—with as much enthusiasm as for the widely-sung *corrido* "A Fistful of Dirt"/*Un puño de tierra.*

It is not simply that bands in the region could find work more easily if they used North American amplifiers, guitars and organs, the brand names of which are prominently displayed on stage. But that was a criterion used to assess the "qualities" of musicians!; and even if the best organs were really made in Japan, they were not after all manufactured in *Mexico,* and the instruction manuals came in English. The special appeal of Fase Cinco, an appealing feature for the Chihuahuans who hired us and danced while we played, was that we were able to produce a north of the border sound and north of the border image and experience.

But while the combination of northern Mexican and United States styles that we developed together was as much fun for us to play as it was for audiences to listen to, it also introduces something of a dilemma. Was I distorting or modifying a popular cultural expression of the northern Mexican musicians with whom I worked by teaching them songs recorded in the United States by Ry Cooder, the Sir Douglas Quintet, Ray Sharpe, and Gram Parsons? Was I subjecting the Chihuahuan peasants for whom we played to yet another form of cultural imperialism from the United States?

BRINGING THE STATE BACK IN

The answer to both these questions is "No." And that answer will be explained before concluding with a more direct discussion of how to consider *norteños'* popular cultural expressions in relation to the States that rule in Mexico and the United States. That I wound up playing with Fase Cinco is the contingent result of the other musicians wanting me to play with them coinciding my interest in learning and playing *musica norteña*. While I did that, I also learned some North American songs I had never before thought to play, some of which were already part of Fase Cincos' repetoire. I was not tampering with traditional, "native" forms so much as doing "my informants'" biding by singing the songs. Overriding that, however, was the fact that working with the band provided me a different and more compelling way of engaging people than sitting before them with a notebook in my lap.

At another level, a lapse into paranoic *hubris* is required to impute such a power and subtlety to the imperial project of the United States with the suggestion that we (ethnographers) *cannot help* but be the agents of our state. To do so gives U.S. capitalism more credit than is it's due. Subtlty is the drawing card neither of capitalism, nor of United States intervention in Mexico and the rest of Latin America; as Branford and Kucinski argue in *The Debt Squads* (1988) the chief drawing card for United States bankers, the International Monetary Fund (IMF), and the World Bank is simply the bottom line.

The central point of this paper is that the people who create these musical expressions, and dance to them, are not simply elements of some generic "Mexican peasantry" dominated above all (or in the last instance) by the Colossus to the North. Rather, they are inhabitants of a particular geographic, political, cultural and historical space for whom the relationship to the Center of Mexico has for centuries been an antagonistic one. Their dances and the music performed during them provide one context in which they can play those two (United States and Mexican) cultural points of reference off one another. They exploit their facility at reproducing and transforming North American styles to the end of marking their difference from, and declaring their independence of, the Center of Mexico, and the Mexican state. During the dances, which are collective performances for/by musicians and dancers alike, people may address and recognize their identities as *norteños,* as inhabitants of the border, and that is not a passive process imposed from above or from without.

Their popular musical expressions, in other words, are formed out of the willful appropriation of elements they select from an alien musical (and cultural) idiom *to empower themselves.* This indeed is one of the oldest and most overlooked functions of music in general. The seemingly accidental combinations of elements that occur in situations of complex political-cultural domination such as exist in northern Mexico, coincident with attempts by the subjects of that domination to liberate themselves, is a phenomenon that merits more careful examination. Lacking the time to go in to it any further, I would instead like to put it on the table as part of a possible future research agenda that would permit us to critique essentialist *constructions* of authenticity that are themselves an historical product of the present.

What is being produced or stated through the medium of these popular musical expressions? The point, it would seem to me, is that through particular musical expressions Namiquipans seek to empower themselves in relation to the state. What is crucial is less the *authenticity* of the popular culture, its incontrovertible "Mexican-ness" for example, than the manner in which its expression during the dances we played involved a restatement, a re-presentation, and a re-formulation of the relationship of popular culture (however authentic or unauthentic) to the forces in society against which it is ranged. The musical expressions of this subordinated social group—agriculturalists or peasants of northern Mexico—give voice to streams of experience and consciousness (Guha 1982b; Chaterjee 1983) that are not reducible to nonpopular forms, even as they involve borrowings from, and transformations of, the latter.

In other words, the study of popular culture cannot be conducted by situating the analysis on some middle-ground *between* accomodation and resistance. That would make it appear as though popular cultural expressions are simply *more* or *less* positive responses to dominant structures, forces and genres, either in a muted way (accomodation), or in a strong way, through negation (resistance). The evidence from northern Mexico suggests, to the contrary, that even when apparently burdened with stylistic and formal elements manifestly derived from dominant or alien cultures, the popular musical expressions have to do with neither accomodation, nor with resistance in the sense that sees them as two sides of the same coin, but with the articulation of a reflexive and relationally stated collective identity. This expression is achieved through the popular appropriation and revaluation of elements and instruments of self-identification derived from (what is ostensibly) outside of their own experience.

Our work of examining the expressions of workers on the margins of capitalism (or even at its center) should be oriented by an attempt toward breaking down wooden dichotomies such as accommodation vs. resistance or dominant vs. popular culture, and instead focusing on the field of change and process between either end of the polarity. The general set of relations between culture and its total context of production as outlined in this essay has not so much to do with music per se, since one could just as well examine popular culture by focusing instead on, say, agricultural practices, historical memory, the formation of popular or community organizations, even electoral behavior, and make a similar argument. The proposition that we would do well to be critical of essentialist *constructions* of authenticity that are themselves an historical product of the present acquires an immediacy and force in the consideration of Namiquipan popular culture in light of the community's relation to the Mexican state.

Dances in rural Chihuahua are events during which northern peasants articulate their relationship to the Mexican state and to a regional sense of identity. By appropriating the contents of North American music and assigning new values to elements of that idiom of self-expression (i.e., asserting that the idiom is their own, its elements different from those promulgated by the state), these people empower themselves. While the language is appropriated from the north, and to that extent "unauthentic," a new range of possible meanings emerges in the context of performance, and this is achieved without the people falling into the trap of recreating a kind of power identical—even if negatively—to that of the state. Their popular musical expressions involve not only a contestation of the forms and forces of oppression and domination, but also an *internal* celebration of the people's distinctiveness. Consequently, the self-empowerment achieved through the collective imagining of their own identities and social possibilities forms a radical, and original, kind of resistance to the state.

4

Artistic Creations from the
Work Years: The New York World of Work

In this chapter[1] I explore the processess by which retired workers interpret their past jobs and work roles through expressive creations, such as sculptures, drawings and paintings, to formulate and maintain a coherent sense of identity in old age and to adapt to retirement. These autobiographical visual statements, which depict the work scene and/or continue the use of occupational materials and work-related skills, provide access to the nonverbal thoughts and perceptions of retirees about the meaning of work as a significant component of identity formation in old age.

Anthropological writing on life history discusses autobiography as a process of self-creation in which people claim the right to define themselves in a coherent, socially acceptable frame (Langness and Frank 1981). Myerhoff, in her study of the aged in Venice, California, stresses the self-definitional and transformative power of autobiography, in which elderly people who exist on the margins of mainstream America use the retelling of life stories to shape self-images and establish a sense of meaning and self-esteem (Myerhoff 1978). Life continuity does not arise spontaneously, but must be achieved through the construction and interpretation of experiences (Myerhoff 1978:108). Kaufman further reveals the symbolic, creative process by which "the self draws meaning from the past, interpreting and recreating it as a resource for being in the present" (Kaufman 1986:14):

> Identity is not frozen in a static moment of the past. Old people formulate and reformulate personal and cultural symbols of their past to create a meaningful, coherent sense of self, and in the process they create a viable present. In this way, the ageless self emerges; its definition is ongoing, continous, and creative.

It was the writings of psychiatrist Robert Butler that first explicated the psychological dynamics of this self-creative process (Butler 1963, 1967, 1975). According to Butler, the elderly reevaluate their lives through reminiscence, which permits the revivification of past experience, the reexamination of old, unresolved conflicts, and the reintegration of repressed events. Events from the past are reinterpreted in light of present experience. The inevitable challenges and crises of aging, such as retirement, the death of a loved one, or an increasing awareness of finitude, often initiate this life review. Such challenges can simultaneously trigger creativity, and the elderly may burst forth with creative works in music, art, or memories. For the medium and content of the new found artistry, these older artists may reach back into youth or middle years, to family and/or work experiences.

A unique opportunity to examine this creative life review process as it relates to past occupational experiences and adaptation to present social context—in this case, retirement—was provided by a folk-art exhibition I co-curated entitled "The World of Work."[2] Here were displayed artistic creations that directly depicted the New York work scene, employed occupational materials, and/or continued work-related skills. The artistic productions of seven of these retirees, enriched by life history interviews I conducted, provide the data for my analysis of the subjective meaning of work as a component of identity formation in old age.

In this chapter I argue that for these older artists, late life creative expressions concerning past jobs reveal and parallel the content and the process of the life review. The data suggest that the consuming, often repetitive physical and psychological processes of retirees' art-making, which focus time and again on work-related themes, parallel the similarly consuming, repetitive processes and content described in classic accounts of the life review (Butler 1963, Kaminsky 1978). Here the nonverbal visual language furnishes insight into the way the individual deals with the subjective realm (Edwards 1986). For these retirees, artistic activity releases and is released by their work-related reminiscences. Artmaking elaborates their past experiences and perceptions into aesthetic artifacts and thereby gives them an objective existence. The occupational folk art creations of retirees manifest their reexamination of unresolved conflicts and reveal needs for self-definition and validation that are not always articulated verbally. These artistic creations objectify the subjective, nonconscious and nonverbal realm and make inner thoughts, perceptions and processes visible. Artmaking expresses and provides access to mental perceptions and processes that are not always at a conscious level of awareness. The examination of work-related folk art suggests that the genres of verbal expression are not always adequate to the task of the life review and that the autobiographic construction of life history may take other forms of self-definition.

I further suggest that past work roles and work skills can also be analyzed as influencing adaptation to retirement and as affecting a retirement life style. As events from the past are reinterpreted in light of the present social context, so experiences and perceptions within the retirement period are influenced, to a large degree, by one's former occupation (Phillipson 1982; Walker 1986; Guillemard 1982). In other words, work roles affect retirement; and retirement, in turn, affects the reinterpretation of one's former occupation.

Below I examine in detail seven case studies which illustrate how occupational folk art provides new understanding of the interrelated meanings of work and retirement and of the processes by which past work becomes a component of the self-construction of identity in old age. This interpretation is underscored further by the presence of three unifying themes revealed in these case studies. These common themes are a concern with the intergenerational transmission of experience, a fascination with precise, remembered detail, and a search for a continuous sense of self within the discontinuous experiences of work and retirement.

DIRECT DEPICTIONS OF WORK EXPERIENCE

John Hartter reluctantly retired ten years ago, at the mandatory retirement age, after working for twenty-nine years as a water use inspector. However, he says he "never really retired, mentally, from the job." In his papier-maché sculptures, Hartter relives unresolved past experiences, provides a detailed recollection of the job scene, and uses humor to come to terms with the indignities and disappointments of his former occupation. In one sculpture, Hartter shows a startled inspector turning on his flashlight to read a water meter and suddenly confronting a huge water bug, crawling up over the side of the meter and covering most of the dial. Another (see figure 1) shows the same inspector on his knees, on newspapers, struggling to read a meter wedged behind a toilet in a cramped, dirty public restroom. In Hartter's sketches, water meter readers are also shown crouched in basement crawl spaces, fending off cobwebs and standing in flooded basements up to their seats in water. Despite the difficulties faced by his inspectors, in the sculptures and drawings, they always appear clean and neat; projecting a presentable appearance on the job was always one of Hartter's concerns.

On another implicit level, this sculpture showing the awkward placement of the meter (originally located behind a high-tank water closet, the top of which is used as a flower container) protests a Taylor-like time-discipline schedule requiring an assigned number of meters to be read each day.[3] Water Department efforts at organizational efficiency, Hartter believes, failed to recognize the realities of flooded basements and hard-to-locate meters, and discouraged the initiative and ingenuity needed to discover unmetered water usage.

It is important to know in this context that Hartter, during his working years, devised many innovative techniques to more accurately gauge water usage. Although these efforts were highly praised, he laments that the devices were never adopted by his superiors, and that in retirement he has not been consulted on the preparation of occupational manuals for training new employees. He also laments the downgrading of required experiences and training required for the job; employees now only read meters and lack the technical expertise to investigate more complex problems. Conversations with fellow water department retirees still center on their high level of interest and expertise, in contrast to bureaucratic administrators who were indifferent to their suggestions for improvement.

A sculpture that depicts Hartter's reminiscences about the changes he experienced over his work life (see figure 2) is entitled "The Rewards of Seniority." In this sculpture, a heavyset, pipe-smoking, overall-suited master mechanic oversees a scrawny young

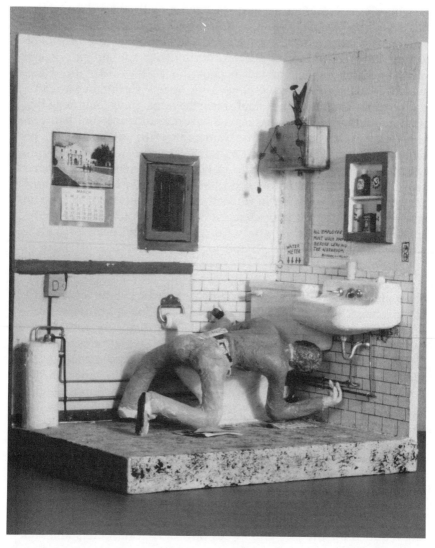

Figure 4.1. A Difficult Meter Reading. John Hartter, artist. Nancy Wells, photographer.

apprentice, who is learning to thread pipe. A kind of Norman Rockwell nostalgia is evoked as the master sympathizes with the young apprentice. Throughout Hartter's art, there is a careful concern with small detail, attesting to his patience, creativity, and playful curiosity. His concern for making things function correctly and completing a quality job are all traits which carry over from his work style and reveal the search for continuity.

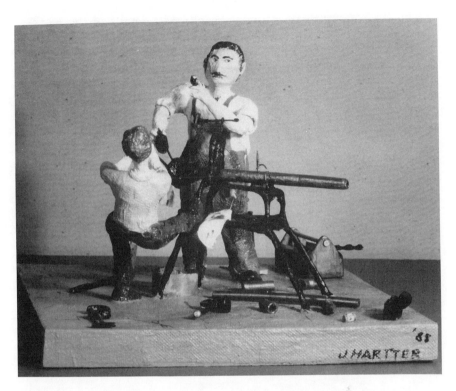

Figure 4.2. The Rewards of Seniority. John Hartter, artist. Nancy Wells, photographer.

Hartter's artistic elaborations of past occcupational events reveal his humor and the pleasure he takes in storytelling. They also bear testimony to the adaptive value of late life creativity (Butler 1967). Hartter is constantly making sketches of past unresolved events for future art projects and is thereby continually reexamining these experiences. His sculptures reveal the conflicting nature of his employment remembrances and his need to sort and integrate his memories. He recalls positively the companionship and mutual respect of fellow workers, his technical knowledge, expertise, independence in problem solving in a variety of tasks, and satisfaction in his work accomplishments. Yet he also remembers the unclean, unsafe, and difficult working conditions, and the disappointments and constraints of the bureaucratic hierarchy. The sculptures reveal his efforts to challenge and subvert these contradictory experiences through the humorous depiction of actual incidents. Careful, patient inclusion of small details of the work-site enable him to reinterpret these actual events and ambivalent feelings against his background of acknowledged competence and sense of mastery in urban water systems, and also against his newly demonstrated skill in artistic expression.

Ike Waksenbaum's sculptures reveal a parallel effort to reestablish dignity despite a distasteful job and to justify his life work as an exterminator as having value and honor. In one piece (see figure 3), Waksenbaum's miniaturized pest control operator, dressed in a cutdown version of Waksenbaum's own former uniform, holds a metal canister of insecticide at the ready. Waksenbaum describes this sculpture:

> The pest control operator is **power.** He can do a lot of things. He can go into an apartment, he can get the master keys to everyplace he wants to go. You have to be loyal, trusty too. And they need you. It's one of the headaches at the Housing Authority, the pest. The superintendent calls you in and he says, "Please help me, do something." They respect this department very much. The exterminator really does a hell-of-a-good job. Pests are an emergency. This is like a statue of my years I was with this department and I'm proud.

To deal with the difficult task of artistically depicting the concept of "pest control" and the irony of making art from killing, Waksenbaum created an enlarged papier-maché waterbug and then placed a miniaturized man on its back (see figure 4). The rider attempts to control the creature by reining the bug's antennae just as a rodeo cowboy might try to ride and control a bucking bronco.

Waksenbaum employs images of potency and utility to counteract and transform the stigma of his past employment and to justify engaging in this "dirty" work to earn a living. In relating his life history, Waksenbaum recounted being part of a select group chosen to go to Washington to rid the White House of rats. Again he proudly associates himself with power, utility, and competence in order to cope with internalized and societal ambivalence about the nature of his past work.[4]

A third artist, Jacob Lasher, who retired due to disability after thirty-eight years as a cutter in the textile industry, now sews "yarn paintings" that depict his beloved cutting and sewing rooms in a textile factory. Like Hartter, he has found difficulty in retiring mentally from the job:

Figure 4.3. Dedicated to Retired Exterminators. Ike Waksenbaum, artist. Nancy Wells, photographer.

You can't just stop what you were doing for thirty-eight years and quit cold. I did like working in the factory because I was never set up for office work. I had to be active and see something that I'd done and accomplish something. I was a cutter. I would see the garment go through and I had that feeling.

Figure 4.4. Riding and Controlling the Bugs. Ike Waksenbaum, artist. Nancy Wells, photographer.

Lasher's pictures are mythologized, generalized remembrances of a job he was forced to leave because of his disability and because of changes taking place in the textile industry. He recalls:

Figure 4.5. The Workers' Advancement: Inside View of Factory (Unionized) Cutting Room. Jacob Lasher, artist. Nancy Wells, photographer.

The union's wonderful as far as I was concerned. But then things started happening. Little by little the line fell out, and imports, and going into automation took a lot of the work away. And then we had to make in seven months what another person made in a year. Things stated falling off and it wasn't good. Automation came in and the imports ruined us, took a big bite out of the industry.

Lasher's pictures are memory paintings of a time when both he and the textile industry were strong and healthy. These positive images of his past help him deal with the late life losses of disability, illness, and forced retirement. Interestingly, there are no human figures in his cutting room scene (see figure 5). It is an image of work tables, machinery and bolts of cloth, empty of human workers. In this piece, Lasher has created a textile world romanticized for all time, for in it there are no mortals who can become disabled, die, or be laid off.

Work images also inform the artistic productions of Clara Johnson, whose family migrated from the rural southern countryside to the urban North.[5] As a result of this odyssey, Johnson was

Figure 4.6. The Johnson Family, Brooklyn, Year 1940. Clara Johnson, artist. Nancy Wells, photographer.

forced to deal with dramatic economic changes and the resultant feelings of discontinuity and disjuncture (Elder 1982). Her first memory paintings, for example, show her family and neighbors working on the farm where she grew up in South Carolina.

Another Johnson painting (see figure 6) shows the family and children in the kitchen of the Brownsville apartment where they lived for fourteen years after moving to New York City. Like Hartter's sculptures, her pictures are precisely remembered and her patient inclusion of exact details allows her to relive, not merely recall, her memories. This domestic scene of women's work reveals her pride in the fulfillment of her adult role as mother of her own family as she sits, resting, near the water heater in the lower right-hand corner. The presence of both her elderly mother (upper left corner) and her own young children suggests an intergenerational continuity that prevailed despite environmental dislocation.

In a third painting (see figure 7), Johnson shows herself in her urban work role as a hospital reception clerk. She recalls:

Figure 4.7. Work Day at the Hospital. Clara Johnson, artist. Nancy Wells, photographer.

I worked in the hospital for seventeen years. I was a desk clerk, the first person when you walk in, throwing the questions and everything at your face. That was me.

All Johnson's years of experience in the hospital are distilled in this one painting. She places herself in the center at the reception desk with all of the hospital equipment around her in the halls: a gurney, carts, oxygen tanks, wheelchairs. At the top of the painting, rooms filled with patients multiply into the distance.

The sequence of Johnson's paintings reveal her review of past life experiences. She depicts herself engaged in various types of work in different locational contexts and at different phases of her family's domestic cycle: her life as a daughter in the South, raising her children as a young wife and mother in New York City while caring for her elderly mother, and as a widow going out to work in an urban hospital after her husband's death. These pictures form a visual life review, and reveal Johnson's search for coherence and effort to develop a sense of continuity of self and family through the storytelling details of her paintings. Her life transitions are depicted in terms of interrelated changes in work status and family relations under different landscapes.

As occupational sociologist Rosabeth Moss Kanter reminds us, work and family are too often seen by social scientists as "separate worlds." Kanter notes that there is a myth that "in a modern society work life and family constitute two separate nonoverlapping worlds, with their own functions, territories, and behavioral rules" (Kanter 1977:7–8). Mrs. Johnson's pictures bring these two domains together and reveal how work and family careers are mutually interlinked through the individual life cycle and as generation succeeds generation, all within the context of changing historical conditions (Hareven 1978, 1982b; Elder 1978; Kleinberg 1983).

Johnson's paintings, such as one of her childhood school, are also meant to instruct her grandchildren about her past and to convey to them specific, significant experiences and places of her life. Her biography is made legitimate through the visual depiction of her reminiscences, which are viewed, enjoyed and cherished by her family as well as by fellow senior center members (Breytspraak 1984). We may say that Johnson's self-appointed task of guiding the next generation is similar to Hartter's desire to author training manuals. Johnson, like Hartter and many other retired folk artists, fulfills the Eriksonian task of generativity—to establish and guide the next generation—as she assumes in her art the traditional role of the elder as repository and preserver of memories and traditions and as "teacher of the lessons of experience to future generations" (Coleman 1974). Her paintings are both a legacy for her grandchildren and a desire for continuity beyond her own life span. As Myerhoff notes, "one means of anticipating death and reconciling oneself with it, is to create memorials for those who remain behind" (Myerhoff 1978:115).

CONTINUITY OF TECHNIQUE AND MEDIUM

The creations of a second group of artists reveal a continuity of medium and/or technique with their former occupations. Their art may be interpreted as an effort to cope with their present social position as retired workers, even more than with any ambivalnce they may have toward their past work roles.

Carlo Bergomi uses the same techniques he employed as a master pastry chef to create, in ceramic, wedding cakes covered

Figure 4.8. Three-Tiered Wedding Cake. Carlo Bergomi, artist. Nancy Wells, photographer.

with roses (see figure 8), grape-enclustered vases and china baskets like those he once made from caramelized sugar. He says of the cake sculpture, "This I worked on like it was a piece of dough; I did it the same way as I used a piece of dough."[6]

Bergomi has achieved stature from peers at his senior center because of these unique creations. His trade skills as a pastry chef-cum-ceramicist clearly impress both members and staff. By continuing to employ the techniques that connect him both physically and psychologically to his past work as a pastry chef and cake finisher and baker, Bergomi has maintained the coherent sense of self, based on technical mastery, he achieved throughout his occupational career. In our consumer society, where older people who do not contribute productively are often looked down upon, Bergomi, now in his eighties, has maintained esteem by continuing the creative skills which link him to his productive past and to the time before Sara Lee and Entenmann's.

Isadore Tolep, in his drawings of trees, deals with a similar psychological problem: that of coping with the social devaluation that occurs at retirement, when individuals are seen as ending their useful productive life and experiencing the onset of dependency and physical and mental debilities (Luborsky 1987). In advanced industrial society, time is fragmented in relation to age and work, and the elderly are cut off from productive roles and made to feel socially irrelevant and incompetent (Östör 1984).

Tolep, who retired as the manager of a large knitting mill, describes himself as "the head man," the person to whom all the employees used to turn, and as someone with a thorough knowledge of knitting machines, who could fix any section that broke down. He also excelled as a colorist and designer of children's sweaters. In coloring, he says, "I was one of the best there was." Yet when queried about the possible continuities in technique and skills between his art and thiry-five years in knitting, Tolep snapped, "Forget about my work. That's over."

Nonetheless, an examination of his art reveals that his drawing line (see figure 9) simulates a knitted stitch, and the bands of color which stripe his drawings echo the stripes on the children's sweaters he once designed.

Tolep now concentrates on drawing trees, and is disarmingly frank about his feelings of mastery. Proudly pointing out his excellence in the coloration of trees, Tolep rephrases Joyce Kilmer: "I think my trees are as good as anybody can make a tree."

On a second interview, when greater trust had been established, Tolep confessed deep feelings of loss on retirement—loss of position, of work associates, of a sense of mastery, and of social and occupational status. The death of his wife soon after his retirement was an added blow. But now, having achieved public recognition of his art work, Tolep has regained a sense of self-pride and group worth: "When I ran my mill, I was the head man. I was somebody. Now people tell me my trees are as good as anybody can make a tree." It took Tolep ten years to reconstruct this sense of self-assurance.

For both Tolep and Bergomi, the process of achieving social validation and integrity of self-concept after loss of work roles at retirement has been accomplished in two ways: through continued use of work-related skills, and through the recognition of peers.

For older folk artists, as for all artists and workers, it is not only achievement in one's own job or career, but public recognition that enables the individual to build self regard. Just as the verbalized life review is often greatly facilitated by the guidance of an

Figure 4.9. Trees. Isadore Tolep, artist. Doris Francis, photographer.

empathetic listener, a witness who legitimates the meaning of the life story being recreated, so the visually constructed life reviews of older artists require similar validation in public exhibition where their autobiographic creations can be viewed and acknowledged by an audience. Such community exhibitions also give public recognition to the retiree for continuing to realize the American work-related values of productivity, achievement, competition, and pride in performance.

Louis Bernstein, a retired printer who lives alone in a windowless basement apartment, ingeniously arranges for his own public recognition.[7] Bernstein continues his lifelong love of paper and printing by constructing sculptures from scraps of paper; the tinfoil from cigarette packs, cream cheese wrappers, and the styrofoam trays from home-delivered Meals on Wheels are typical materials. His art utilizes favored techniques from the complete inventory of printing skills he has mastered: scoring, embossing, and typesetting. To combat a lack of public standing and recognition, Bernstein links himself to personages of transcendent power, authority, and historical significance by creating silver and gold

Figure 4.10. Queen Elizabeth's Crown. Louis Bernstein, artist. Martha Cooper, photographer.

replicas of the crowns worn by Queen Elizabeth, (see figure 10) the Pope, Haile Selassie, the Czar of Russia, and so forth. He describes the consuming transcendent nature of his work process:

> Since I came here, I was alone. If I didn't do that, I couldn't stay here, because this kept me busy. Sometimes I would start maybe six, seven in the evening, you know, after I had supper.

So I'd stop and look, "Oh my God, it's seven in the morning!" I didn't even know the night passed me by, because when I did it, I put everything in me. Everything in me to make my artwork to be a perfection. If it's not perfection, I don't want to do it.

Extending the traditional use of paper for correspondence, Bernstein also executes small, three-dimensional sculptures which he has mailed to Princess Grace of Monaco, former President Reagan, and other luminaries, on occasions of birthdays or in cases of accident or illness. He notes:

When the Queen sees my art work, does she know it comes from a tray of chicken, that it comes from an egg carton?[8]

In exchange for these paper sculptures, Bernstein's mailbox is filled with calligraphed thank-you notes, written on engraved stationery and sealed with elegant stamps. "Dear Mr. Bernstein, I am commanded by the Queen to thank you for your beautiful handmade card." Bernstein has achieved through his paper sculptures his own social recognition and the reflected appraisals of a special audience.

SUMMARY AND CONCLUSIONS

To summarize the seven case studies just described, all of the artists deal with the theme of continuity as they struggle through the making of artifacts to establish an intergrated sense of self against the discontinuous experiences of work and retirement. In their folk art creations, these artists self-consciously document and display their own interpretations of themselves, and thereby achieve a sense of coherence and recognition of the self over time (Myerhoff 1984). Their concern with precise detail and careful techniques echoes back to past work environments and skills, and thereby links them both physically and psychologically to former work places and work roles. The display of these work-related artifacts evokes acknowledgement and recognition for their achievements similar to that formerly provided by work peers; it also demonstrates their continuing need to transmit learned work knowledge and experience to successors thereby forging links to future generations. As the transmitters of memories, experiences and traditions, they integrate working praxis with intergenerational obligations. Their autobiographic, aesthetic statements reveal how past work roles and skills are interpreted to form a significant component in the reconstruction of a continuous sense of self-identity in retirement.

It is useful here to link this discussion to the literature on the alienation of the worker in industrial society (Harper 1987; Burawoy 1979; Noble 1979; Heilbroner 1975; Braverman 1974; Sennett and Cobb 1972). In case studies, anthropologists and folklorists have examined how employees in repetitive, dehumanizing routines also manipulate occupational materials and techniques to gain autonomy in their work lives (Jones 1984b), to counteract alienating conditions and to overcome feelings of powerlessness, meaninglessness, isolation, and self-estrangement (Blauner 1964). Some workers in automotive and steel plants, for example, produce "homers"—aesthetic creations made secretly from workplace materials and tools, such as chess sets made from bolts and nuts, jewelry from paint drippings, or knives from scrap steel (Lockwood 1984). This covert, extra-occupational activity allows workers to foster self-definition at the worksite by taking control of their leisure time—breaks, lunch, after-hours, or often just the few seconds gleaned from perfection of a job skill technique. Work is no longer just a job, and leisure a significant activity done away from the worksite. Rather, work and leisure are integrated as the workers strengthen their own identities through their creative participation in the occupation and thereby gain a more positive self-perception. The appreciative response and assistance from fellow workers add to the sense of accomplishment and social integration.

The retired workers discussed above have similarly employed forms of aesthetic expression as a resource to enable them to better control their lives in the work and retirement setting of the twentieth century. During their working lives, they experienced the rapid transformation of industrial processes and the decline of their traditional trades with the substitution of new processes and materials (Braverman 1974). Now, with the emergence and institutionalization of retirement, they must also cope with their own economic marginalization and social devaluation (Phillipson 1982). Often, too, they retired reluctantly. In industrial society, there is a sharp discrepancy between individual capacity and cultural/legal definitions of age (Myerhoff 1984). They and their work experience have become outmoded, redundant. It is within this context that the necessary autobiographical tasks of the later years and the formulation of a coherent sense of self must be achieved. They must also control and organize their increased free time according to their own inclinations (Guillemard 1982). In their autobiographical representations, these retirees exploit their past occupational roles and skills as a resource for adjusting to this post-work period. In making art, they challenge ambivalent feelings and subvert memories about conflicting past work experiences and strengthen and reaffirm their identity with their former occupation. In retirement, a new integration of work and leisure is achieved; these retired workers now "work to create" (Jones 1984a).

Work is a subject which dominates their artistic autobiographies. Old age is interpreted against the context of earlier life experiences and the social conditions affecting them (Hareven 1982a). Past jobs and work roles are interpreted as a source of subjective meaning and contribute to identity reformation in old age. The accomplishments of their productive years are, for many, a source of gratification and positive self-esteem. As seen through the lens of late-life experiences, their work lives include pride in performance and mastery of technique, a sense of control, and a feeling that work was a means of self-expression and psychological sustenance (Harper 1987). This is their present-day account of their past occupational reality (Kaufman 1986), despite changing historical conditions and the rationalization and fragmentation of work processes. Nonetheless, questions remain concerning the implications of new work technologies and organization, and the upskilling/downskilling controversy about the changing meanings of work for the increasing numbers of older persons—both men and women—during the expanding period of retirement (Pahl 1988).

In conclusion, the processes and manifestations of reconstructing of a continuous sense of a self in retiremnt have much to contribute to our understanding of the subjective meaning of work throughout the life cycle, of the relationship between work and leisure, and of the influence of work on the other spheres of an individual's life—in this case, retirement (Phillipson 1982). Analysis of the autobiographic, visual statements of retired workers suggests an important—but untapped—resource for identifying and understanding life experiences associated with work, and for informing the debate about alienation, deskilling and the rationalization of work in capitalist society.

ROBERT McCARL

5

Exploring the Boundaries
of Occupational Knowledge

My subject in this paper is boundaries, specifically the boundaries that enclose, separate, and ultimately differentiate the individuals and subcultures involved in any work culture. Folklorists
have long been interested in the relationship between inter- and
intra-group lore, and I propose to elaborate on that interest in light
of current shifts in folklore theory and methodology (Limon 1983;
McCarl 1990). This approach builds on previous models of occupational folklife that stress the central importance of work technique
as a shaping force in work culture, and combines that approach
with a more Marxist, dialectical model (McCarl 1978).

One of the key tenets of Marxist analysis is that "the mode of
production in material life determines the general character of the
social, political, and spiritual processes of life" (Marx 1972
[1859]:161–162). This carries with it the explicit realization that
man's attempt to come to terms with a changeable and dynamic
universe forces him to think and act in a variety of ways over time
and space. Yet this influence of the material world on man's

thought and action is not simply deterministic, one has a multitude of technical and social options for solving these economic requirements. The dialectical relationship between the *forces* of production (the skills, arts, and techniques of work), and the *relations* of production (the social arrangements that direct the forces of production and allocate its output on and beyond the shop floor) are what I hope to explore here. My thesis is that technique performances in work culture are the primary means through which workers express themselves to knowledgeable insiders within the work group. Yet having made these essentially individual statements through technique performance, the social hierarchies within and beyond the forces of production cause the individual to seek allies and gain power through a symbolic manipulation or transformation of the social hierarchy in verbal form. Put more simply, people interact with tools and machines based on the precedents of inherited knowledge, yet their social positions within the work group may be altered through their representations of self through both work performance and narrative critiques of that performance.

I have been exploring and writing about the importance of work technique as a "shaping principle" or primary activity in work culture since the early seventies (McCarl 1974). Early in my research, I drew my theoretical approach almost directly from the shop floor, initially a sheet metal production shop in Portland, Oregon. It seemed to me then (as now) that the techniques learned and employed by welders comprised a sophisticated constellation of movements, rhythms, shortcuts and "tricks-of-the-trade" that were understandable only to insiders, almost completely unknown to management and yet responsible for the excellent piece-rate salaries commanded by these industrial craftsmen. Later work with a number of other trades led me to my fire fighting research which I continue to pursue. Yet having started from an almost microscopic appreciation for the communicative importance of work technique in the sheet metal shop, to the varying levels of skill exhibited or withheld during a fire fighting attack, I began to recognize the need for a theoretical model that placed the entire range of expressive culture (verbal arts, techniques, customs, and stylized movements) in a broader theoretical context (McCarl 1985:159–172). Current discussions regarding a more reflexive approach to ethnography have led me to an interest in better understanding a more critical approach to work culture and the following discussion is the result (Myerhoff and Ruby 1982:1–39; Marcus and Fischer 1986:137–165).

Michael Burawoy provides a number of useful insights regarding the strategic use of work technique in his book *Manufacturing Consent* (Burawoy 1979). He describes the labor process as having " . . . two analytically distinct but concretely inseparable components—a relational and practical aspect" (Burawoy 1979:15). He then extends this dichotomy into a discussion of the fetishism of commodities whereby workers extend their practical experience of the forces of production into a combination of real and imagined social relations between people as people and people as fellow commodities in the capitalistic system (Burawoy 1979:16–18). Perhaps most importantly for this discussion, he then makes the following assertion:

> Lived experience presents what is socially produced as 'natural' and beyond human control. It is unaffected by knowledge and the consciousness individuals carry. It makes no difference whether the occupant of a place in production be Karl Marx, John Rockefeller, or Joe Hill, the fetishism of commodities will be equally real to all (Burawoy 1979:17).

To make this approach more complete we need to step outside of the worker's perspective to carefully examine our own role in observing and documenting these skill and narrative performances. If we as researchers are as bound by this combination of the real and the imagined labor process, how does it affect our occupational culture? Robert Heilbroner states that it is the job of the dialectical observer to discover distortions in social and political life so that our systematic misconceptions can be traded to see essences where previously we saw only appearances (Heilbroner 1980:61–67). At the same time, Jose Limon urges folklorists to "understand folklore as a conditional expressive repertoire of residual and emergent practices" (Limon 1983:48). I will discuss these issues by examining two occupational narratives: the first by a black fire fighter and the second by a female fire fighter in the city of Washington, D.C. I will conclude with some preliminary observations concerning the impact that a more dialectical approach can have within a specific work group.

The accounts given here were collected as part of a National Endowment For the Arts-Folk Arts-funded study of fire fighters in Washington, D.C. The project (conducted 1979–1980) concluded with the publication of a booklet ("Good Fire/Bad Night") that was distributed to the fire fighters through Local 36, the District of Columbia Fire Fighters Union. A subsequent monograph based on this material was published in 1985 by the Smithsonian Institution Press (McCarl 1985). The primary focus of the project was ethnohistorical. I was attempting to document work traditions in a changing urban occupation, return that documentation to the fire fighters themselves and assist them in using my findings as the basis for community dialogue.

The first account provided here is narrated by a black technician (tillerman on a truck) with ten years on the job at the time of the interview. The setting is a study room in a quiet corner of the fire house and the context is somewhat tense in that I was working for the white-run local, and this narrator was active in the opposing black fire fighters association:

Mc: What's your major concern about the department today?

B: I think that my biggest beef on the job is that some . . . somehow or another it just seems like that the officers, it's something about officers. Now I was in the service myself and I had men under me, and its just now something that seems like, the officers, not all officers, it seems like some officers in the fire department I don't like the way they handle things.

Mc: Handle authority?

B: Yeah, right . . . that's just like, today. We got with a guy with two stab wounds in his chest, you know? So I rush in and immediately I look at the guy . . . and apparently, I don't know maybe the ambulance guys slipped up on something or overlooked something . . . but the minute I looked at the guy I knew that the guy was in trouble. It was just a matter of time, you know, his eyes was comin' into a stare . . . it was glossy. I looked at his chest, his chest (takes quick breath) just every now and then, you know. And I felt his pulse and his pulse was very weak. And immediately I looked up and said, "Al, call in a code," you know right away, because I knew that was the first thing to do. Two stab wounds in the chest—should have already been called in. But I don't know what the ambulance was doing before we got there, maybe it was already called in, I don't know. So it just so happened that the hospital was waitin' on us when we got there, they had the whole team. And the guy went out in the back . . . he stopped breathin right in the back of the ambulance, they was workin' on him back there. And then when I came back at the house, the sergeant tell me don't do that again. I said, "Don't do what?" He said, "I'm in charge on the scene. Don't you call in no code." I said, "But sergeant, it was a factor of life or death . . . " So I told the sergeant that and he said it don't matter, from now on he calls in all codes. So that's the kind of thing I think about now between officers and me and it seems tougher here in a company like 8 Engine, almost all black with new white officer like the sergeant we got now.[1]

This account illustrates simply the narrator's evaluation of his individual performance. All fire companies develop shortcuts and cooperative techniques that allow them to act quickly in emergency situations. The narrator's suggestion to Al, the wagon driver, that he call in a code is just such an example. Looking more closely at the depiction of technique, however, we also see that the actions of the other members of the company, the truck man, bar man, hook, and so forth, are disregarded. This focus on self is typical of fire experience stories and it reflects a concentration on the specific division of labor within a fire company (the driver recalls the traffic, the bar man the lock, etc.) while it also reflects only imperfectly the complexity of these performances and the momentum these acts give to all of the other expressive forms in the culture. Individual actors are recognized as such when they call attention to themselves or the flow of the attack is interrupted, but otherwise they become their assigned specialty: Haligan bar, hook, tiller, and so on.

Immediately following this and most technique performances (the practiced efficiency of calling in a code and transporting the victim to the hospital) the narrator is confronted with social considerations that force him to characterize and locate his performance along a variety of rhetorical lines. Having accomplished what he and the other members of this predominantly black company feel is a good job, he must subvert his narrative about the action by addressing his lack of attention to the chain of command, and more importantly, his failure to defer to the wishes of a new white officer. He is a black fire fighter in a predominantly white, male fire department, run by a black fire chief in an ethnically polarized city, and he has some interesting choices when it comes to verbally depicting this technique performance. He could tell it at the black fire fighters' association meeting as an example of discrimination; to a fire fighter of any race or sex as an example of the perversity of officers; or to a folklorist as an illustration of how polarized the races have become in the department. My point here is that the story provides the narrator with a variety of opportunities to rhetorically move across group boundaries within the culture but actual technique performance itself remains knowable and useful only in highly restrictive ways (Fernandez, 1979:39–60). To state this another way, the oppositional quality of verbal art to symbolically transform social relations is limited only by the creativity and abilities of the narrator; while the oppositional quality of the technique performance is simply no performance at all or a partial performance used to make an overtly oppositional statement. As trade unions learned long ago, the only true weapon that workers have is to collectively withdraw their labor and knowledge as a vehicle for change.

One cannot negotiate a social position at the work face of a job, he or she either knows it and does it (thereby participating in the forces of production), or does not. Both the relational and instrumental dimensions of the labor process (to use Burawoy's terms) form the basis for judging the appropriateness of individual work action, but the performance of the techniques themselves provide little if any opportunity for secondary, symbolic interpretation. They are, as Bateson terms them, "primary process" (Bateson 1972:130–131), and as such they provide a very limited opportunity for misinterpretation. As discussed below, this is not the case with regard to the narrative performances which characterize these work actions.

My second story was narrated by a woman fire fighter who had been in the department less than a year when I interviewed her. She had been forced to sue the department to finally gain entry into the training academy and although she was very open in our conversation, she was also very much aware of who had employed me to do the study and what I was up to in my project:

S: I think that the only way they would feel that you are a great fire fighter is if you go in and single-handedly brought out ten people at one time and lost both arms and legs then they'd talk about it. But if you go, just go in and do your job, just like they're goin' in and doin' their job, then that's not good enough for them, you gotta be great. And of course they pat each other on the back all the time. Build up each other's egos. . . . First time we had a fire, and it took a few fires for them to find out I could carry my weight, for them to at least settle down a little bit. While at first a lot of them just ignored me as if I wasn't here, and I know it was because they didn't know what to say to me: "What on earth am I gonna say to this woman?" So they just chose to pretend I wasn't here. But they settled down a little bit and I think that when they found out that they won't die because of me, you know, and that it doesn't make that much difference that I'm a woman, you know, the company's still run the same.

We've had a couple of second alarms. We had a fire at the GSA building, that was a second alarm . . . it was a lot of people pushing and shoving, that's the main thing I can remember. I hadn't been in the company that long. This is not something; fire fighting is not something that you walk into the fire house today, and tomorrow you say you like it. It might take years before you can actually get to the point where you can say you really like your job. It took me three months before I really understood what was happening, you know, what everything was that was going on and then things started to fall into place for me. I . . . know . . . a lot of guys coming back from the fire . . . said I was scared especially at the GSA fire because that was really a bad one. I didn't have the experience because for one thing I really didn't know what was going on. All I knew was that I was following the people that was in my company. I was doing what I was told to do. We put the fire out. We all had our masks on, so that wasn't a problem. And I was always with someone so I was never frightened of being alone or not knowing where to go. Ah, it was very hot, and we were holdin' on to each other's coattails. And I didn't get very frightened. I mean I probably would have had I known how bad it was. But I didn't.[2]

This account underscores the primacy of technique by its virtual absence. Unlike hundreds of fire accounts collected in this project, this narrative reveals the narrator's tremendous frustration concerning the reasons for her lack of informal knowledge. Unlike black and white male fire fighters, there is no female fire fighting tradition from which she can gain informal support. In cities across the country, women are creating an emergent work tradition that reflects a cultural isolation almost unimaginable to outsiders. Women in the fire service must perform life-threatening techniques that can only be learned through experience and informal critique, yet they are continually denied access to that body of knowledge while they are judged as if they had it. Although women have entered the relations of the work culture, in order to enter the culturally determined forces of production, they must master the complex skills of this trade almost totally on their own.

The oppositional narratives exchanged by women fire fighters not only counter the daily barrage of sexist language, cartoons, physical harassment, and even clothing of the trade with verbal style and wit, but also have resulted in an emerging female subcultural perspective toward this previously all-male culture and its techniques that is just taking shape. Perhaps most importantly, this example illustrates that the tension between the conservative techniques of work and the many layers of social hierarchy that interpenetrate those processes create ideological struggles of some complexity on the shop floor itself. The ethnic, gender, generational, and even regional subcultures of the work force may negotiate ideological and social positions in the union hall or grievance hearing room, but the demands of work technique on the shop floor return each and every worker to the instrumentalities of work. As Burawoy states:

> The production of things is simultaneously not only the production and reproduction of social relations but also the production of an experience of those relations. As men and women engage in production, they generate a world of appearances (Burawoy 1979:16).

One might add, that ethnographers and documentors of work culture are also locked within this "imaginary" world since our work is no less affected by the capitalistic system and its continual commodification of human creativity. Perhaps the greatest challenge we face is the continual reexamination and articulation of the results of this process on our lives and our relationships with the people we "study".

The accounts given above provide opportunities for rhetorical movement because they combine a recognition of the importance of material considerations, while they also depict those technical concerns in social terms. These narratives aren't war stories ("There I was trapped between the fire and certain death"), nor are they simply complaints about racial or sexual discrimination. They represent a tension between the technical and social demands of fire fighting that links the physical constraints of work with the more visible and manipulable human universe in which it is judged. The stories are important as products of performance, yet we lose sight of their wider importance if we neglect to see them as vehicles for change. Even though that change itself is narrowly constrained by our present economic system, we as professional researchers continue to describe people (informants) and human processes (performances) in objectified, empirical terms that have little to do with day-to-day life.

Folklorists have often documented the emergence of social structure in work techniques—the fool's errand assigned to the hapless apprentice sent for a nonexistent tool is the most common genre (Hand 1942:143–144). Yet this view of work culture is primarily normative—it reflects a perception of lore as a stabilizing influence that recognizes but doesn't respond to change. We are probably closer to cultural reality when we view work culture not as a superorganic entity, but as a human experience made up of actions and thoughts inherited from the past that are in constant dialectical relationship with those of the present. The sediment of past experience and the contexts in which it was and is judged provide points of reference against which (using the fire service as an illustration) Mason and Catholic, Protestant and Jew, Irish and Italian, black and white, and now male and female workers attempt to rhetorically adjust social reality to technical demands (McCarl 1985:95–112). There are, however, additional contexts in which these movements will be interpreted. I will turn my attention to these contexts to conclude this paper.

A retired fire chief once suggested that I view a fire house as a microcosm of its city and neighborhood—no better and no worse. And just like an all white neighborhood that has been newly integrated, the department as a whole carries on its daily business while extremists on both sides try to settle cultural conflict through various legal and illegal means. Behind the surface of these seemingly irreconcilable differences is a core of leaders who maintain informal control of the forces of production at the level of technique performance. These leaders seek out and find covert ways to tap the interests and energies of their subcultural constituents through oppositional narrative, compromise, and sometimes simple dishonesty. It is their ability to know and be able to manipulate the various limits within which knowledge can be brokered between subcultures that keeps the department from simply exploding. Affirmative action and sexual harassment charges may be formally adjudicated in the courts, but unless and until these various subcultures and their respective leaders come to informal terms with these issues, they will continue to provide the basis of most intercultural contact within the work setting. The irony in the fire service is that technological change (high rise buildings, subways, toxic, and nuclear chemical disasters) are forcing the development of new techniques at a rate faster than even the best training can accommodate. This two-ended candle will continue to burn until informal leaders become a part of the urban decision-making process or until a major catastrophe with serious loss of life illustrates how willingly we place material over human concerns.

A folklorist or historian entering this culture in order to document and present it to outsiders should realize the glacial nature of change in a work environment. There are no quick fixes for any of the cultural conflicts and issues involved, and perhaps the most useful role we can play is to document the folklore resulting from conflicts between residual and emergent traditions without compromising the covert strategies of informal control in the culture. We cannot adequately characterize the actual performance of work technique, which ensures its informal control, since technique is a primary process only knowable to the actor in action, but we can, however, provide a historical context within which current conflicts can be perceived against a temporal background of parallel confrontations that have been overcome and which contribute to the current manifestation of the culture. The oppositional narratives told by black and women fire fighters are socially revolutionary because they challenge the white, male status quo. Beneath this relational conflict, however, is a technical tradition that only partially responds to these social pressures, if at all. As documenters we must strive to depict both the social flux and the mutable aspect of this dialectic. If we anticipate a static picture of culture or history, we misrepresent the essence of this world, portraying it in oversimplified and normative terms.

In conclusion, I think that a dialectical view of folklore, one which examines informally passed communication generated from technical activity evaluated through a variety of subcultural audiences, has the potential for reinforcing the humanistic tradition of our fields. It may also provide us with a better appreciation of the political implications of our research.

Returning to the examples cited above, the broader question or essence that lies behind our misconceptions about this culture begins with our perception of who fights fire in our society. A fire fighter is paid to put his or her life on the line to protect life and property. Yet in Washington, D.C., the last two fire fighters who died in the line of duty were killed in an abandoned warehouse and an abandoned adult theater—neither of which had sprinkler systems. As city governments cut corners by closing companies or buying cheaper equipment, merchants refuse to adhere to the most basic fire codes, and the public denies fire fighters the right to strike or even voice complaints about working conditions, we need to ask ourselves what these insights tell us about our own cultural values. Are things more important than people, and if so, should we be reinforcing this materialist view of culture or history by further objectifying cultural members in our books, films, and academic articles? Or can we help to abolish these distortions of reality and stereotype to penetrate to the cultural dynamism beneath the surface?

In partial answer to this question, we might look to the tension between the forces and relations of production in our various disciplines. It is too easy to be manipulated by powerful members of social hierarchies who have only their own political or economic agendas in mind. Union leaders, managers, government and private granting agencies, and academic or public bureaucracies can never know the realities of the forces of production at the workplace experienced by insiders, but they can profit from insights we might provide them in our attempt to depict the insider's point of view. Perhaps we need to work closely and long enough with cultural members to be trusted by an informal leadership who we recognize as existing in the tensions between emergent and residual traditions. The technique performances of black and women fire fighters, for example, will become a part of the collective residue of experience in that culture. The narratives and emergent forms of expression that will cause that change through an opposing perspective, however, provide us with a challenge to perceive cultural expression not as our employers would like it to be, but as it really is. Now that we have recognized the power of folklore and ethnography to change culture as well as preserve it, we have to accept our responsibilities as participants rather than passive observers in the struggle. Objectivity is an illusion we will no longer be allowed to entertain as the people we study demand an increasingly active role in the images of their lives and work that we present. Each time I walk into the fire house in Washington, D.C., the first question is, "What do you want this time?" My answer must honestly depict the product I want to make of their lives, the reasons why I am making it, and a damn good justification for their involvement.

6

Eating Out of One Big Pot: Silk Workers in Contemporary China

The silk weaving shop was kept dim so that weavers could discern any mistakes in the weave. Shades covered the tall windows of the cavernous room to block the glare of the sun, and only one bright bulb hung down over each loom. These iron jacquard looms were oddly beautiful in the dimness, with the rows of bulbs throwing off a shimmery light onto the thousands of fine silk yarns in the warp. But the deafening cacophony of shuttles pounding furiously back and forth across several hundred looms kept weavers' attention on their production quotas. Most weavers hovered over the four looms each of them must watch, to change the weft bobbin or fix a broken yarn. They stayed during their meal times, eating beside their looms to meet their quotas. The men and women in the Number One Weaving Shop were especially burdened because they wove the most intricately patterned of the silk quilt covers ubiquitously used in marriage dowries. Fixing a mistake could take hours, even with the help of the shift leader. Still, some of the young male weavers, inveterate chain smokers, took regular cigarette breaks in the tiny office off the shop floor, which also offered some respite from the noise. Weavers sometimes wandered briefly over to another area of the shop, to visit a friend. One machine repairer liked to flirt with the young women weavers, as did the floor sweeper, who tried to get them to go dancing in the evenings at the newly opened dance clubs.

Quotidian life of the mid-1980s in this silk weaving factory of Hangzhou, an east-central coastal city that serves as China's silk capital, has been fundamentally transformed by the recent "imaginary," or symbolic vision, of economic development in China known as "economic reform." Formulated beginning in 1978, this vision of reform that the party-state has instituted has one essential goal in urban industries: raising workers' productivity. No longer portrayed as the bearers of a revolutionary consciousness, workers, under the current regime, are loudly and publicly blamed for the ills to which industrial production is said to have befallen during the Cultural Revolution (1966–1976)—and implicitly during the entire Maoist era.[1]

The Cultural Revolution, I often heard during my fieldwork in China (1984–1986), had inculcated a lazy work ethic in workers. Silk industry cadres, factory managers and intellectuals from the nearby university, reflecting (and creating) dominant representations, metonymically captured this sense of laziness for me by invoking the four-character idiom *chi daguo fan,* "eating out of one big pot."

The idiom is a metaphor that resonates with notions of family. Eating out of one pot happens—literally—only within the family. To "share a stove" (or pot) in China refers to a joint household sharing both their living quarters and their food.[2] However, within the family it serves as yet another metaphor for sharing out of the family food and money pot, without a close calculation of how much each individual has contributed. Among some silk workers' families, unmarried children who had entered the silk factories had begun to give a set amount of money each month to their parents. But in most of these families, children did not directly offer cash. It was understood they would occasionally contribute goods, while their parents' support allowed them to save the necessary money to marry.

The link of finances to food within the family makes this phrase a powerful representation for work relations in China. When used to refer to factory workers, eating out of one big pot means that no matter how much or how little workers produced, they all

ate the same "food"; that is, received the same wages.[3] Those who
continued to work hard, I was told, were not given their just des-
serts, for the factories concerned themselves with the overall
amount of production but did not record how much each individual worker contributed to that production. Therefore, so the current dominating critique goes, workers learned to slack off.

The metaphor has still deeper meaning for factories. The work
unit in China has, until recently, operated in a fashion analogous
to the family. State-run factories hand out ration tickets for a variety of foodstuffs; factory cadres give workers permission to marry
and supplements for the newly married couple's one child; and the
factory "looks after" (*zhaogu*) elder workers prior to retirement by
transferring them to less exhausting jobs within the factory with
no reduction in pay and after retirement by providing a pension.

In changing the organization of production under economic
reform, state bureaucrats and factory managers have simultaneously reinterpreted these meanings of work that are embedded in
the labor process. The current reform attempts to abolish this phe-
nomena of eating out of one big pot is simultaneously a move to
restructure relations within work units from family-like interactions to ones based on impersonal measurement, rules, and regulations. In criticizing workers for eating out of one big pot, the state
has argued that work should now be understood in terms of "productivity." State bureaucrats and factory managers now hope to instill in workers a disciplined[4] approach to work through the
institution of new, hierarchical wage and bonus systems, with differential rewards and punishments.[5]

To understand the changing labor process in China under
economic reform, it is necessary to understand this complexity of
cultural representations of work and how these meanings are inextricably tied to everyday practice. One cannot separate the labor
process, or organization of production, or divisions of labor—call
it what you will—from the cultural meanings through which
workers and managers come to construct their significance.[6] For
"productive inequalities"[7] do not stand apart from human consciousness and agency, as a congealed set of determinate structures. One discerns this interconnection most vividly through
attention to historical shifts in these representations as they are
embedded in the organization of production. Thus, my argument
focuses on the contrast between the Cultural Revolution and economic reform.[8]

This essay addresses current social relations of production in
China's urban industry by examining the cultural construction of
work in terms of productivity. In the discussion of productivity,

however, my concern is not primarily with production statistics. While statistics have their use, they fail to enlighten us about the social process through which workers have experienced these changes. Statistics taken by themselves tend to obscure the dimension of human agency and gloss over the issues that provoke the most intensity of feeling. To paraphrase the English historian E. P. Thompson, behind these seemingly objective statistics lies a complex structure of human relationships, a structure that legitimates certain types of conflicts and inhibits others (Thompson 1966:205).

My discussion of workers and productivity therefore begins with the assumption that productivity stands for something more than simply a concept self-evidently tied to measurement and quantification. More significantly, it represents a discourse on the values that the state and factory managers currently attach to what they measure, specifically on those dealing with age hierarchies, the division between mental and manual labor, and gendered work relations. Attempts to increase productivity have both refracted and given rise to a constellation of cultural meanings and practices diametrically opposed to those of earlier socialist work relations in China.[9] Moreover, this discourse, at once a social and ideological process, is one in which workers and managers have been reconstructing workers' subjectivities; that is, what it means to be a "good worker."

This process is one in which workers challenge and sometimes resist the domination of reform. Workers' contestation of production pressures stems not from mere laziness, as state cadres and factory managers would have it, but from their experience of past practices, the memory of which serves to raise serious questions about the state's current fixation with productivity.[10] Some workers continue to claim the importance of other aspects of their lives currently dismissed as hindrances to "efficiency," and in so doing, implicitly call into question whether productivity should be the exclusive goal of production.

In any analysis of China presented within a Western context, it is crucial, I feel, to emphasize ordinary people's agency in the construction of social life. Western scholars too often assume that social relations in China are a natural effect of the state's intentions. We would do well, instead, to understand contemporary China through the concept of hegemony; that is, an ongoing process of the creation of meanings and values that has to do with lived experience, the practical consciousness of everyday life and what we might call ordinary common sense. As Raymond Williams has argued of this Gramscian concept, hegemony is a process tied to unequal power relations such that dominant discourses shape people's interpretations and practices, but they never determine them.[11] An emphasis upon hegemony also enables us to move beyond recent attempts to find "resistance" in quotidian consciousness and activity. For, if hegemony involves consent, if only partial, then one must attend to the complicated ways in which workers' practices involve both accommodation and resistance, both subversion and acceptance. These are not political positions in any simple sense, but rather constitute subjectivity as a site of intersecting, and sometimes contradictory, discourses.[12]

A word is in order here about the concept of socialism. The problem of how we represent the nature of socialism is inherent in the narrow focus on workers' productivity and the reintroduction of hierarchical wage systems, for these goals were criticized in the Maoist era as signifiers of the social inequality and inhumanity in socialism's theoretical opposite, capitalism. Western scholars often highlight the contradictions in the Chinese Party/state's theoretical stance, yet they rarely attend to the dichotomies within our own representations of socialism. These representations veer from socialism as the ideal solution to the human alienation of capitalist societies or, in the anticommunist rhetoric, to the hell we might end up in if we fall out of capitalist heaven.

Western Marxist scholars have long been critical of socialist governments,[13] but only recently have such scholars produced ethnographic and sociological studies of what have become known as "actually existing socialist societies."[14] These studies offer important insights. Yet they still leave us without a method for comprehending socialism and capitalism as discursive categories that people also use in meaningful and consequential ways. What do we conclude, for example, about a situation in China where the state encourages factory managers to adopt so-called capitalist methods to pursue profits but when they do so, accuses them of not having the proper socialist spirit? Capitalism and socialism clearly do not exist simply as objective social systems but as discursive categories, always ideologically construed, in countries that pride themselves on being socialist as well as in Western democracies.[15] The specific content of these categories is worked out not only on an abstract level but in the context of everyday life with its mundane problems and contradictions. Thus the meanings of socialism and capitalism in urban industry in China are not instituted from above by the state, but are currently taking on new shapes as workers and managers struggle over the new reforms. There is not space within this essay to address more than the specific context of

Chinese industry, but ultimately any examination of China should juxtapose their interpretations against ours.

EATING OUT OF ONE BIG POT

The state's determination to put an end to eating out of one big pot is a fundamental repudiation of Cultural Revolution ideology and politics. In the Hangzhou silk industry, challenges to hierarchical divisions of labor during that time (especially from 1965 to 1973) took several forms. Many, though not all, managers in the silk industry are "sent down" (*xiafang*) to work at menial jobs within the factory. Additionally, wages were frozen, and workers who started jobs in the factories were paid the same wage, regardless of their assigned job task. Finally, bonuses were nonexistent, for material rewards were considered to be a hindrance to the development of a socialist work ethic. Serious political battles broke out in the factories over these issues, battles which led to massive disruption in factory life.

Many workers were, of course, active during that period. They actively challenged managerial authority, through "speak bitterness" sessions where they humiliated managers, sometimes beating them as well. At other times, due to structural constraints in the flow of raw materials, workers did not engage in consistent production. While it is obvious, then, that workers did not remain fixed to their production positions, what makes eating out of one big pot an ideological characterization is its imputation to workers of a natural disposition towards laziness. This negative interpretation of workers' identity is above all a renunciation and inversion of Cultural Revolution class relations, in which workers held the dominant political voice in many factories, if only for a short period. It is equally a rejection of the collectivist ideal of the Maoist era, in which workers were not ranked or measured individually.

THE POSITION-WAGE SYSTEM

The new wage and bonus system, introduced into the Hangzhou silk industry in the spring of 1985, is known as the "position-wage system" (*gangwei gongzi zhi*). Designed to raise workers' productivity through differential rewards and punishments, this new system applies to workers but not to cadres and is based, not on seniority as with the old system, but on the job position or category. Jobs are divided into five main categories: (1) weaving;

(2) warp preparation; (3) weft preparation and inspection; (4) transport; and (5) miscellaneous—sweeping and machine cleaning. Weavers are in the top category and receive the highest wages, with the other categories following at a distance of five yuan from one another. Workers just entering the factory were put on this new wage scale. They did not start at the wages set for each category, however, for it will take them six and a half years to reach these wages. As for workers already at the factory, older workers above the scale will keep their original wages until retirement; those not yet receiving top wages will gradually be given raises.[16]

Bonuses for workers in the silk industry are based on piecework. After workers fulfill a set quota, which represents their basic wage, they earn the rest of their income through the bonus. Quotas are set such that workers must exceed them to make a living wage—that is, the wages for each category include the bonus. The problematic nature of the bonus portion of the wage is reflected by the fact that most workers in the silk factory say that their bonus gets deducted if they fail to reach the maximum amount rather than that they made on extra amount. The wage then actually has two components: one fixed and one variable. They label this latter portion the bonus.[17]

The position-wage system is said to be the answer to ridding factories of the phenomenon of eating out of one big pot. As such, it is cast as a way to liberate industry from the constraining political categories of the Cultural Revolution and thereby allow work to return to its so-called "natural" rhythms. Silk Corporation cadres and factory managers explain and justify the new system in the context of a wider discussion on individualism and individual responsibility now current in China. Those individuals who are willing to work hard, so the ideology goes, will get ahead. They thus present it as judging workers on an individual basis, blind to any attributes other than their productivity. However, we can see hegemony in process in this new system—hegemony as I have defined it earlier as a lived process of the production of meanings and values, tied to unequal power relations—because, if we examine the situation more closely, we can discover that the very notions of "hard work" and productivity are not neutral but are based on changing interpretations of age, status and gender.

CONTESTED DISCOURSES

Yang Zhuren,[18] a Party cadre at a state-run silk weaving factory and someone with whom I had numerous conversations, explained to me the dominant interpretation of age in relation to productivity informing the gangwei system:

> The previous system wasn't appropriate. With textile workers, when they are old, the quality of their work is not good. They say of textile workers, "They mature early, they contribute early, they deteriorate early." When someone has just entered the factory, after a few years, around twenty years old is when they produce the highest quality. But they were getting the lowest wages. It was not fair. . . .

This representation of youths as the most productive workers stands in radical opposition to the former notion that older workers, as masters (*shifu*) in their trade, should be rewarded for their knowledge and experience. In one sense, this reverence for youth reflects a more general notion prevalent in China today: that people are their most creative and can offer their greatest contributions to the advancement of society in the early years of their career.[19] There is much talk now in China of the need to "juvenize" (*qingnianhua*), to encourage older people, especially cadres who occupy leadership positions but do nothing, to step aside for more capable people stuck in junior positions. This discursive elaboration of the positive qualities of youth represents a fundamental challenge to the kind of seniority still prevalent in the Party and most workplaces. Furthermore, emphasis on the greater capacity of youths draws on an implicit assumption about a direct relationship between biology and productivity. This idea has much credibility in the present social and political milieu in which science has replaced Marxism as the theory to which people turn for answers to current dilemmas.

The new position-wage system rewards youths relative to elders in that those who entered the factory only a few years ago will receive the same wages as those who have worked in the factory for twenty or thirty years. Additionally, in the future, older workers will not receive wage increases after they have reached the top of the scale. This system, based on changing interpretations of productivity, does not simply reward individual workers who work harder as compared with their fellow workers on a one-to-one basis, as implied in the policy to end eating out of one big pot. It rewards a category of workers—youths—based on the hegemonic representation of youths as possessing a greater potential capacity to produce. That youths do not always produce more became clear when I asked one assistant director of a collective silk weaving factory which types of workers had their pay docked most frequently. She promptly replied, "Mostly it is the 'naughty' boys. After work they go out and play. They play late, so they have no energy to work the next day." But the fact that youths' actual work performance does not always reflect the current belief in their capacity has in no way diminished that belief as it becomes part of the position-wage system.

The very definition of productive in relation to age is thus going through a fundamental transformation as the new position-wage system gets put into place. But this transition is far from a straightforward process of imposing a dominant ideology onto the factories. Managers and workers in the local silk factories, through the experience of their everyday work lives, are interpreting and contesting the meaning of the new reforms. Managers in upper level positions in the factory tend to agree with the view expressed above by the Party cadre that youths are more productive. But lower level managers, such as workshop supervisors, have mixed sentiments. On the one hand, they too want to find the best way to raise productivity, which may have to mean greater incentives to youths. On the other hand, they argue with the managers above them on behalf of older workers in their shops who complain to them that their wage increases are too low in comparison with those given to the younger workers. The older workers, angered that the new system no longer recognizes seniority and thus interrupts their expected life trajectory, feel that they should be rewarded for the many years of hard work they did in their own youth.

One older worker, Yu Shifu, explained the inequities as she saw them: she had begun work in the silk factory at the age of fourteen, in the early 1950s, when the factories were first formed. She had fought to become a weaver, and had worked hard as a weaver ever since, for thirty years. In the past, older workers could transfer to less strenuous jobs without losing any wages in their last few years before retirement. She had looked forward to the job transfer to which she felt she was entitled, for she had given the factory a lot over the years, and factory management should "look after" (*zhaogu*) her. But with the new wage system, transfer to another job category means a cut in pay. This worker was upset about the changes. These new changes, she said, *xin butong* (literally, won't go through my heart; my heart won't accept them). These arguments and discussions in the factories force us to rethink the relationship between culture and economic relations: the hegemonic interpretations informing the new wage system are taking shape through the lived experience of workers, cadres, and managers that leads them to continuously interpret and contest the reforms. Generational hierarchy is not a mere idiom through which divisions of labor are constructed, but lies in the very heart of them.

In addition to the cultural category of age, the new wage and bonus system is equally infused with changing interpretations of the status of various job categories. This is especially evident in the current attempts to reinstitute weaving as a job task of higher value than prep or inspection work. Some managers now claim that the skill level and labor intensity of weaving are greater than those of these other tasks. Historically, weaving was considered a highly skilled job. But now the entire textile industry is seen as one of low skill in comparison with the more highly technological industries that have been introduced since 1978. The silk industry does not have the ring of modernization to it and in a country that wants to look modern as fast as possible, these older industries lack the flash of computers and nuclear power plants. The silk industry does, however, bring in a substantial amount of foreign currency from its export of silk. Forty percent of their production is for export.

Despite this shift in notions of skill within the broader context of industrialization, managers can justify the identification of weaving as a skilled job in the silk factories and assign it to the highest wage category because weaving takes more time to learn than prep or inspection work; it is associated with more complicated machinery; and more discrete tasks are involved in weaving than in the other jobs.

Weaving occupies the highest wage category not only because of the skill level it is now said to have relative to prep and inspection work but also because it is considered the most productive job. But its productivity is not determined by measuring and comparing the value of labor added onto the silk cloth at each stage of the production process. Rather, weaving receives higher pay because the work is said to be more "bitter" (*ku*) than the other jobs. Bitterness and suffering were once considered positive socialist epithets. Now, however, their heroic glory has faded, and few people take it as a matter of pride that they do this kind of work. In this sense, the notion of productivity is defined by the idea of bitter work.

The "bitterness" of weaving, as I learned during the time I spent at one silk weaving factory, is due to the fact that almost all mistakes found in the finished cloth are blamed on the weaver. The weaver is not necessarily always at fault, as both managers and workers readily admit, but it is too difficult to trace the mistake to any other source. In the weaving shop, an argument ensued one day between a weaver and a prep shift leader over a mistake in a piece of cloth still in the weaver's loom. The weaver insisted the mistake must have been the result of poor thread preparation, but because he was unable to convince the prep shift leader to agree with him, he had to take the loss. More than any other workers in the silk factories, weavers regularly have their pay docked for falling short of the new, more stringent quality standards. Weavers thus find themselves more burdened with responsibility for the finished cloth. In this sense, their work is more "bitter". Productivity is thus additionally defined in terms of accountability for mistakes.

Under the new wage system workers are rewarded differentially but again according to category of worker and not merely according to individual effort. A particular prep worker, for example, could conceivably work harder, in terms of actual job performance, than a particular weaver, even though the latter's task is considered more bitter than the former's. The new wage system is about inducing workers to work harder, but based on categories constructed from changing interpretations of, in this case, status. "Skill" and "productivity" are not transparent economic categories that are self-evident and analyzable without taking into account the ways in which they are discursively construed.

Managers and some workers agree with these changes, but other workers contest the new status relations reflected in the position wage system. At one state-run factory, I happened to walk out of the factory reception office one afternoon at the moment when the dining hall workers—about ten of them—marched into the Labor and Wages Office. I, along with several others, stood outside the window of that office and listened as these workers proceeded to berate the head of that section. Their actions amazed me, because they recalled the Cultural Revolution and therefore, I thought, would be politically dangerous. The factory director then squeezed his way into the room and they turned to berate him. Again, this contradicted everything I had read about hierarchy and the power of the Party in China. But the dining hall workers were quite angry about the new wage and bonus system just introduced into the factory. They were angry that, with this new system, they would now receive lower wages than other workers and their jobs would be of lower status because they were fixed at the low end of the pay scale. The managers responded that if they wanted higher pay they could go be weavers. The dining hall workers insisted their job deserves recognition for the hard work involved. After several hours of heated discussion, the argument finally wound down. The dining hall workers, only temporarily mollified, left the office, dispirited and dissatisfied with the results.

The dining hall workers' resistance to the dominant interpretations of the wage and bonus system stands as directly oppositional practice. Other workers have accepted the new cultural representation of themselves as in need of raising their productivity but they do not always act on it in the way the state intended. In the weaving shop of the factory I worked in, there was a thirty-one year old unmarried man named Sun who did the lowest paying and lightest job in the shop—sweeping up the garbage. He complained that his wages were scarcely enough to support him—he ate them all every month. But he had no interest in learning to be a weaver to earn higher pay. He lived with his retired parents, who gave him money for the requisite fashionable clothes and cigarettes *de rigueur* among young unmarried male workers. Quite by accident one day, I came across him selling the latest clothes from Hong Kong on the free market. Free markets have been opened since 1978 and unemployed youths are encouraged to establish what are known as "individual enterprises" (*geti hu*) in these free markets. However, workers with jobs in state-run factories are not permitted to set up individual enterprises. But this worker had struck an agreement with his shop supervisors that if he showed up for work every day they would overlook his entrepreneurial activities. His sideline enterprise nets him three times his wages in the factory, but he did it not only for the money; he liked to use his brains, he told me, and "because it lets me lead a life better than the common worker. I can eat things they can't afford to eat, and I can go places they can't go. I want to be like that." Young male workers like Sun have inculcated the state's praise for high productivity, but they have deployed these meanings in unintended ways. Their high productivity, that is, does not always go to the state. Anthony Giddens has emphasized the importance of unintended consequences of praxis for the social reproduction of relations of domination (Giddens 1979:59). These unintended consequences highlight the complexities of resistance.

The status notions informing the new wage categories among workers in the silk industry also inform the division of labor between managers and workers, a division that has become increasingly salient under the current reforms. Here too, these changing interpretations are tied to larger social processes in which "social position" as a concept has once again been given positive value in China and the social hierarchy of the Cultural Revolution has been overturned and replaced by one where intellectuals now have the most prestige. In the current milieu, where intellectual work is much more highly valued than the "mere" execution of ideas, the division between mental and manual labor has grown even greater. Yang Zhuren insisted that the differential compensation for managers and workers is based on the fact that the value of their labor is not the same. The value, or productivity, of mental labor is, however, difficult to measure. The assistant director of a collective factory—a woman I often sought out because I admired her sense of purpose about her work—told me that cadres are paid according to the "heaviness" of their responsibility. When I asked her to spell out the details of how they measured that heaviness, she replied, "For example, if the director of the factory gets Y100 . . . then the section head gets Y80." The degree of responsibility is thus decided by the job title. But no exact correlation between job title and degree of productivity can be drawn.

Prior to 1986, the differences in wages and bonuses between managers and workers were not marked, still a holdover from Cultural Revolution practices. Yet the highest reward in an office job lies, not in the wages, but in the job itself. Every worker hopes to be promoted to a desk job, where he or she no longer has to stand up all day; where everyone works only the day shift, instead of the four-shift system for production line workers (two days on day shift, two days on evening shift, two days on overnight shift, and two days of rest); and where the workload, from a worker's point of view, is significantly lighter. From worker's viewpoint, then, a manager's responsibility might be heavier, but the workload is not. Nonetheless, in the winter of 1986 a new wage and bonus system for cadres was introduced, a revision of the grade-level system (*dengji zhidu*), that will create a larger gap between the incomes of managers and workers.

These cultural interpretations of status and skill underlying the *gangwei* wage system are themselves infused with particular notions of gender. We can see this gendered interpretation of productivity through the fact that the position-wage system applies only to work increasingly considered women's work—that is weaving, prep work, and inspection work. Tasks such as machine repair and transport (truck driving) are considered skilled manual labor and are defined as men's work. The manager/worker divide also coincides with divisions of labor between men and women in the silk industry. Some women can be found in silk factory management, but the majority are men and management is becoming more of a male domain under the current reforms.

To appreciate fully the gendered implications of these new reforms, a brief review of the recent history of the silk industry and its sexual division of labor is in order. Prior to Liberation and in the first few years after the 1949 Communist Revolution, silk production in Hangzhou still took place almost exclusively in household workshops. Generally speaking, men did the weaving and ran the household business and women and children prepared the thread. In 1954 the state merged these household workshops into state-run factories. Men entered the factories with their looms and continued to do the weaving. Most of the women from these household workshops who entered the factories continued to do the prep work. A few of these women, however, struggled to become weavers. For them, it meant higher pay, a skill, and more control over their labor. One should also note that during this time, and really up to the current economic reforms, a substantial number of managers rose up from the ranks of weavers.

With the 1958 Great Leap Forward campaigns to bring more women into the workforce, and the division of tasks so that weaving and machine repair became separate jobs, women began to do more of the weaving in Hangzhou silk factories. Beginning in the 1960s, silk weaving and prep work were gradually deskilled and devalued, although the technology remained virtually unchanged during this time. Women increasingly predominated in silk production. Wages were lowered both absolutely and relative to the more prestigious industries men began to enter.

By the mid-1960s, the silk industry was experiencing a decided feminization of its workforce. This trend towards feminization of silk production work has continued apace, with a slight reversal in the period immediately after the Cultural Revolution. At that time, urban youths could inherit their parents' factory jobs as a way to return to the cities from what they viewed as their countryside purgatories. Young men entered the silk factories again. They took up jobs as weavers, machine repairmen, and transport workers. The male weavers I spoke with during their cigarette breaks laughed at my suggestion that they might ever do prep work. They said they would be too embarrassed. Their hands are too rough and they don't have the patience, they explained.

With this brief and perhaps a bit breathless jog through recent Chinese history, we should make note of two points. One is the historical contingency of the emergence of this gendered teleological division of labor. This is not a teleological tale of the evolution of functionally superior technological systems. Instead, I want to emphasize that the development of this gendered division of labor has depended on a number of background conditions, both within China and related to China's place in the world economic system, including the nationalization of industry, the initial closing of the borders to Western trade, the disastrous economic conditions after the Great Leap Forward, and the social effects of the Cultural Revolution. Secondly, the industrialization process that has shaped this gendered division of labor has not evolved according to an inner structural logic, or inner structural contradiction, but has depended on political and economic conditions in China.

Since the early 1980s, only women have entered the work force, and only women from the countryside. Virtually no urban youths desire jobs in the silk industry any longer because of the low pay and poor working conditions. As urban workers can now test into the factory of their choice, no one from Hangzhou—male or female—has shown up to work in the silk factories. To resolve this labor crisis, managers have turned to recruitment of peasant women, most of them relatives of current factory workers.

Under the economic reforms, an increasingly rigid distinction is being drawn between the production line jobs of weaving, prep, and inspection work, which have been construed as manual labor and those jobs now more highly valued as skilled technical labor and mental labor—machine repair, transport, and managerial work. Concurrent with this process is a transformed sexual division of labor: the manual labor tasks are now becoming defined as women's work while the technical and mental labor are considered men's work. This sexual division of labor is taking shape through gendered interpretations of work capabilities such that women and men are said to have different capabilities uniquely suited to these divergent tasks. One cadre told me that the new wage system is for tasks considered boring, low skill, but that need energy. Women in China are believed suited to these kinds of tasks—they are said to have the requisite patience, they are said to be less complaining about boring work; they are said to have nimble fingers, which, according to this ideological construction of biology, uniquely suits them to prep work. On the other hand, they are said not to be suited to machine repair. Machine repair work entails climbing up on top of the machines and this is said to be inconvenient for women. Because gender capabilities are defined in opposition to one another, men are thought to be good at machine repair because men are said to be uniquely capable of technical tasks. A few

women in the silk industry have job assignments as machine re-
pairers, but this in no way calls into question the fundamental beliefs that adhere in the sexual division of labor. To the extent they
are seen as capable, these women are thought to resemble men.[20]

Representations of the appropriate managerial qualifications
are also gendered. Women are said to lack the intellectual capabilities of men and the necessary leadership qualities. They do not
know how to resolve disputes or how to make the necessary social
connections, or *guanxi*, so essential for getting anything done in
China. Male cadres would invariably tell me that managerial work
is inconvenient for women due to their family responsibilities.
Given the sexual division of labor of childcare and housework in
China, their claim has some validity, but only if that division remains unchallenged. With telling omission, they do not raise this
objection for women doing production work on the shift system.

These gendered interpretations of women's physical and intellectual capacities serve what Foucault has called a regime of
bio-power (Foucault 1980:139–144) in which women's bodies are
culturally inscribed in a way that makes them objects to be manipulated and controlled. Through these gendered representations of
women, factory management can then attempt to subject women
to the microtechnologies of factory work discipline in order to raise
their productivity.

Many women workers, through their daily practical experience of living in a world structured by gender, accept these reciprocally confirming yet still hegemonically construed representations of their gendered selves as fundamentally tied to family responsibilities and to biology. That is, the objective structure of the
gendered division of labor becomes part of their lived subjective
experience. This subjective experience can, however, be applied to
originally unintended purposes—in this case, resistance to the new
pressures for higher productivity. Women take off from work more
often than men for family reasons—to prolong a maternity leave,
care for a sick child, or breastfeed a newborn. Young mothers look
forward to the extra hour they can take each day to breastfeed their
babies for the first year after birth. Xiao Tang, a shift leader in a
weft prep shop, told me, after her return from a supposed visit with
her newborn, that she does not breastfeed, but that she likes to
visit her mother during that hour. In these quotidian strategies to
lessen the burden of their silk work, women themselves reproduce
aspects of the larger culture. This resistance thus paradoxically re-
inforces the sense that women are less productive than men.[21]

Wage differentials, as I have emphasized, are justified under the reforms because they are said to reflect individual differences in productivity. When we think of productivity, we assume it has to do with something measurable, like piecework. And the bonuses do reward piecework. But, more importantly, the position-wage system reflects an enshrinement of a distinction between mental and technical labor versus manual labor. Weaving is no longer the category for gender distinctions or for struggles over control of one's labor. Now the divide stands between management and production workers—management categories are about men and production categories are about women. Women workers now contrast themselves with management, not weavers, when they raise issues of working conditions or better jobs. These reforms represent a critical reshaping of the classification of work that more or less elides with gender. The productivity of women's labor is now going to be evaluated on a different, and lower, scale than men's because women's work has become equated with manual labor. Since the jobs that men do are defined as the more productive ones, men inevitably come to be seen as more productive than women. These representations of men and women will continue to appear as common sense truths as long as this gendered division of labor prevails.

CONCLUSION

The economic reforms in the silk industry, as exemplified by the new wage and bonus system, are thus not a simple, straightforward policy to reward individual workers who work harder. We have seen that the criticism of workers for shirking their responsibilities and living off the labor of others is an ideological representation entailed in a rejection of the Cultural Revolution. But the new wage policy is much more complex than a mere attempt to solve even that issue taken as a problem *prima facie*. It signifies a fundamental shift now in process in notions about the nature of work and productivity. This new hegemony is far from a coherent, articulated system of meaning. Productivity, at present, stands as a trope for a range of interactive concepts: bitterness, responsibility, skill, and status, some of which are at times contradictory. The notions of hard work and productivity are further based on beliefs about categories of people: "youths," "managers," "men" and workers in jobs considered bitter and essential to the production process. These kinds of people are now said to be more productive by definition. The whole notion of productivity as tied to the division of labor under this new system is thus not a neutral concept. It is infused with beliefs about age, status, and gender.

This brings us back to the issues I raised at the beginning of this essay. The case of economic reform in the silk industry forcefully demonstrates the point that labor processes are processes of cultural interpretation through everyday practice. One can begin at the broadest arena of relevant meaning: the relationship between socialism and capitalism. The current struggles over work relations and their meanings implicitly suggest that "socialism" and "capitalism" are representational constructs always relationally— and thus relatively—defined. I am not denying that socialist societies and capitalist societies exist. What I do want to stress is that capitalism and socialism exist primarily as politically resonant signifiers, not as objective structures. To paraphrase Laclau and Mouffe, "socialist societies" or "socialist relations of production" are not abstract entities but the "[loci] of a multiplicity of practices and discourse (Laclau and Mouffe 1985:102)". In the current period of economic reform in China, workers and managers strategically deploy these categories in their arguments about the labor process.[22] If we analyzed these arguments using objectivist models, we would have to dismiss them as rhetoric in the pejorative sense, which would take us back to the outdated understandings of ideology as mystification. We need to recognize that these interpretive struggles over meaning are simultaneously struggles over "material" needs.[23] Socialist societies are always ideologically construed, not in the abstract, but in the course of quotidian practices. As Party cadre Yang once mused, "It's not clear what is reasonable. These questions of political economy are a matter of controversy. A socialist economy can use capitalist methods. Some say this will make ours a capitalist system. The country's leaders say we can't change into a capitalist system. But if we don't watch out, we will."

Recognition of the importance of situated interpretations is equally critical for understanding how everyday practices inform the labor process. An argument that the significance of work relations arises purely from the shop floor would have normalized the very values of age, gender and mental/manual divisions that workers currently contest. Only by placing the silk industry within the larger cultural field of meaning in China can we begin to understand why economic reform angers older workers, makes the shop office a site of frustration, or naturalizes women's biology. There is nothing inherent or necessary or even comprehensible about how a silk factory would establish these meanings unless we broaden the cultural context.

Power, lodged in productive relations, does shape the discourse about the new wage and bonus system. But that power is not emanating from one direction only. As Anthony Giddens has pointed out, subordinate actors' very involvement in social relationships gives them a certain power (Giddens 1982). Workers in China, as a dominated group, nonetheless display great creativity in challenging and transforming the dominant interpretations of the economic reforms, and the final configuration of those reforms will be an outcome of these struggles. Pierre Bourdieu has made this point by emphasizing that ideologies are inscribed with a history of power struggles for the legitimation of particular visions of the social world (Bourdieu 1985). Thus ideological, or symbolic, struggles constitute an ongoing process in which these visions become articulated through the practical consciousness of social actors as they go about their quotidian activities.

Yet, we need to move beyond the search for a pure stance of resistance, beyond discussions of whether this or that action or state of consciousness truly constitutes resistance if it does not lead to revolutionary action. That approach assumes that social actors bring essentialized a priori identities into social relationships. The lives of China's silk factory workers under economic reform highlights the multiple and sometimes contradictory ways that workers interpret and therefore act upon these recent changes. If older workers complain, they also reproduce the sense that hierarchies based on age should exist. If "manual" workers contest the new wage hierarchies, they, too, sometimes accept the notion that intellectual work constitutes labor of higher value. If women question gendered divisions of labor within the workplace, some of them have embraced motherhood as one of the few alternative subject-positions possible for them.

Nonetheless, it is important to stress the agency involved in these social relations of work and meaning. We have seen how "even" in socialist societies ordinary people actively create meaning and hence their social worlds. My fortunate arrival in China at a time when the new wage system was just introduced led me to recognize that workers in the silk factories are never passive recipients of state policy. Certainly the dining hall workers' angry explosion should remind us of that.

TAMARA K. HAREVEN

7

The Festival's Work as Leisure: The Traditional Craftsmen of Gion Festival

INTRODUCTION

The debates about the role of work in modern society and about the relationship between work and leisure have dominated thought and scholarship in western society since the industrial revolution.[1] These issues have become especially acute in "post industrial" society. The editors of this volume have rightly introduced a more complex view towards these issues, by drawing on the anthropology of work and on social history. Rejecting the dominant view of work in modern society as dehumanizing, they emphasize the constructive role of work in identity formation, and in providing self-esteem and honor. When viewed as distinct from "labor," work is being recognized as having a positive impact on the formation of individual and social identity. My own study of textile workers in New England has also demonstrated the laborers' strong attachment to their industrial work as part of their identity and sense of community (Hareven 1982).

The role of work in identity formation is particularly significant in Japanese society, where the organization of work has become regimented to an extreme, and where *work* and *leisure* in large enterprises have become highly regulated and controlled by management, in order to shape a collective group identity that conforms to the company's ideals and dictates. Under these circumstances, leisure is not an antidote to work, but rather part of the company's control over the workers' entire time budget.

This paper examines a highly traditional festival in modern Japan, where workers are able temporarily to reverse their streamlined roles and to achieve once a year a self-identification in a nonregimented work process. While festivals usually serve as occasions of leisure and joyous transgression, their organization and successful execution requires exhausting work, elaborate organization, synchronization of delicate time schedules, and extraordinary skills (Abrahams 1982). Even traditional festivals that are enacted in contemporary society are regulated or controlled by state and municipal bureaucracies, insurance requirements, traffic regulations, and police. Thus, while festivals are intended to provide a release from the pressures and routines of daily work, they generate work pressures of a different character, which bring to the foreground the leadership and skills that are essential for their successful production and maintenance.

Festivals in Japan have had the special role of enforcing the status quo, and of upholding the existing hierarchy of class or age through their special rituals. Festivals have also provided, however, certain groups or social classes with the opportunity of temporarily reversing their roles and of expressing their group identities (Bestor 1989; Soeda 1973). Such role-inversions were controlled, or initiated in the past by the ruling classes. They were used as occasions that enabled peasants or members of lower classes to vent their frustrations in a controlled, ritualized way, and then acquiesce to the authorities.

In contemporary Japan class divisions are less rigid than in prewar Japan, but boundaries based on occupation, income and social status are still clearly observed. The Gion Matsuri (Festival) discussed in this paper provides the craftsmen engaged in its production with the opportunity to transcend, at least temporarily the boundaries of their class, to gain a sense of identification with the community, and to achieve honor and self respect, through their use of their indispensable traditional skills in producing the Festival.

The Festival's work is no ordinary labor, and the service of the community members and the craftsmen is no ordinary service. The Festival is homage to the Gods who visit the community during these celebrations. The craftsmen's labor, and the community member's labor, is *O' Kamisamano Shigoto* (labor for the Gods). Even though the craftsmen receive some pay for their services, this pay is considerably lower (by about one third to one half) than what they would be receiving for their usual work. In this sense, the craftsmen view themselves as volunteers. They take their vacation time from their regular jobs during the Festival and contribute their time and labor to the Festival intensely. Since vacations in Japan are extremely short, the craftsmen actually forego their main vacation for the sake of the Festival.

This paper discusses the role of the traditional craftsmen in Kyoto in constructing and moving the Gion Festival's giant floats *yama* and *hoko*. It examines their relationship to each other, and to the community members who employ them once a year, utilizing their special skills during the Festival.[2]

THE MOVING MUSEUM

The Gion Festival, one of Japan's three biggest and nationally famous festivals, has been celebrated annually by the residents of the Muromachi district of Kyoto, since the ninth century. (Yoneyama 1973). During the Festival, each neighborhood sponsors and produces one "float." (a *hoko* or a *yama*). The festival culminates in a procession of thirty-two giant "floats". They consist of two types: the *hoko* are three-story, towering structures which are moved on giant wheels and pulled along the streets by close to one hundred pullers for each. The *yama* are smaller one-story structures and are carried through the procession by twenty to thirty pall bearers. The *yama* and *hoko* which resemble miniature shrines, are decorated by magnificent carvings in wood, lacquerware and metal, and are hung with ancient tapestries, rugs, and dyed fabrics.[3] As the *yama* and *hoko* move in the parade through Kyoto's main downtown streets, Kyoto people refer to them as the "The Moving Museum."

The townspeople in the *Yamahoko Cho* district who have produced and maintained this Festival were traditionally the wholesalers of kimono. Since World War II, the district's population has become considerably diversified in occupation and businesses, but wholesalers of kimono and related accessories still keep their shops and residences in certain sub-neighborhoods of this district.

Following World War II, most of the traditional houses and shops on Shijo Street were replaced by modern, tall office and bank buildings. There are hardly any dwellings left on the corner of Shijo and Karasuma Streets—the focal point of the Gion Festival. The former residents moved out to the suburbs and the older ones died carrying their knowledge with them. In several of the thirty-two neighborhoods, a few original families still reside in their historic houses, or at least keep shops there. Even in these communities though, the exodus to the suburbs continues. Soaring land values in this central area of Kyoto have attracted real estate speculators, who drive out the local residents, sometimes through pressure and threats of violence. They replace the traditional two-story wooden houses with highrise "mansions" (apartment buildings) and parking garages. The *Yamahoko Cho* is thus embroiled in a continuing struggle to maintain its traditional streepscapes and its original community.

The Gion Festival was already recognized as one of Japan's major festivals in the Edo period. In exchange for the Festival's cultural and religious contribution to the nation, the Tokugawa Emperor recognized Kyoto's maintenance of this Festival as a form of "tax." Kyoto was exempt, therefore, from certain national taxes. Because of the Festival's national importance, the other districts of Kyoto City that were not involved in the Festival were obligated to contribute to the *Yamahoko Cho* (The Gion Festival's district) through a fixed tax in money or labor for the maintenance of the Festival. This obligation was eliminated during the Meiji period (Yoneyama 1986). Nevertheless, residents of other districts, the merchants' and hotel and tourist service associations have continued to contribute to the Gion Festival on a voluntary basis, because of the Festival's importance to Kyoto's cultural life and tourism. The Yamahoko Cho district, that puts on and maintains this Festival struggles financially, and the Festival's Central Committee (Gion Matsuri Rengo Kai) are engaged in a continuous effort to raise financial and volunteer support from various associations within the city.

Even though the Gion Festival is produced in one district of Kyoto only, it is shared and celebrated by the entire city and by hundreds of thousands of visitors, who watch the parade on July seventeenth, on Kyoto's main downtown streets. Since its early origins, the Gion Festival has therefore attracted numerous visitors from other parts of Japan. (Until World War II there had actually been two parades: one on the seventeenth of July and one on the twenty-seventh, each parade encompassing the *yama* and *hoko*

Figure 7.1. The Hoko in the parade of the Gion Festival on Oike Street in Kyoto. In the foreground Nivatori Boko, followed by two other hoko in distance. The pullers are moving the hoko forward, and the two *ondotori* are directing its movement with their fans. The musicians are on the top tier. © Tamara K. Hareven, photographer.

of one half of the district. Because of traffic problems and the financial efforts involved in producing two parades, they were merged after World War II into one held annually on the seventeenth of July.

The Gion Festival has become in recent years one of Kyoto's main tourist events. Among Kyoto's three nationally famous festivals—Aoi Matzuri, Jidai Matzuri (Festival of Ages), and Gion Matsuri, the Gion Festival stands out as Kyoto's greatest tourist attraction. The Festival brings hundreds of thousands of tourists (domestic as well as foreign) into Kyoto, and serves as an important source of income for the city's tourist industry.

According to tradition the Gion Festival's initial purpose was to avert a plague which was devastating the population of Kyoto. In this respect, the Gion Festival is one of numerous Summer festivals in Japan, which occur after the various Spring festivals and before the Bon Festival (ancestor worship) in August. When the Gion Festival first started, the townspeople paraded a primitive *hoko*—a symbolic weapon that was intended to fight evil. Initially unadorned, it was shaped as a metal pole with a pointed end on the top, and was carried around in religious processions. The primitive *hoko* used for the Gion Festival were subsequently enveloped and embedded in fancy ornaments, and were finally surrounded by the structures of the towering floats which are used in the procession today.

What had originally been a magical weapon intended to fight the evil that besets the community, was transformed into a display of the merchant bourgeoisie's pride and wealth, expressed in an elaborate display of artistry. The tapestries and carpets which are used to cover the four sides of the towering structures, have become symbolic of Kyoto's connection with China and Western Europe. From the seventeenth century on, the *hoko* and *yama* were decorated with carpets imported from Iran and India, and with tapestries woven locally, as well as imported ones from Belgium, France, and China. (One of the magnificent Belgian tapestries depicting scenes from Homer's Iliad has survived as a unique specimen of that genre, which cannot be found in Belgium anymore.) Since the Yama Hoko Cho district's main merchandise had been Kyoto's handwoven brocade, the display of tapestries and precious rugs on the *hoko* and *yama* is one of the Festival's main characteristics and claims to fame.

The construction of the Festival's floats (*yama* and *hoko*), requires a variety of traditional skills, which are gradually becoming extinct. These towering floats are built from wooden beams which are knitted together only by an elaborate rope mesh. No nails or pegs can be used. Magnificent lacquerware, bronze and gold ornaments are fitted together as in a jigsaw puzzle, and mounted upon the skeletons of the floats. The tapestries and various artistically dyed fabrics are then hung and fixed with metal clasps. Finally, the wheelmen mount the huge wooden wheels, so that the *hoko* could be moved in the procession. The turning of these wheels around street corners requires the kind of special skills used for maneuvering carriages in the Middle Ages. During the parade, the *yama* and *hoko* move through the streets of Kyoto as a result of coordination of the efforts of the carpenters, wheelmen, conductors (who signal when to move and when to stop), and the men who pull the *hoko* forward with heavy ropes.

Before World War II, residents from surrounding villages, who were tied to the townsmen in the Gion Festival district by various obligations, used to perform these highly skilled services. Nowadays the community members who produce the Festival have to hire the few craftsmen who have retained these skills, or who learned them from the older generation. During the year, these craftsmen work in ordinary occupations such as high-rise construction jobs, factory work, or as salaried men or farmers. Once a year, they leave their regular jobs and carry out the Festival's labor. Despite its arduous and dangerous character, these craftsmen consider the Festival's work as a form of leisure. The Festival offers them a special opportunity to practice and display their skills in front of millions of viewers on the streets and on television. Their reunion during the Festival with fellow craftsmen and community members enables them to socialize together once a year and to maintain a sense of the Festival's community.

Since the skills needed for the Festival are becoming exceedingly rare in modern Japan, the craftsmen use their knowledge as a means of managing the procedures and social events of the Festival beyond what would be considered their usual status. The community members who are responsible for the Festival depend increasingly on these craftsmen's knowledge and performance. Without them it would be impossible to construct the *hoko* and to move it safely. Even the slightest mistake in the turning of the wheels or in the coordination of the rope pulling, could cause severe accidents. In view of the delicate coordination and balancing required in holding up and moving the giant structures, these craftsmen are indispensable during the Festival. The power of knowledge also enables craftsmen to participate in special social events, such as the final party following the Festival from which members of their class would have been excluded in the past, because of their lower social status.

This paper is based on extensive interviews of the craftsmen as well as the community members and leaders in the various neighborhoods involved in the Festival, which I have carried out over the past five years. My original purpose in studying the Gion Festival was to understand how the communities that are responsible for the Festival produce it and carry on its traditions, despite the pressures of rapid modernization. Over the past five years, I have conducted repeated, open-ended interviews of the community members and leaders in six of the thirty-two districts of the

Festival, and of the various craftsmen who work with them. I have followed the preparations in each community, starting each year from July first, when the Festival's work is officially launched.

THE FESTIVAL'S WORK

The entire Festival's work is carried out by three groups: the community members, the hired craftsmen, and the volunteers. The community members are obligated to contribute fixed amounts of money and a certain amount of labor each year in carrying out the Festival's work and in managing it. They take turns in carrying the responsibility for various tasks and the management roles. In reality the community members contribute both financially and in time investment way beyond their required share. Most family businesses in the community close down after July first, and barely reopen by the beginning of August. Men and women work day and night on all the details and the preparations. The craftsmen, on the other hand, are hired as "experts" for a specific time period, to carry out their specialized tasks. They are paid at least a minimal fee for their labor.

The construction of a *hoko* and *yama* involves three teams of craftsmen each with its specialized skills and responsibilities: The carpenters (*daiku*) construct the *hoko* from wooden beams and poles which they knot together with elaborate heavy ropes. They use no nails or any other type of pegs in this process. The carpenters' work culminates in the construction of the roof which is made of elaborate carved wood and lacquer segments, which fit together as a puzzle. The construction of the *hoko's* skeleton always begins on the tenth of July and is completed within two days.

The "helpers" (*tetzudai*) work closely with the carpenters. They assist the carpenters in the construction of the *hoko*, in building the roof and tapestries and the various ornaments, and finally in moving it through the streets. The carpenters as well as the helpers have special tasks during the parade itself, as will be described below. The third group, the wheelmen (*kurumakata*) are in charge of mounting the giant wheels of the *hoko* and in moving the *hoko* during the parade. After the parade they are responsible for dismantling the wheels and for preparing them for storage.

The three groups of the craftsman work in close coordination with each other. They all take their instructions from the *Oyakata*—the contractor who is responsible for all three groups to the community leaders. Under the main *Oyakata* there are usually two subcontractors, one for the carpenter and helper groups, and one for the wheelmen. The subcontractors are responsible for recruiting the workers in their group and for supervising their respective tasks directly. In some cases, the two subcontractors also negotiate and communicate directly with the community leaders.

The organizational structure of the craftsmen thus varies from one community to another. In some cases, one main *oyakata* of the carpenters is in charge of the entire production and the two subcontractors are responsible to him. In other cases, each oyakata carries out his respective tasks in coordination with the others, but is responsible to the community leaders independently, and controls his own men.

Each *Oyakata* seals his contracts for his work with the community leaders on the first of July each year. It has been customary for the chief *Oyakata* and for the two subcontractors to attend the *Kippuiri*—the opening meeting for the preparation of the Festival's work on July first. Even where there is a chief *Oyakata*, the two subcontractors appear at the *Kippuiri*. In that ceremony, the community leaders, dressed in *haori*, the formal black kimono which is customarily worn during special celebrations, kneel in front of their deities. The *Oyakata* and the subcontractors wear business suits rather than their usual working clothes. Each subcontractor presents his contract to the community leaders, detailing the amount of work to be accomplished, and the price for materials and labor. The community leaders and the contractors bargain over the fees. Since the same *Oyakata* serves the same community year after year, the fees were actually agreed upon long ago. They involve only a slight increase each year due to the increases in the cost of living or in the price of materials. Once the community leaders and craftsmen reach an agreement they consecrate it in an *O'miki* ceremony in which sanctified *sake* is drunk in front of the community's deities.

The community members' promise to each other and the craftsman's promise to the community is no ordinary promise. It represents a sacred promise for a sacred task—service for a festival that celebrates the special presence of the deities from the Yasaka Shrine in the community. The community leaders and the contractors promise each other that they will do their best to produce the Festival as effectively this year as in the past: *"Kotoshi Mo Yoroshiku Onegai Shimas,"* "This year please do your best again." The promise is then consecrated with the communal drinking of sanctified *sake*. The community leader in charge of the Festival's organization for that particular year (they take turns), carries a small lacquerware table with a silver *sake* flask and cup. He kneels in front of each member in turn. He then bows and hands the member a cup and pours the *sake*. The member drinks the *sake*, returns the empty cup, and bows. The leader then provides him with a snack of dried squid. The member eats part of it, wraps the remainder in Japanese paper and tucks it into the pocket inside his kimono sleeve, for good luck. The leader moves on to the next person and the next; including the contractors. All participants kneel in the typical Japanese position until the ceremony is completed.

THE CRAFTSMEN'S PERFORMANCE

The craftsmen's activities could be roughly divided into four stages: construction, rehearsal, parade, and dismantling. The first stage, the *Hokotate*, entails the construction of the *hoko*, the mounting of the ornaments, the attachment of the wheels, and finally the hanging of the tapestries on the *hoko* in preparation for the parade. This entire operation, starting from the bare beams and ropes to the erection of the *hoko* with its sacred pole, is accomplished in three days. The second stage (*Hikizome*) involves the rehearsal for the parade on July thirteenth, during which the *hoko* is pulled only a short distance within the neighborhood. Next comes the climax of the Festival—the parade on July seventeenth, and finally the dismantling and putting away of the various parts of the *hoko* and treasures in storage for another year.

During the first stage the carpenters and the assistants construct the skeleton of the *hoko*. They then assemble the *Shimbo* from its parts. It consists of a tall pole which is topped by a young pine tree. A small effigy of the deity is attached to the pole. The *Shimbo* represents the most sacred section of the *hoko* and is, in fact, a metamorphosis of the original *hoko* into ultimate splendor. Following the mounting of the *Shimbo*, the community members assemble around it. They decorate the pole with branches of the *Sakaki* tree (a sacred tree used in various *Shinto* rituals), which are bundled into two large bouquets. Community members and guests each pay homage by tying numerous small pieces of sacred white Japanese paper to the branches, which symbolizes the presence of the deities. (Women are also allowed to participate in this ritual). By the time this task is completed, the branches look as if they were covered with snow. An elderly community member then purifies the pole by scattering salt over it, and by pouring *sake* over the deity's effigy. The *hoko* and its *shimbo* are now ready to stand up.

The chiefs of the carpenters' and assistants' teams pull up the *hoko* to its erect position while the people assembled around the *hoko* watch in awe. This process, requiring delicate balancing, is accomplished with the help of a winch and a metal cable. As the chief carpenter coordinates the pulling, the *hoko* rises slowly. It then rests temporarily suspended at a forty-five degree angle to the ground. Then it continues to rise higher and higher, until it stands perpendicular to the ground, soaring three stories high. Community members and by-standers all applaud. The craftsmen then prop the *hoko* with the necessary stabilizers and guards in order to support it in its standing position.

Next, the wheelmen attach the giant wheels to the *hoko* and fasten them with metal screws. They then cover the screws with brass caps, on which the emblem of the *hoko* is engraved on the center of each wheel. They also attach the ropes required for the pulling of the *hoko*, one on each side. Next, the carpenters, the assistants, and the community leaders attach and hang the various ornaments in preparation for the trial run—*Hikizome.*

Hikizome is the rehearsal for the parade, two days before the event, carrying important ritual meaning in its own right. Technically it is to test whether the *hoko's* operations work smoothly and whether the *hoko's* tower and pine tree will clear the electrical wires overhead. *Hikizome* also provides, however, an opportunity for the community members and the craftsmen to enter the Festival's mood and to anticipate the main celebration yet to come. It is the first chance in the Festival's proceedings for the craftsmen to display their accomplishments to the public, although the audience is quite small at that time. During *Hikizome* the craftsmen still wear their work clothes, and the community leaders wear ordinary clothes. Only the main community leader, (*Chonai Kaicho*) is dressed in formal black kimono (*haori*). *Hikizome,* unlike the parade on the seventeenth of July is truly a community event, in which women and children and old men participate in the pulling that moves the *hoko*. During the parade, however, the *hoko* is pulled by teams of young men (mostly university students who are paid for their services, or by volunteers in some instances).

The musicians, wearing their *yukata* (traditional summer kimono) with their *hoko's* emblems printed in blue and white, climb into their special space on the top of the *hoko* and start playing the Festival's processional music with their flutes, cymbals, and drums. The helpers and carpenters, assisted by community members and children, seize the long ropes and pull the *hoko* as the wheelmen, using metal levers curved at the edge like a spatula, start prodding the wheels from behind. During *Hikizome* the *hoko* travels only a short distance, at the most one and a half city blocks. Then it is pulled back to its original location.

Most of the neighborhoods in the Festival's district have very few, if any, children residing in the area. Numerous children are brought, therefore, from other neighborhoods by their teachers or parents, especially for *Hikizome*. The adults tug on the rope together with the little children, their faces transformed with the pleasure of pulling the *hoko*. *Hikizome* on the thirteenth, much more than the parade on the seventeenth, is truly a folk event. In a sense, it is The Festival.

After *Hikizome*, the carpenters and helpers stabilize the *hoko*, prop it up, set the rail guards, and construct the special wooden platforms adjacent to the *hoko*. From these platforms, community members and volunteers will be selling good luck tokens and various memorabilia during the three days preceding the parade, especially during the evenings. While the carpenters construct the platform, the electrician mounts numerous lanterns strung on ropes like pearls. These illuminate the *hoko* at night with soft, ornamental lights. When walking in the Gion Festival's district at night I would suddenly see the soft glow of these tapestries of light, like fantasy ships in the night.

Following the successful rehearsal, the wheelmen and carpenters return to their regular jobs. They reappear again in the Festival's district at the crack of dawn on the seventeenth, when the preparation for the parade begins. During the three days between *Hikizome* and the parade, the *hoko*, adorned by most of its ornaments and hung on its four sides with its ancient tapestries and carpets, stands on display in the center of its neighborhood. Each *hoko* usually stands in front of the community house, where the neighborhood's deities are stationed during the Festival. The community members place the statues of the deities on an altar surrounded by the display of the communities' Festival treasures, especially the tapestries and carpets that will be hung on the *hoko*. Many of the textiles are too old and too fragile to be carried in the parade, but the public can still enjoy viewing them in the exhibition.

During these last three days before the parade (*Yio-yoi-yoi Yama, Yoi-yoi Yama,* and *Yoi-Yama*) hundreds thousands of visitors wander from one community to the next to watch the exhibitions of treasures in each *hoko* and *yama* and to buy good-luck tokens braided from bamboo leaves (*chimaki*) blessed by the priests of the Yasaka (Gion) Shrine, and various other memorabilia. During these

Figure 7.2. Iwato Yama - close-up of the top tier. The musicians are perched on the top banister playing the flute The master of the carpenter and his assistants are on the roof. Next to the tower the statue of one of the community's deities is standing in full view.©Tamara K. Hareven, photographer.

three evenings the traditional musicians play their haunting beat on the upper tier of the *hoko*. Thousands of people walk the short distances from *hoko* to *hoko*. They listen to the lively rhythmical performance of the musicians; climb into the top of the *hoko* through a special stairway; admire the ancient ornaments and buy the memorabilia and good-luck tokens.

The streets are lined with hundreds of peddlers' carts, selling fast food, such as broiled squid, candy, octopus pancakes, sweet bean cakes, corn on the cob, along with various trinkets and toys, beetles, goldfish, and ornaments for the children's aquarium. The entire district of the *Yamahoko Cho* takes on the character of a carnival. The climax of these festivities occurs on *Yoi-Yoma*, the night of the sixteenth—the third night, and the last one before the parade. On that evening the crowds are so thick that the streets connecting the various *hokos'* locations and even *Kyoto's* main wide street *Shijo*, look like a sea of people.

During these three days the *hokos* and the sales tables are staffed almost completely by community members and volunteers. (In recent years, however, neighborhoods whose population has been depleted are hiring students to help in the sales). Children dressed in summer kimono (*yukata*), chant songs in unison, inviting the passersby to buy the good luck tokens. Communities that have no resident children left, "borrow" children from other districts in Kyoto, in order to keep this ancient atmosphere alive.

The Parade

The climax of the Festival also sets the grand stage for the craftsmen's performance. In the early morning, prior to the parade, the carpenters and the assistants mount the final ornaments on the *hoko*, hang the tapestries on its four sides, and prepare it for movement. They then change into their parade outfits: narrow breeches, white happi jackets with the symbol of their *hoko* printed on it, and special bands tied around their foreheads. The *Oyakata* of the carpenters and his main assistant climb to the top of the *hoko's* tower, where they sit on the roof during the entire parade each on one side of the pine tree. Clutching on to the ropes, they issue orders to the conductors (*ondotori*) and to the wheelmen, instructing them when to move and when to stop. From their lofty positions they also watch the electrical wires overhead, and signal to the *ondotori* each time the *hoko* tower is likely to be entangled in the wires.

Six of the carpenters' and helpers' team dress up in the conductors' special *yukata*, (summer kimono) adorned with the dramatic designs and symbols of their particular *hoko*, and serve as conductors (*ondotori*). Uninformed viewers who see the two *ondotori* in their dramatic kimono directing the movements of the *hoko* with their rhythmic and skillful movement of the fans, imagine them to be the highest ranking community leaders. In reality, they are carpenters and helpers. The two conductors (*ondotori*) are perched on a narrow platform in front of the *hoko*, directly above the wheels. With one hand they hold on to a rope, suspended from a canopy above their heads and with the other they signal to the wheelmen and the rope pullers, directing their movement. Each *ondotori* holds in one hand a large gilded fan with the *hoko's* symbol engraved on a silver background on the other side. The silver and gold colors flash in the bright light so that the leader of the procession could see the signal. The *ondotori* move their fans in unison, in incisive and stylized rhythms. Like in a kabuki dance they signal the *hoko's* movement and stopping. At the same time, they chant the orders "*Yoi-yoi-ya-ma.*" The wheelmen respond to the instructions and start pushing or stopping the wheels as directed. The *oyakata* of the wheelmen, who walks on the street in the middle, in front of the two wheels, transmits the orders to the pullers, who then proceed to pull in synchrony as the wheelmen prod the wheels.

The wheelmen wear narrow black pants and the typical Japanese workmen's black cloth boots and black ornate happi jackets with the symbol of their *hoko* imprinted on the back. They flank the wheels on each side, as well as behind and in front of the *hoko*. Except for the *oyakata* of the carpenters, who rides on the very top of the tower, the wheelmen's tasks are most complicated and dangerous during the parade. They have to push and prod the wheels with great precision, or else the *hoko* might roll backwards or forwards unexpectedly, and run over the wheelmen or the community members who march in front of their *hoko* dressed in Samurai garb (*kamishimo*). The chief wheelmen has the dangerous task of crawling under the *hoko* between the two front wheels, just as the *hoko* is set in motion, while two or three other wheelmen prod each wheel forward from the side. The chief wheelman jumps out just as the pullers begin to pull the *hoko* forward. The slightest miscalculation in timing could cause him to be run over by the giant carriage.

The parade starts sharply at 9:00 a.m. on the corner of Shijo and Karasuma Streets—the heart of the downtown, and currently Kyoto's main banking center. At 8:50 a.m., Naginata Boko (the

Figure 7.3. Funa Boko - This is the only *hoko* shaped as a ship. On the bottom right hand side the two master wheelmen are prodding the wheel in its forward movement. The wheelman in the very front has to retreat immediately as the *hoko* moves forward. On the bottom left side five wheelmen are prodding one of the hind wheels, and one *ondotori* is standing above the left wheel. ©Tamara K. Hareven, photographer.

most sacred *hoko* that always leads the parade) begins to move backwards from its home position to the corner of Shijo and Karasuma Streets. *Ochicosan*, a young boy consecrated as a messenger to the gods, is carried up the ladder to the top of the Naginata Boko. This sacred child is positioned on the top tier of the *hoko* in front of the musicians. He signals the beginning of the parade with his drum. Immediately, thereafter, the other *hoko* on Shijo Street begin to move towards Naginata Boko, and line up on Shijo Street. Next, the other *hoko* from the side streets emerge each into Shijo street in the order prescribed by the lots that their leaders had drawn in Kyoto's City Hall on July 2. The order of the *hoko* and the *yama* in the procession changes every year in accordance with the lots, except for Naginata Boko, which always goes first, and for several other *hoko*, which for historic reasons have a fixed place in the parade. Once all the *hoko* and *yama* are lined up on Shijo street, the procession begins.

The *yama* and the *hoko* advance on Shijo street which is lined with spectators on both sides, until they reach the checkpoint for *Kuji Aratame* (the "inspection of lots"). At that point, Kyoto's Mayor, dressed in the purple robe and tall hat of historic nobleman, and various dignitaries sit on a platform erected especially for the ceremony. When each *yama* or *hoko* arrives close to the Mayor's station, it stops and awaits its turn. Three community leaders of the first *hoko* march forward in a line. Two deliver to the Mayor's assistant a bunch of the good-luck tokens (*Chimaki*) which had been blessed for that *hoko*. The chief community leader steps into position facing the Mayor, who stands under a parasol.

The community leader, dressed in samurai garb, and following the stylized steps and arm movement of a Kabuki dance thrusts the lacquer box containing the certificate, which affirms this *hoko's* or *yama's* place in the order of the parade, toward the mayor's face. The Mayor reads the certificate aloud, and grants the *hoko* permission to move on. The community leader then displays his acrobatic skill—waiving the handle of his fan, he ties the silk string around the lacquer box containing the certificate. He bows to the Mayor, and then turns to face his community representatives and *yama* or *hoko*. Again, with the movements of a Kabuki dance, he waves his fan to signal to the head wheelman to move forward. The next *hoko* arrives, and so on until all *yama* and *hoko* have passed the Mayor. *Kuji Aratame* is one of the most media-attractive events in the parade. Television and press cameramen swarm at this station. The community leaders as well as the craftsmen, conscious of the broad coverage, display their skills and magnificent costumes to millions of viewers.

The most important test for the craftsmen and the most dramatic opportunity for displaying their skill occurs, however, at the two points where the *hoko* has to turn the corner to the next street: one on the corner of Shijo and Kawaramachi Streets, about one third of the way through the parade; and again on the corner of Oike and Shinmachi streets, just before the end of the parade, when all the *hoko* and *yama* go down narrow Shinmachi Street back to their home neighborhoods.

The turning of the corners (*Tsujimawashi*) on those two occasions requires the greatest concentration, skill, and fine coordination among the carpenters, helpers, pullers, and wheelmen. The slightest error in turning can cause the *hoko* to loose its balance and topple over. (Each *hoko* carries on its top about forty musicians, most of whom are young children and teenagers. The success of this operation rests on the coordination of all groups of craftsmen involved, but it depends most definitely on the wheelmen. The turning of the wheels around the corners is accomplished by using the ancient technique of wet bamboo slats. As the *hoko* reaches the intersection it stops. The wheelmen line up the bamboo slats on the pavement in the direction to which the *hoko* is expected to turn. They then pour water over the polished bamboo, so that the wheels can slide over it. Next, the master carpenter on the roof issues instructions to the *ondotori*. They, in turn, signal with their fans to the master wheelman, and he orders the wheelmen to turn. The wheelmen, with their feet planted firmly on the pavement, and their palms pressed against the side of the wheel, push the wheel; and at the same time, the pullers rush across to the opposite corner and pull the ropes in the direction into which the *hoko* is to turn.

The wheels slide over the wet bamboo slats, and the *hoko* turns the corner. Usually the *hoko* is led only by two *Ondotori* [conductors], but because of the formidable task of turning, their number doubles during this operation. While the *hoko* is waiting to be turned, the musicians play merrily the most rhythmical pieces of the Festival's music. During the turning, the musicians stop their music and beat the drums only, as thousands of viewers lined up behind the ropes hold their breath. At the moment of turning even the drums stop; the only audible sounds is that of the *Ondotori* chanting their orders rhythmically to the wheelmen and rope pullers, and the creaking of the wheels, as the *hoko* turns. Once the turning is accomplished, the musicians resume their music and the *hoko* is on its way. The energetic but controlled thrust of the wheelmen against each giant wheel of the *hoko* has become one of the most popular photographic poses of the Gion Festival. "I only wish that sometimes they would take the picture of our faces," said the *Oyakata* of the wheelmen of one of the *hoko*, "they always take our picture from behind."

The first *hoko*, Naginata Boko, reaches the corner of Oike and Shinmachi Streets by approximately 11:30 a.m. From there it takes about another hour and a half until the *hoko* returns to home base. "For us there are really two parades," said one of the craftsmen, "The real parade is on Shijo street; there we do everything carefully and in style. The second parade is on Kawaramachi and Oike

Figure 7.4. Fune Boko and another *hoko* in the midst of turning on Oike Street into the narrow Shinmanchi Street. The wheelmen arrange the bamboo slats in preparation for sliding the wheels over them. ©Tamara K. Hareven, photographer.

Figure 7.5. Iwato Yama - Mr. Wada, the master wheelman of this *hoko* (facing) is arranging the bamboo slats in preparation for turning. His son (back) is assisting him. On the right hand side the two older *Ondotori* are guiding the Hoko from below, while a young Ondotori is given his first opportunity to direct the *hoko* from above. ©Tamara K. Hareven, photographer.

(the two main streets lined with seats for the tourists). There we just take it easy and get it over with."

Following the brief lunch rest, each *hoko* moves towards the street corner awaiting its moment for turning the corner. As the *hoko* moves down the narrow Shinmachi Street, one can have a glimpse of the Festival's historic atmosphere that has been lost on the wide streets. On Shinmachi Street, there is hardly any space between the *hoko* and the doorways to the houses on each side. From their second floor windows the residents hand out beer and juice cans to the musicians on the top of the *hoko*, and receive in return *chimaki*—the good luck tokens that are hung on the door lintels, and that protect one's house from evil. By the time the last *hoko* turns down Shinmachi Street around 2:30 p.m., most of the community members and craftsmen have marched and exerted their efforts on Kyoto's hot streets for about four to five hours. The craftsmen started three hours earlier, and their tasks are not yet finished. The task of dismantling the *hoko* is still ahead of them.

Dismantling

Despite the exhausting march in Kyoto's humid heat, no one rushes to dismantle the *hoko* immediately upon its return to its home neighborhood. Elated by a sense of accomplishment, and saddened by the realization that the *hoko* is about to vanish for another year, the craftsmen slow down the *hoko* as it reaches its home street. Community members who did not participate in the parade, especially women, children, and older people applaud the *hoko* when it arrives: *"Gokurisama! Gokurisama!"* (You did a great job!). The wheelmen and pullers now move the *hoko* up and down the block, as they had done during *Hikizome* (rehearsal), and the musicians play with renewed energy. Gradually, the *hoko* comes to a stop. Despite the arduous task accomplished, no one seems to be in a hurry to stop. The musicians continue to play for the benefit of their community members. Finally, the music stops, and the last beat of the drums and cymbals echoes in the quiet street (no traffic is permitted yet on the street). The musicians climb down the steep ladder. Everybody on the street welcomes the musicians and the community members, and the craftsmen who have returned from the parade. The women hand them cups of cold green tea. After the public performance in the parade, the community now has its private celebration.

The Festival is successfully over, and "Thanks to the shadow of the Gods, no one was hurt!" Everyone voices their sense of relief and satisfaction with the year's accomplishment. The community members unburden themselves of their Samurai hats, and the wives rush to sort the mushroom-like hats and the straw sandals to pack them in preparation for next year. The community members and the musicians go to the traditional restaurant on their street or to the community hall to have their communal lunch and cold beer first, while the craftsmen embark on their next arduous task—the dismantling.

First they take down the statues of the Gods and carry them into the nearby community member's house designated as a temporary shelter for the gods. The Gods stay there until the next day, when they are undressed and they and their costumes are safely tucked away into the camphor wood boxes and stored for another year. Next the craftsmen strip the *hoko* of its finery—the carved wood, gilded metal and lacquerware ornaments and the magnificent tapestries. Some of the community members assist the craftsmen by receiving these parts and by storing them temporarily on the elevated floors of the nearby houses or stores, in preparation for packing.

Next, the wheelmen remove the wheels and with the help of a crane, they hoist the wheels onto a truck, and drive them to the municipal warehouse, where they are stored until next year. Kyoto's municipal government has built a special complex of warehouses that look like mausoleums with their giant safe-type iron doors for the storage of the *hoko* and *yama* parts and for all the Festival's treasurers. Each community has one warehouse in this complex in Maruyama Park. Next, the carpenters and the helpers dismantle the *hoko's* roof, which consists of finely carved wooden lintels and magnificent hand painted lacquer panels. Community members, including women, help put these treasurers in the temporary shelter until the next day.

At this stage, it is almost 4 p.m. The community members emerge from the dining hall, slightly swaying from the long exertion and the beer. The craftsmen, followed by the wheelmen, enter for their meal and cold beer. (This would be their first meal since 7:00 a.m. In 1989, the Festival's Central Committee banned the eating of boxed lunches during the parade.) After the meal the wheelmen return home, but the carpenters and their helpers still continue the Festival's labor. If the weather is good and no rain is forecast, they cover what is left of the *hoko* and return to their homes until the next morning. If the weather is bad, or there is a possible threat of rain, they stay into the evening and continue to dismantle the *hoko*, until only its skeleton is left.

Figure 7.6. The community leaders of Iwato Yama are marching in the parade in front of their *hoko*. They are dressed in Samurai garb, carrying their traditional straw hats. ©Tamara K. Hareven, photographer.

Early the next morning, the carpenters, and the assistants return to the *hoko* site. They complete the dismantling while the community members—men and women, dust off each piece of wood, polish the lacquerware and the gilded panels, and remove the smudges from the tapestries and other textiles. They then wrap each piece in its designated wooden box, and prepare it for the municipal warehouse.

Meanwhile, the carpenters and helpers disassemble the *hoko*. They cut down the young pine tree that was the crowning glory on the *hoko's* roof. Next they slash the rope work that they had knotted so painstakingly during the construction. Anyone walking through the *Yamahoko Cho* district between 11 a.m. and 12 a.m. on the eighteenth of July can see piles of cut rope on the pavement surrounding remaining beams of the *hoko*. The heavy beams are the last ones to be transported on the truck to the municipal warehouse. The craftsmen complete their work, put away the last pieces, and change their clothes. They submit their bills to the community leader and go off to lunch together.

On the nineteenth, however, the contractors (*Oyakata*) of the craftsmen and wheelman meet again with the community members for their final celebration. The *Uchiage*—final party, sometimes nicknamed *Ashi Arai* (literally "washing your feet") takes place in a famous traditional Japanese restaurant. On that occasion, the beer and *sake* flow from "bottomless" containers and the meal is lavish. (Prior to the festival each *hoko* amasses a huge number of *sake* bottles which are donated by various individuals and companies, and are dedicated to the Gods. The *sake* is consecrated during the Festival, and is drunk during that final party in order to "make the gods happy.") During the party the men enjoy the company of *Maico* (young geisha), something the craftsmen could never afford nowadays in their own circles. The craftsmen thus consider the party a much higher reward than the modest financial compensations they receive from the community.

THE FESTIVAL'S PILLARS

Ennoshitano Chikaramochi is a Japanese expression that has no precise counterpart in English. It means the "power from below" that upholds a house, an institution, or the entire society. The craftsmen who construct, maintain, support, and move the giant floats of the Gion Festival in Kyoto are often perceived as "the power from below." Their contribution is indispensable to the production and effective performance and maintenance of this Festival. Who are the craftsmen of the Gion Festival? Most of them do not reside in Kyoto City, and none of them reside within the Gion Festival's district (*Yamahoko Cho*). They are recruited from the suburbs and villages in the periphery of Kyoto. Many of them are engaged as construction workers on highrise buildings (*Tobishoku*), and travel around in Western Japan, from one construction site to the next. Others are carpenters, metal workers, farmers, factory workers, and self-employed craftsmen. Some of them work together year-round in the same carpentry team and under the same *Oyakata* as during the Festival. But the majority see each other only once a year, when they meet for the beginning of the Festival's work. "We are like Tanabata" (the two legendary stars that meet only once a year; they had once been lovers on earth but after their transformation into stars, they meet on each July 7), said one of the carpenters, "Our paths cross only once a year during the Gion Festival."

For many of the craftsmen the Gion Festival thus provides a special form of continuity and permanence. The same team members meet once a year for the Festival. During my five years of study of this Festival I have met the same craftsmen each year. (After my fifth appearance on July 1, they have also come to view me as a permanent participant, and as one on whom they could count for the annual reunion.) The community leaders do not maintain any contact with the craftsmen and their *Oyakata* during the year. "We do not know his address," said one community leader about the *Oyakata*. "He will show up for the *Kipuiri* on July 1, just the same as for the past twenty years."

Some of the craftsmen, who are now in their sixties or seventies, have been working for the Festival for forty or fifty years. Many are second- or third-generation in the same family, serving the same *hoko*. Most of them have learned the Festival's traditional skills from their fathers or uncles, or from their fathers' friends. The younger members of the teams active in the Festival today are still learning from their older relatives. Mr. Aotani—the *Oyakata* of the carpenters and the helpers in Iwato Yama—a *hoko* south of Shijo Street, is second generation in that capacity. His father had been the *Oyakata* for the same *hoko* until his death. Aotani accompanied his father in the Festival's work since his childhood, and apprenticed with his father in his youth. He learned the Festival's skills from his father along with his ordinary carpentry skills. Now Aotani leads the carpenters' and helpers' teams for the same community, and also employs his own son and nephew.

Aotani's wife recalled an incident concerning Aotani's mother, when his father had served as *Oyakata* for Iwato Yama in his time. The senior Mrs. Aotani was appalled that her husband was riding on the top of the *hoko* during the parade. That meant that he rode higher than the deities (whose statues were immediately under the roof on which he was sitting). Mrs. Aotani dealt with the problem by preparing each year a completely new set of clothes for her husband, including underwear and socks, to be worn during the parade only, so that he would be pure when he was close to the Gods. The current Mrs. Aotani continues to follow the same practice. "I do my best," she said, "and if an accident happens, at least I know I did all I could."

The *Oyakata* of the wheelmen for the same community, Mr. Wada, now in his early fifties, is the oldest son in his family. His grandfather had been the first generation in his family to work for Iwato Yama. Wada lives in Shiga prefecture, one hour's drive by car from Kyoto. He is the contractor of a team of highly skilled plasterers, who construct and repair the walls of the traditional gardens, homes, and temples, including the Imperial Palace in Kyoto. The team consists of Wada, his three brothers and his two sons. During the Festival, Wada, along with one brother and his two sons, works on the wheelmen's team for this community (*Iwatoyama*). Two other brothers work for Tzuki Boko—four blocks away, on Shijo Street.

When the Tzuki Boko team experiences difficulties, Wada runs over to Shijo Street, and advises his brothers; conversely, when Wada is short-handed, his brothers come over to help him. Usually, only Wada's oldest son had worked in the Festival. In 1989, Wada initiated his younger son (twenty years old) to the Festival's work. Wada introduced to me the shy young man with great pride. He told me that his wife, anxious over her younger son's exposure to danger, made his costume by her own hands, rather than have him borrow one of his brothers' or uncles' costume. This was in order "to please the Gods." During the parade the young man assisted the wheelmen by handing them tools and by carrying bamboo slats and water. He was not yet allowed near or under the wheels.

The *Oyakata* for the carpenters and helpers at Kanko Boko, Mr. Nakamura, in his late fifties, works normally as a construction worker. An orphan since his early teens, Nakamura was "adopted" by Mr. Sugiyama, the chief *Oyakata* for Kanko Boko, and was trained by him in ordinary construction and carpentry work. Sugiyama also trained him in the Festival's work, and since then they have been working together for Kanko Boko. Sugiyama claims that Nakamura was a juvenile deliquent in his teens and was tempted to join a gang. His initiation into the Festival's work gave Nakamura a sense of continuity and permanence. The commitment he formed towards the Festival then led him to embark on a more regular work-life on Sugiyama's construction team. Last year, Nakamura introduced two of his sons to the carpenters' team. Now all three work together and Sugiyama is grooming Nakamura as his successor as chief *Oyakata* for Kanko Boko.

Even the other members of the teams who are not related to each other or to the *Oyakata* through kinship ties have known each other for many years through their regular jobs, or by living in the same neighborhood. The Festival's work has placed them into a strong in-group relationship—into a symbolic community that is reconstituted without fail each year, once the Festival's work begins. The Festival's work provides the craftsmen with a special community, which transcends the boundaries of neighborhood, territory and status. Many of the older craftsmen and the community members have known each other's fathers and have known each other as young men. "We have watched each other grow older year after year."

A sense of continuity is not only an important factor in the craftsman's satisfaction and motivation. It is the key to the Festival's survival. The initiation of young men into the Festival's work and the transmission of skills to the next generation is one of the main concerns of the Festival's older craftsmen, especially of the *Oyakata*. Those who are unable to recruit their own sons, or who have no sons or nephews, encourage unrelated, but promising young men to join. "It was after the war (World War II), and life was still very dull around here. We were living here in the countryside and we were looking for some entertainment in the city," recalls Mr. Kida, *Oyakata* of the wheelmen of Kanko Boko:

> At that time they revived the Gion Festival for the first time since the War. My former classmate told me that he is helping an old man with the wheels of Kanko Boko. He said it was fun and it gives you a chance for entertainment in the city. I went along and I started to learn from him. Here I am, still doing it. But nowadays it is difficult to interest young men in this kind of work. They now earn enough and they can go on their own into the city and play around as much as they like.

Kida has no sons. After the old wheelmaster who trained him died, Kida started recruiting young men from his own village. Mr. Yamamoto, now in his early forties, was trained by Kida in this manner and is second in command. The wheelmen's most intricate work during the turning of the street corners now rests primarily on Yamamoto, a slender, short man, with enormous strength and the agility and the grace of a ballet dancer.

The older craftsmen and the *Oyakata* have few incentives to offer to the young men whom they recruit, other than sociability and the chance to perform in public. The sense of loyalty and the religious devotion, which are important to the older men, are less appealing to the younger ones. Perhaps the greatest incentive for the younger men is the speeding up of the training period, so that they will have a chance to perform in public during the parade.

Traditionally, apprenticeship in Japan has taken a long period out of a young man's life, during which he had to perform only menial tasks while learning from the master by observation or osmosis. Since the rapid modernization following World War II, the apprenticeship process was accelerated in all areas, except in the very traditional crafts such as weaving and the potteries. In the Gion Festivals' teams, the older men teach their young recruits with great dedication and care. They enable them to try to perform on their own within a short period after their initial training. They teach young carpenters and helpers the complicated conductor's (*Ondotori*) movements and chants, so that the young men would have the more glamorous role of wearing flamboyant costumes and of performing on the *hoko* during the parade.

The young men who had trained for this role in early July were allowed to perform as *Ondotori* (conductors) while the *hoko* moved on Oike Street. "We are giving the younger men a chance this year," said one of the middle aged *Ondotori* who was walking on the street behind the *hoko*.

> Of course we wouldn't let them do it on Shijo Street. [Where the more solemn and formal part of the parade takes place.] It is a good chance for them. After we turned the corner to Oike Street, we handed the fans over to them, and said "you do it now." We are walking behind the *hoko* so that the young men wouldn't feel that we are looking over their shoulders. But Mr. Nomura is there watching from the corner of his eye in case there is any trouble.

The following year, the two young men were allowed to be *Ondotori* during the turning of the street corner—when four *Ondotori* were leading together. The other two were their veteran teachers. After the parade, the *Oyakata* of the carpenters of that particular *hoko* asked me if I would send him copies of the pictures of the young men performing as *Ondotori*. He made it a special point to request the pictures of the young men, even though he was aware of my habit of sending him every year multiple prints of the pictures of his team members' work, which I took on various occasions of the Festival.

THE POWER OF KNOWLEDGE

Sugiyama, Nakamura, Aotani and Wada, and their many colleagues in other *hoko* carry the keys of the survival of the Gion

Festival. In their knowledge of the traditional skills also lies their sense of confidence, which allows them to rise beyond the confines of their class in modern Japanese society. Their special knowledge and skills are disappearing rapidly from modern Japan, as are other traditional crafts.

Most of the technical knowledge needed for the Gion Festival is based on the oral tradition. There are, of course, historic documents describing various organizational or traditional aspects of the Festival, but there are no technical manuals illustrating the details of construction, manipulation and movement. Some of the older *Oyakata*, such as Mr. Sugiyama, have developed their own manuals and diagrams consisting of informal notes which they modify and revise over the years. But there is no standard manual offering systematic guidelines. All the training of new apprentices takes place through observation and personal explanation. Prior to World War II the community leaders themselves carried a good deal of the knowledge about the construction, decoration and movement of the *hoko*, as well as about the history, symbolism, and rituals of the Festival, as part of an oral tradition. This knowledge has diminished considerably because of the erosion of the original communities in the *Yamahoko Cho*.

In every community, however, there still are some old men who carry on the oral tradition. These men work together with the master craftsmen and share their knowledge. In the Kanko Boko neighborhood, on Shijo Street for example, where not even one original dwelling or shop has survived, five old men, former residents of this community, return every year from the suburbs and cooperate with Mr. Sugiyama the *Oyakata*, with whom they have worked for over forty years. They pool their knowledge and offer him advice; but they always accept his decision on all technical matters as the final word.

Sugiyama and the other *Oyakata*, who carry the vanishing skills and knowledge required for maintaining this Festival exert special influence within the Yamahoko district—an influence and respect that transcend the usual status in Kyoto society. Some of the *Oyakata* stretch this power by trying to control various ceremonies connected with the Festival that are not central to the construction or maintenance of the *hoko*. Mr. T. for example, the *Oyakata* for one of the major *hoko*, expects complete submission from all the craftsmen under his command. He also orders the community members and leaders who carry out supportive and ceremonial tasks. Some of these members are the wealthiest men and heads of the most prestigious shops and families in Kyoto. Mr. T.

also dictates to the firemen when they should visit the *hoko's* exhibition space for inspection, and sometimes keeps the priest from the Yasaka shrine waiting on the street, while decoration of the *hoko* is in progress. In daily life, Mr. T., a building contractor, would have never had a chance to order the leaders of this *hoko* and he would have had virtually no social contact with them. Mr. T. has also become a favorite media subject. His face frequently appears in the newspapers and on television as the man who "singlehandedly carries the burden of that *hoko*."

Other *Oyakata*, such as Sugiyama, Kida, Aotani, and Wada are more modest in their exercise of power. They use their knowledge and skills as a resource to be shared with the community leaders, rather than as an instrument of aggrandizement. The community members collaborate with them and adhere to their judgment, especially on matters of safety and efficiency. One of the remarkable characteristics of the work procedures of these craftsmen and the community members is their style of collaboration and communication. An outsider approaching a *hoko* during its construction process could distinguish the craftsmen from the community members mostly by the fact that the craftsmen are wearing helmets ("hard hats") and baggy pants, with the tight leggings and boot characteristic of the construction trade. Otherwise, it would be difficult to tell apart the wealthy kimono wholesaler from the construction worker, as they work side by side. The *Oyakata* stands or sits next to the work area and supervises every activity. One rarely hears, however, an *Oyakata* or a community leader utter direct orders or instructions. Most of the work is carried out implicitly, based on mutual understanding of the tasks and procedures. New workers or volunteers watch carefully until they find their own tasks.

Most of the exercise of power by the traditional craftsmen is subtle but firm. While the younger craftsmen enjoy the opportunity to display their power and prowess, the older ones enjoy their special role in providing the continuity necessary for keeping the Festival alive, despite the hazards of modernization and the pressures of bureaucracy. For these older craftsmen the chance to serve in the Festival also fulfills an important religious function: it is their opportunity to serve the Gods.

DISCUSSION

The Gion Festival thus provides the rare opportunity of witnessing the temporary status reversal brought about by the special needs and challenges which the community members encounter in producing and maintaining the Festival. The transformation of the traditional *Yamahoko Cho* neighborhoods into a district of banking and business companies, and the accompanying depletion of the neighborhoods of their former residents and small shops has made the community members who still reside in this area dependent on the service of craftsmen from outside the district.

The community members who produce the Festival once a year are "modern" men and women, who work and live in modern settings, and who utilize modern technology (cars, telephones, electricity, for example), even for the Festival's work, whenever possible. The Festival's organization and events are timed precisely by modern schedules, and comply with the rules of contemporary bureaucracies, such as the municipal, prefectural and national government, insurance regulations, and police.

To the uninformed eye, the relationship between the craftsmen and the community members could be considered an ordinary form of sub-contracting in normal business relations. In such terms, it would mean that the community members hired the craftsmen to perform a certain job on an annual basis, in exchange for pay. Their relationship would not be different from that of other organizations or individuals who contract with craftsmen directly, or with an *oyakata* for certain services. In reality, however the relationship between the craftsmen and the community members is of a highly symbolic nature. It is deeply intertwined with the Festival's rituals, with labor for the Gods, and with the symbolic community that emerges during the Festival and recreates itself each year. Once a year the craftsmen identify with the Festival's community in which they achieve symbolic membership and status. (cf. Turner, 1969). They become part of this community by different means than the ordinary membership in an urban neighborhood (*chonai*) in Japan; they achieve temporary membership through work and participation in the Festival's effort.

The craftsmen who work in the Gion Festival are not, however fossils from another age. They are "modern men" who function under the constraints of the streamlined world of work and the bureaucratized society of modern Japan. They employ their traditional skills as a means of counteracting, at least temporarily, the larger processes of modernization and bureaucratization. Through their work in the Festival they express their identities as traditional craftsmen with special skills.

8

Work and Worship:
Changing Images and Changing Lives
in West Bengal

In 1956 the state government of West Bengal in India decided to build a steel plant on what were then the lush green paddy fields of a rural agricultural region.[1] In this area of strongly entrenched landlord interests, land acquisition presented a major problem, as did provision of housing and jobs for the uprooted, largely local villagers. As negotiations with the local representatives proceeded, a major unanticipated stumbling block presented itself in the form of a permanent shrine to the god Siva that stood on the site slated for clearance and construction of the industry. Siva is worshiped primarily, though not only, to enhance fertility, and this shrine attracted villagers from miles around. While any number of trade offs in the form of compensation and privilege were possible with regard to loss of land and livelihood for the villagers, when it came to the shrine the village and government representatives found themselves at a stalemate. The local representatives were adamant that it could not be moved and a compromise was only reached when the state agreed to leave the shrine intact, opening the gates to the factory grounds annually for the celebration of Siva Rattre, the major yearly ritual. The concession was an important one since women, who constitute the majority of visitors for this festival, are not ordinarily permitted on the grounds of heavy industrial sites.

Some participants in the negotiation might have expected that with time, and the growth of industry, interest in the shrine would wane, eventually to be forgotten. But, quite the opposite occurred. Over subsequent years, as the region developed into a major industrial urban belt, so did the importance of the shrine, until today tens, if not hundreds, of thousands of people including the work force of the surrounding industrial belt flock to the factory each year to make offerings and sacrifices in the hope of being granted children, particularly sons.

The experience related here is but one example among many of how ritual continues to thrive in the face of industrial development. This article explores ritual expression and symbolic representation as they relate to new forms of organization created by emerging patterns of production and reproduction, wage and non-wage labor that have transformed the regional economy and polity.

By now there is mounting evidence that the process of industrialization is far from a simple unidirectional path, characterized by a standard set of related economic, political, social, and ritual changes. The inadequacy of this model, drawn as it is from western capitalist experience, was evident as early as the 1950s and 1960s when anthropologists began to document "situational behavior" among migrants and workers in Africa (Mayer 1961, Mitchell 1969) and "compartmentalization" among industrialists in India (Singer 1972). Their studies explored adaptations to what were often conflicting and contradictory values and norms of the urban/industrial workplace in one instance, and those of "traditional" kin and community in another. Similarly, Third World workers in general have been characterized as "only partially proletarianized" (Leys 1971:315) or "semi-proletarianized," having supposedly failed to make the anticipated full transition to a "traditional working class" (Laite 1981).

There is then, a reluctance to move away from the familiar western frame of reference and to comprehend changes in the Third World, in terms of apparent deficiencies, instead of the very complex relationships between the various domains of social life that manifest themselves differently in each society. Within the conventional framework, the elaborate rituals of worship and ceremonial display on the factory grounds in West Bengal are but vestiges and holdovers of preindustrial beliefs and practices. However, as Nash has shown in her work on Bolivian miners, "assumptions about traditional and modern systems of belief often fail to capture the complexity of selective changes in symbol systems" (1979:162). The preconquest beliefs she describes provide the basis for Bolivian miners' formations of identity and resistance to oppressing, alien, industrial forces.

The following discussion contends that ritual and symbolic representation figure centrally in the process of industrial social change. The world of representation among Bengali factory workers is a contested domain in which symbols constitute potent weapons in the struggle over transformed and continually changing class, caste, and gender identities. While these identities are readily explained and contained in the multitude of dichotomous categories that form the underpinnings for conventional theoretical understandings of industrialization, modernization, and development, during the past few years they have been scrutinized by feminist anthropologists.

Categories such as modern/traditional, public/private, production/reproduction, with their heavy freight of associations, apply across all historical time and social space. Feminist anthropologists point out that the domains of public and private are *not* coterminous cross-culturally; they show that power and authority are not simply distributed along the lines of public/private, or male/female. Moreover it can be argued that in the domestic domain, the privatization of the world of women and reproduction is the creation of, rather than a background to capitalism (Mies 1986). Capitalism creates and recreates "housewife-like" forms of non-waged work and petty commodity production upon which the wage system depends (Bennholt-Thomsen 1981, 1984; Mies 1986). Furthermore, a number of studies now show how relations of interdependence among women engaged in nonwage work form basic structures for survival, (Stack 1974) and contexts for politicization (Susser 1982).

This critique assumes change to be a constant, social forms and meanings to be continually in flux, so that old organizational forms can, as Cohen (1974) has shown, fulfill new functions and take on new meanings. The terms of my discussion then shift to the structure and meaning that new and old forms take at specific times and places, under varying conditions.

In what follows, I discuss changes in ritual performance and symbolic representations found in two arenas: that of the factory

and that of the residential town of Rajmath, in the context of regional economic and political changes. I review four major ritual
complexes as they have emerged in recent years: (1) the celebration
of Biswakarma, creator of the universe, (2) The Durga-Kali ritual
complex, (3) the worship of Laksmi, goddess of wealth, and (4) women's household rituals. The primary focus is on the first three, on
the yearly festivals connected with the worship of these deities,
while the fourth is touched on only briefly and serves to show
how, as men gain control over major areas of ritual representation,
the performance of womens' rites creates the organizational basis
for an extensive network of support in times of need. These rituals
are referred to using the Bengali term *puja,* and the major occasions
are characterized by the acquisition of a clay image of the deity,
either through purchase from, or traditional exchange relationship
with, persons of the potter caste (*Kumar*).

The discussion is framed by several questions, the answers to
which suggest the varied ways in which accommodation and resistance are continually being worked out through the medium of
symbolic expression: (1) Which deities are chosen for worship? (2)
How are the deities represented? (3) Where does the ritual take
place? (4) Who are the participants in the celebrations? (5) Who has
control over the presentation and representation of the deities?

BACKGROUND

The population of the town of Rajmath comprises the former
inhabitants of ten villages relocated in 1956 to a nearby field when
the aforementioned steel plant was built. This region soon thereafter became the second major urban industrial complex in the
state of West Bengal. Known as Chandinagar, its population grew to
500,000 within ten years. From a relatively stable agricultural region under the control of the local small elite landlord class, this
industrial stretch quickly became a hotly contested political field,
an arena for radical working class politics and the center of major
political upheaval.

Initially Rajmath was largely shielded from the momentous
changes taking place in the burgeoning metropolitan area by leading members of the local landlord class, who, by virtue of key positions they held in government and industry, retained power in
their hands. This situation changed with the emergence of competitive unionization and electoral politics. The change was foreshad-
owed by shifts in the structure and composition of class and caste
relations brought on by industrialization.

In this region, class and caste roughly coincided. Formerly one-quarter of the population were of the landlord class, primarily Brahman by caste, one-quarter were small-landed agricultural workers of the middle range agricultural and artisan castes, and one-half were landless agricultural workers, largely Untouchables. Some members of the landlord class were able to start businesses, and those with connections were to profit handsomely as contractors of materials and labor. Most of the able bodied men, however, were absorbed into the industrial workforce. As persons of different castes worked side by side in similar jobs, the once congruent structure of caste and class began to shift, and bonds of clientage formerly linking families of different castes were broken.

While men worked in the factory for eight-hour shifts and tilled what remained of their fields, women were unable to obtain jobs in the formal labor market. Not only were they barred from work in the factory, but they found that men were preferred, even for secretarial jobs. And, where women of the agricultural classes had once worked together with men in the fields, now there was pressure in the name of status and purity to relegate them to the home, to domestic and reproductive labor. Previously the cultivated fields and household formed a unified field of agricultural production, now public and private domains became increasingly differentiated, as did gender roles.

In an economy to which cash income was quickly becoming of critical importance, the relegation of women's work to nonwage labor meant that women's labor power took on less value, and women, perceived increasingly as a burden, became difficult to marry off. Once a more equal exchange, marriage now became less so as dowry came to be a requisite for being given away. Dowry, or "demand," as it is called, long customary among those of the landlord class who could afford to confine their women, spread rapidly among the former agricultural laborers, forcing families into debt. It spread like a tide, which even the organized efforts of various caste councils (*samaj*) found themselves unable to change. During this same period, dramatic changes occurred in the ritual life of the population. They took place in the factory, in the residential town of Rajmath, and in the homes.

THE FACTORY

While Siva, symbolizing potency and reproduction, drew the attention of women from far and wide, ritual activity organized inside the factory by men, focused on Biswakarma, creator of the universe. Only a short time before, Biswakarma was exclusively worshipped in small foundries and associated with the highly specialized caste of Blacksmiths (*Lohar*). Now he had become popular in heavy industry. In the classical text of the Mahabharata he is mentioned frequently as having fashioned the weapons and tools of warriors out of bone. And, as each deity has its respective animal carrier, Biswakarma is depicted with his carrier the elephant (see figure 1).

Today, the yearly ritual celebration of Biswakarma has become one of the most popular throughout this industrial belt. In the steel plant each department collects money, vies to buy the best image, and in competitive spirit, stages various social activities such as dramas. As with all images, at the end of the puja, it is paraded with fanfare through the streets to its ultimate destination for immersion into the body of water—a pond or river—that symbolizes home.

The significance of this appropriation of the deity, Biswakarma, by a large scale industrial organization can only be fully appreciated in the light of the broad representation of castes that constitute the workforce of the industry. From Rajmath alone a nearly full spectrum of castes participates. Once associated with the ascriptive status of caste, Biswakarma now has come to represent a new working class culture.

Contrary to expectations, however, industrial management not only suffers the existence of these festivities, but together with the trade union helps to organize them. Perhaps this can best be explained by the festivities providing a means both to make otherwise arduous and distasteful factory work palatable, and also to help instill a competitive spirit among the workers. It has become part of the process whereby formerly agricultural laborers are ushered into the culture of the workplace. As Willis (1981) describes for working class youths in Britain, culture penetrates ideology, in this case the ideology of industrial labor, enabling internalization of a new working class culture. Rather than being simply a tool of management, however, the festivities take on a life of their own as they provide the occasion for a new form of collective action essential to organizing on the basis of class rather than caste.

THE TOWN

In the residential town of Rajmath, similarly striking changes in patterns of worship have occurred, only two of which will be

Figure 8.1. Biswakarma. Clay Image of the Creator of the Universe, with his carrier, the elephant. Eva Friedlander, photographer.

mentioned here. The first is the increasingly widespread observance of *pujas* surrounding the Durga/Kali complex, and the
second concerns changes associated with the observance of Laksmi
puja.

The Durga-Kali Complex

The ultimate power in Bengali cosmology is expressed in Ma Sakti
(*sakti* = power), a power that can be used either as a positive force
for creation, as represented by the goddess Durga (see figure 2), or
as a negative force for destruction, as represented by the goddess
Kali (see figure 3). Both the rituals associated with Durga and Kali
have spread widely since industrialization. Worshipped primarily
as Durga, Ma Sakti sits astride her carrier, the lion, brandishing ten
weapons in her ten hands, at once the slayer of Ravanna the
demon, and the mother of the gods who surround her: Ganesha,
associated with business, Laksmi with wealth, Saraswati with
learning, and Kartik, the soldier, with warfare. The archtypical
mother, she upholds virtue against evil. But, she is also a daughter
and hence makes the annual autumnal visit to her father's house
for four days, finally to be sent back to the Himalayas where she
resides at her father-in-law's house. As for Durga, so for the women
of Rajmath, and increasing numbers of women in Bengal, who
travel ever further for a suitable marriage. They leave their father's
house for their father-in-law's house upon marriage, returning but
once a year for a few short days at the time of Durga Puja. For the
wives of the new factory workers, this journey between the two
houses is one with which they are painfully familiar. Protectors of
virtue, they are destined to be forever outsiders, moving between
the two.

Prior to industrialization the sponsorship of Durga Puja, the
major yearly ritual in West Bengal, lay largely in the hands of the
dominant landlord families, Brahmans by caste. Establishing a permanent image in the family temple for the yearly celebration required the ability to mobilize a wide network of kin, the resources
to pay for related ritual work, and a regional clientage that would
attend the associated rituals and festivities. In turn, the *puja*
served to solidify and strengthen the power and influence of the
family in the region.

Other sectors of the population also occasionally tried to
sponsor such a *puja* in an attempt to raise their caste rank. A sign
from Durga was usually the precipitating factor. She would appear
in a dream asking to be worshipped and given a permanent home

Figure 8.2. Durga. Clay Image of the Goddess of Creation. Eva Friedlander, photographer.

in the household. In one village, an image, known to be particularly powerful, was established by the Bagdis with the help of their Brahman patrons. The Bagdi caste held a marginal position between the respectable and untouchable castes, but had managed to raise themselves to respectable rank while still in the village. Sponsorship of a Durga Puja marked their separation from the Untouchables. Within the first decade after industrialization, other castes similarly tried to install a Durga in their temples, but most met with failure.

While these attempts most often were unsuccessful, another development began to change the very nature of the festival. Durga had gained widespread popularity among a much broader sector of the general population in West Bengal than previously, and her worship was now being taken out of the confines of the home and into the public arena. Rather than being sponsored by a family, the ritual and accompanying festivities were now being taken over by neighborhood groups. They came to be known as *sarbajanin pujas* (community rituals) and were organized predominantly by working class men. These public celebrations became especially popular in urban industrial areas, and were the focus of widespread gift giving and growing consumerism. A similar situation without the gift exchange pertained with regard to the goddess Kali, the major related festival held approximately one month after Durga *puja*.

In contrast to Durga, her counterpart, Kali is depicted in the throes of a frightening spate of madness brought on by her son Kartik's death. Insane with grief, she rampages the world, killing and destroying all in her path. Only the desperate act of her husband Siva, who tries to stop her by throwing himself beneath her feet, stems the tide of her anger. With this reversal of the natural order, she is shamed to her senses and realizes with full horror the extent of her power and the destruction she has wrought. Her body adorned with skulls and bones, she is depicted as surrounded by the symbols of death, funeral pyres and skeletons, tongue extended in shame and astonishment to find her husband underfoot. Kali, associated with death, has always been a favorite with dacoits, thieves and persons of generally shady repute, but she is now far more generally popular.

Shakti, then, is represented as mother and creator on the one hand and as wife and destroyer on the other. The image of Durga conveys the critical and central role women play in reproduction and maintenance of the labor force. In Kali, wife and destroyer, the potentially destructive power of wives is conveyed, and a warning issued regarding the need for control lest they wander forth and

Figure 8.3. Kali. Poster Image of the Goddess of Destruction. Eva Friedlander, photographer.

play havoc with the world. At another level the two images reflect the increasingly ambiguous position women hold between their father's house and their father-in-law's house, due to their growing economic dependency and the ambivalence in sentiment towards women that this breeds.

Durga has achieved a kind of mass appeal in West Bengal, and with this has come significant change in the iconography associated with her. The images of Durga can be divided roughly into three types. The most traditional image is highly stylized, with little differentiation except for size and face, between Durga and her four children. They convey a visual unity enhanced by the painted semi circular arc that frames the group, depicting scenes from the Himalayas, her father-in-law's home from where she descends and to which she must return. A more modern image is somewhat naturalistic in form. Standing close to one another the deities are realistically dressed or painted in draped clothes. Distinct from one another, they continue to be loosely united by the painted arc above them. The images used for *sarbajanin pujas*, the third type, have, however, lost this unifying framework and are now presented as separate figures, an expression of the fragmentation of the old kin based social order that is now being transformed (see figure 4).

Laksmi Puja

Similar changes are underway with regard to the significance of the goddess Laksmi and surrounding ritual activity. Associated with agriculture, the production and distribution of rice—the staple food—Laksmi rituals have in the past been, and continue to be, aimed at a plentiful harvest. Performed in the fields and households, the major observances take place on four occasions throughout the year. In addition, they are performed four times a month, and worship of Laksmi constitutes an integral part of other rituals as well.

The goddess Laksmi can be represented in any number of ways: a clay image, a picture (see figure 4),—frequently a poster illustration—simply the figure of her carrier the owl, a brass measure of rice covered in red cloth and decorated with cowrie shells representing an auspicious wedding sari, or by the rice paddy itself. She enters every household in the form of footsteps outlined in rice powder, and these adorn all other festivities as well. Every young girl hears herself endearingly called Laksmi *may*, or daughter Laksmi, as she is growing up, and married women too may be called Laksmi *ma* or mother Laksmi, in praise of their dutiful performance of the housewifely role. Good fortune is said to come from having Laksmi in the house.

Today, however, the need for dowry has meant that girls are increasingly seen as a drain on the household economy and the image of Laksmi is less associated with agricultural production than with wealth in the form of cash or capital. Accordingly, a good daughter is an obedient one, a girl who can be married off easily; the good wife is a frugal housekeeper, and above all the mother of sons, enabling her father-in-law's household to prosper financially.

Figure 8.4. Laksmi. Image of the Goddess of Wealth. Eva Friedlander, photographer.

In picture images today, coins are often a substitute for the inevitable paddy she was once depicted as strewing at her feet (see figure 6); the brass measure of rice may be replaced by a small clay pot with a slit for use as a bank. And, where once performed in the fields and at home, now the major rituals take place at the temple as well.

In addition, however, to the multitude of Laksmi *pujas* that mark the yearly ritual cycle, the primary annual festival dedicated to Laksmi has become a public ritual and the most elaborate one associated with her name. Not unlike Durga and Kali *pujas*,

Figure 8.5. Clay Images of the Goddess Durga, slaying the Demon Ravanna, and her four children, each a separate and naturalistic figure. Used for community *puja (sarbajanin puja)*. Eva Friedlander, photographer.

Figure 8.6. Popular calendar picture of the Goddess Laksmi commonly found in homes.

Laksmi *puja* is also organized by neighborhood men, her image paraded through the streets. These festivities, however, are organized predominantly by upper caste/class men in the town, those who have had the longest involvement with wage labor, and who now, having lost all their land, are the least involved with agricultural production. While for the lower caste/class population still somewhat involved in cultivation, Laksmi *puja* represents women's control over agricultural processes, for the upper class population she represents potential wealth as the bearer of sons and household manager. Here the shift in emphasis from women's central role in agricultural production to reproduction is made explicit.

Several female deities, then, have moved prominently into the public arena, the organization of related ritual activities largely appropriated by men. Their representation is expressive of new structural tensions experienced by women, in turn eliciting fears of unpredictability and the need for control. Durga, Kali, and Laksmi were always present in Bengali cultural life, but they have now become all pervasive in ways they had never been.

Women's Rituals

While these examples provide ample evidence for accommodation by a new proletariat to working class conditions and a growing immersion in the capitalist economy, what they tell about resistance, is less obvious. At one level, the collective experience in organizing across caste lines for neighborhood "ritual work" can be said to provide substantial collective experience that may then be transferred to the political arena. But there is another sphere of representation, the world of women's rituals that draws on an overlapping, yet separate pantheon of deities and spirits. The multitude of rites, such as *Siva Rattre*, with which this article began, richly punctuate women's lives. The express purpose is enhancement of the fortunes of their father-in-law's homes, the birth of sons, their health and wealth, as well as that of other members of the household. But the rituals are also the occasions for communal activity for which it is necessary to gain the cooperation and labor of other women. They are, therfore, the occasion for developing neighborhood ties first in their father's house and later their father-in-law's house. The ever constant mobilization of women to prepare for one or another *puja* and the associated exchange of goods, services, and information, lay the groundwork for a broad network of mutual support. These bonds provide women with the basis to resist some of the abuse which results from growing economic dependency, separation from kin, and the resulting alienation they experience.

CONCLUSION

Ritual expression is, then, not antithetical to the world of industrial labor, nor does capitalist development appear to be ushering in the demise of expressive rites. Rather, if the activities in Chandinagar are any indication, is appears that ritual worship has increased in extent and intensity. As Abner Cohen has stated, ritual lies at the nexus of self and society, its symbols expressive of the designs of the broader society and polity, at the same time that they are linked to the interpretive needs of individuals. According to Cohen, "In these performances, selfhood is recreated in terms of the symbolic forms that articulate the changing organizational needs of the group, and the organizational needs are thereby transformed into categorical imperatives that impel the individual to action through the inner dynamics of selfhood." (Cohen 1981: 155–156) The "group," however, has changed. It is no longer the village caste, or intervillage caste network; nor is it the village. Rather, new forms of solidarity have emerged. In Chandinagar the shifts that have taken place at a ritual and symbolic level express recent changes in relations of power, both with regard to class and gender. At the same time, both in their potential for reinterpretation and in the changing parameters along which participation takes place, these rituals break ground for new forms of collective action.

9

Working Through the Crisis: Resistance and Resignation in the Culture of a Deindustrialized Community

INTRODUCTION

The crisis of de-industrialization in Cape Breton, Nova Scotia was experienced most recently through plant closures during the 1980s. The closures epitomize how processes of uneven development result in the marginalization of regional economies and the way historical circumstances of community development play a significant role in the articulation of social responses to structural changes (Roseberry 1988; Smith 1989). Using the example of Glace Bay, a Cape Breton mining community, this paper will consider the nature of local culture as it has been produced and reproduced historically.[1] Particular attention will be accorded contradictory ideological processes in Glace Bay culture evidenced in workplace, household, and community relations, which demonstrate Sider's proposition that "culture is an active force in history" (1986:7).

In 1987, just before my arrival in Glace Bay, there was an unexpected outburst of militancy in the town's largest fish processing plant, also the largest private source of employment in the town. Paradoxically this resistance occurred at a time when optimism should have prevailed about the plant's more stable future. The plant had been recently modernized and the management was promising more secure employment. However, management's strategies for restructuring the plant's labor process clashed with deeply held cultural values that were previously accommodated under more paternalistic forms of control.

As I argue elsewhere (Barber 1990), the plant workers' militancy demonstrated the potential for resistance contained within local culture practices. By the same token, fish plant paternalism was compatible with resignation, a form of subordination to the interests of capital. The fact that fish plant paternalism was the management system preferred by the Glace Bay fish plant workers attests to the strength of this form of plant organization. The experiences embedded in household and community relations in Glace Bay which have been sustained through the long processes of deindustrialization in the Cape Breton economy, contributed to the shape of production politics in local fish plants, as well as to household livelihood practices.

This paper demonstrates how the mobilization of household strategies in informal economic relations in Glace Bay occurs within an ideological framework which has emphasized a strong sense of community commitment and identity. Forms of intimacy and obligatory social ties in the paternalistic workplace *and* in community relations, can serve the interests of capital and the state in maintaining a labor force relatively satisfied with more marginal forms of employment; the lesser wage income being compensated for through household resource strategies and community relations. These forms of accommodation to the status quo, fueled by ideologies and sentiments which are disparaging of alternative practices, appear to embrace a false consciousness about the relative economic disadvantages experienced by the community as a whole.

On the other hand, these mutually reinforcing sets of relations also allow alternative and sometimes historically radical challenges to external forms of control. Paradoxically, the local forms of fish plant paternalism (and political patronage) provided both the rationale for workplace militancy and the method for mobilization. Thus the consciousness of these plant workers does not follow the more obvious route suggested by periods of radical expression in the town's history (described below); namely that the historical manifestations of community-based radical class consciousness is the explanation for the recent militancy and emergent class awareness. For such is the conclusion which might be drawn from a narrow application of a theoretically anticipated class consciousness (see Fantasia's 1989 critique). On the contrary, this most recent example of worker mobilization underlines a dialectical tension between cultural strategies, which I associate here with resignation and resistance. These strategies are tied to both the material and subjective components of the workplace, household, and local community, all of which are dynamically engaged with the broader structures of political economy.

Owing to certain developments in marxism, theories of the labor process have dominated the study of the relationship between work and class-based mobilizations. A productionist bias still pervades much of this research despite a decade of critique, most notably from feminist theory, that demonstrates the significance of gendered relations of social reproduction. Moreover, theories of the labor process which neglect the broader social environment outside of the workplace, fail to account for the lived experience of social class; the cultural dimensions of the workplace, working at a certain job, *and* the various other activities and relations which are involved in daily living. As Marx noted, the politics of production and political mobilizations are forged through both objective and subjective class-based experiences. Relations of both class and gender are reinforced, reproduced and also, most importantly from the point of view of responses to economic and social transformations, resisted and reacted against through social routines which make up all of daily life. Finally, as this example of Glace Bay well illustrates, the cultural processes and patterns of work which guide the agendas for militant social action and which can expand and/or limit people's perceptions of the possibilities of collective action, are nurtured within household and community relations, as well as at privileged sites of production.

THE NATURE OF LOCAL CULTURE

Historically, Glace Bay and the other mining towns of Cape Breton) were built on hardship and conflict. A series of powerful mining interests sought to prevent and later weaken the collective voice of the miners in order to keep down labor costs as a buffer against unstable markets. Forceful methods were used to suppress the miners' militancy and the Canadian state proved a willing agent of capital in shaping the formative politics and economy of the region. Indeed the state was prepared to kill for capital in this period and even today, a local municipal holiday commemorates the death of miner William Davis, shot in 1925 by untrained but legally constituted company police. Collusion between local and national politicians also allowed for the deployment of the Canadian militia on numerous occasions, most notably during the volatile decade ending with the bitter strike of 1925 (Macgillivray 1980).

The miners who migrated to work in the Cape Breton coal fields during the early years of this century came with two important sets of cultural experience. Many came from the impoverished rural communities in the region first settled in the early 1800s by highland Scots evicted during the brutal Highland clearances. This group brought with them cultural conventions forged out of the extreme hardships of their uprooting and resettlement. Most notably they clearly held strong commitments of loyalty to their kith and kin. Later migrants, more experienced industrial wage laborers arrived from Europe and brought with them practical knowledge of class politics and the union movement. From this blending of culture and tradition emerged a strong, articulate, and disciplined union leadership which harnessed extraordinary loyalty from the rank and file miners; union loyalties were eventually able to transcend potentially divisive cleavages based upon ethnic and religious ties and, significantly, the rivalries stemming from different forms of labor contract and hierarchy in the workplace.

The documented labor histories of this period emphasize that through the increasingly bitter wrangling with the coal companies, the people of Glace Bay and other mining communities manifested an intensification of solidarity, strength, and commitment in their fight for a decent and fair means of livelihood. There is clear evidence of the development of radical class consciousness on the part of more than a few miners (Frank 1979, 1988; McKay 1983) and control over community affairs was wrest by miners from local politicians too willing to perform the bidding of the coal companies (Frank 1981). What had been company towns became labor towns. In Glace Bay in particular, after the battering received by miners and their union in the workplace, the political front shifted more obviously to the community level. The electoral process became one vehicle for a distinctive community-based voice after the disappointing outcome of strike action (White 1978). Thus, Glace Bay was founded in a period which saw shared adversity and suffering as common experience along with calculated strategies of class-based resistance. These circumstances shaped the distinctive characteristics of local culture, a culture marked by a longstanding capacity to weather hardship (an inward-looking set of strategies) and also, traditions of solidarity conducive to collective acts of resistance.

At the time of my research in 1987, the constancy of hard times and the persistence over generations of the struggle, in Kathy MacPherson's words, to put "bread on the table," is every bit as much the legacy of historical events as the social memory of industrial conflicts. Resignation to economic hardship and, on occasion, forceful collective resistance to perceived injustices, the predispositions in Glace Bay working class culture, are underscored through the daily struggles to survive as well as through the collective mobilizations of major labor conflicts. Thus, in Glace Bay, some sixty years after the bloody events of Davis Day in 1925, history bears upon the present not just because of conflict in the relations of production but also through the impact of persistent economic decline upon household economics in the domain of social reproduction. The idea of "getting by no matter what," a pragmatic approach to the difficulties presented by living with chronic economic instabilities, is reproduced as the cornerstone of Glace Bay's culture. This culture is well articulated at the household level.

Miners were able to forge cohesive class strategies of resistance through the social ties of kinship and community, and out of necessity, people relied upon these social ties for household subsistence. Hence, household economic strategies were also tied in with the capacity for resistance on the part of the miners. The resourcefulness and skill applied to daily survival, particularly during the seasons of cutbacks and strikes, required the extended labor of all members of households especially women. In this sense, women's labor—but also other forms of household labor—sustained the protracted resistance of the Cape Breton miners. The very same strategies which were applied to harnessing support for class-based action were also applied to mobilize social, political, and economic resources for household survival. Glace Bay culture therefore, has been historically produced and reproduced to reinforce particularly close knit ties of kin and community and local loyalties, including a reliance upon extended household labor. Historical events reveal these relations were essential to the shaping of working class consensus displayed by the miners, their dependents, and their supporters. Household, community, and workplace dynamics were necessarily intertwined in the processes through which Glace Bay class-culture emerged (in the Thompsonian sense).

Working class culture in Glace Bay today resonates with distinctive attitudes, ideologies, and practices which have been carried forward as part of the class-based "mode of social recognition" defining everyday life in Glace Bay (Williamson 1982:2). As my Glace Bay neighbor Doris MacLeod told me; "people in Glace Bay today who were born and raised here grew into it too," that is they have learned well the livelihood strategies inscribed in local culture where "making do" is a predominant theme.[2] In 1987, the context of daily life, a major component to the "it" Doris speaks about, meant contending with an official unemployment rate which climbed to 25%—an artificially low figure held down by short-term work grants and by the failure of the statistics to capture the employment instabilities of seasonal and casual workers.

LIVELIHOOD

The concept of household livelihood is applied here in the broadest sense of the term. In reflecting on family and households, anthropologists (and historians) have shifted their attention away from classification, typology, and structural comparisons towards a view that the social units we label as households, or sometimes families " . . . are as much about production, exchange, power, inequality, and status." (Yanagisako (1979:199) This production, or resource-focused model of the household resolves several problems evident in earlier approaches. First, it avoids the tendency to conflate family and household as if they referred to the same thing. Moreover, the household resource model avoids the limitations posed by presuming kinship relations to be the distinguishing feature of the productive unit (Harris and Young 1981), and discourages presuppositions about household membership, commitments and activities on the basis of residence and propinquity (Harris 1981; 1982). Finally, by focusing on how resources available to households are processed, it is possible to move away from the implicit biological reductionism which has plagued much of the literature dealing with the functional and structural features of the gendered division of labor within households.[3]

The main thrust of recent critiques of household-focused research has been directed towards what Whitehead (1981:89) refers to as the "black box"; the need to de-construct household relations in what was often portrayed as the socially neutral household.

Through the lack of analysis indicating otherwise, households were perceived as consensual units where the needs of all were catered to (MacKintosh 1988). A related problem preoccupying feminist approaches to the study of households and work concerned the treatment of home-based labor. In an important if protracted theoretical debate, feminist scholars exposed the academic conventions in which domestic labor was rendered invisible, or was located in a domain separated from market oriented forms of work and valorization. Thus activities associated with productive work came to be examined closely whereas activities associated with domestic labor, and the contributions to the household from domestic labor received less attention. Households are by no means consensual units. Household income strategies (the disbursement of the resources of the household, including labor) and the allocation of the benefits and returns from the resources, involve the politics of gender and of age (for example, Whitehead 1981; Sharma 1986; Morris 1990). Furthermore, dualistic models which separate market and nonmarket forms of labor, or formal and informal spheres of economic activity, are of limited application. In these ways various critiques posed by feminist perspectives have guided an expanded concept of work, labor, and resources enabling a more complete understanding of the interrelationships between household-based labor (for the purposes of self-provisioning as well as market-based exchange) and labor in the formal wage sector of the economy (for example, Bradley 1989; Pahl 1984; Redclift and Mingione 1985).

Certainly, in the case of livelihood practices in Glace Bay, the interdependencies between wage labor and domestic labor and formal and informal economy become more apparent when the contributions from community and household relations are drawn out. One novel aspect to household practices in Glace Bay is the intense sociability required to maximize household resources and to gain useful information about a whole range of economically significant opportunities. In short, the work of livelihood in Glace Bay continues to involve "looking out for one's own" and to draw upon meaningful social ties. As noted in a recent study of urban household economies:

> Livelihood is never just a matter of finding or making shelter, transacting money, and preparing food to put on the table or exchange in the market place. It is equally a matter of the ownership and circulation of information, the management of relationships, the affirmation of personal significance and group identity, and the interrelation of each of those tasks to

the other. All these productive tasks together constitute the work of livelihood. A similarly expanded concept of work is implicit in studies of unenumerated economic organization or the informal sector (Wallman 1984:22).

Today as in the past, households in Glace Bay engage in a wide range of economic activities which call upon kin and neighborhood based networks of support. Kin based patterns of household occupancy are also extremely fluid. Not all couples are able to set up and sustain their own households although that might be their first choice in more prosperous conditions. Furthermore, Glace Bay residents join other Cape Bretoners in the longstanding practice of emigration, seeking either temporary wage work or perhaps a better, more financially secure livelihood elsewhere. Here again, kin based networks are mobilized to assist the emigrants in getting settled in their new environment. All of these practices fuel an ideology of Cape Bretoners as warm, hospitable, sociable, generous, loyal, and above all, strongly committed to "back home" and to the idea of returning home.

Glace Bay household economic practices in the formal and informal sectors of the economy are inextricably bound up with cultural expressions of a sense of place and way of life. Such ideologies of commitment to place and people can provide a buffer against the injustices of political and economic processes which have undermined the Cape Breton economy. The local discourse expressing commitment to place emphasizes the positive features of the community, its neighborliness and friendliness and the fact that people help each other out and seek to enjoy life. By socially affirming their commitment to place, the people of Glace Bay foster an outlook which includes pragmatism, loyalty, and a sense of shared hardship, all of which I am posing as part and parcel of the local cultural dynamic of resignation but also of resistance.

A SENSE OF PLACE: LOCAL COMMUNITY

Like many coal districts the mining communities of north east Cape Breton have retained their distinctive character, stark and sprawling. Whereas the nineteenth century coal towns of England and Wales were built with brick, stone, and slate, the coal companies of Cape Breton built simple wooden structures which have survived as the basic architectural form. In the early stages of construction in the town, neighborhoods were built around the pitheads of the mines as well as around the downtown commercial area. At the turn of the century, when Glace Bay's major settlement occurred, the company houses were placed within walking distance of the pithead they served, further testimony to the hegemonic interests of coal companies in controlling their labor force and commanding ready access to the labor power they so brutally exploited.

Today the historical conditions of the settlement of Glace Bay are still represented in these neighborhoods, often named after the mine that determined their existence. While such places as Bridgeport, New Aberdeen, Number 2, The Hub, Sterling, Caledonia, Passchendaele, MacKay's Corner, and so on, are not clearly marked on the official map of the town, residents refer to their neighborhoods by these names. Socially, these neighborhoods continue to function as distinctive little communities. Residents of adjacent neighborhoods such as "the Hub" and "Number 2" can hold strong opinions about the different social attributes of members of the adjacent neighborhood, one street away, despite the fact that there are no visible distinguishing features, nor apparent social differences between the two neighborhoods. This particular pattern of strongly asserted neighborhood identities became apparent in 1987 on those occasions when extraordinary events disrupted the otherwise smooth flowing of daily events. One event which inspired reflections on the social attributes of various neighborhoods involved a violent robbery. This crime was explained away by some townspeople as predictable because, "after all, what would you expect from those people up there." (This prediction was not confirmed by the local police department who felt that the town's crime rates could not be pinned down to the neighborhood level.)

Furthermore, people usually present their place of birth by neighborhood first: "I was born out Caledonia way" or "I was raised in the Hub." Thus, neighborhoods are the focal point of many longstanding and predictable social relationships. Ties of obligations and expectations typically associated with community relations are first and foremost embedded at the neighborhood level in Glace Bay.

One final example of the manner in which the coal mining heritage imposes upon basic community orientations in everyday life concerns social gatherings which occur at the neighborhood level. Because these neighborhoods were first built up as discrete entities, many of them contain a hall large enough to host sizable social gatherings. Such gatherings might take the form of private family functions, such as anniversaries, weddings, christenings, general family reunions and the like, all of which are celebrated extensively in Glace Bay. But the gatherings can also be staged to provide a social event at the neighborhood level, as in the example of the benefit dance which serves the dual purpose of socializing and fund-raising.

The benefit dance indicates that today, most Glace Bay residents recognize the pit-head focused neighborhoods as a place where one has identity and personal support in hard times. For example, a single parent employed at a local fish processing plant was worried about stretching her budget to cover additional expenses relating to specialized medical treatments her son required in Halifax, the provincial capital (some 600 kilometers away). Her co-workers proposed a benefit dance in the community hall of the area where she had been "raised" but was no longer resident. The benefit appeared not to carry any social stigma arising out of such a pubic statement of financial need. It was suggested by the woman's co-workers that whereas her present neighborhood in Reserve Mines would be much less likely to support her cause, people from her "home" neighborhood in the Hub knew her well and would "come out" to a benefit in her assistance. The cost outlay to stage a benefit included a fee for the hiring of the hall and often a disk jockey's services. A small cover charge plus money from the sale of drinks usually covers these costs and allows for modest fund raising. And in fact, announcements in the community newspaper revealed benefits to be a common form of personal fund-raising at the neighborhood level. Locality or one's community base continues, therefore, to have efficacy both socially and economically, a factor which I am posing as crucial to household survival strategies and to class-based mobilization such as that initiated by the town's militant fish plant workers in this historical-cultural setting of long-term economic decline.

SHARING HOUSES AND TRADING SKILLS: KINSHIP AND NEIGHBORHOOD BASED INFORMAL ECONOMY

In Glace Bay, as I have noted above, housing is a key resource in economic strategies. People moved between households giving and receiving aid in response to changes in their own or other's circumstances. Few households in the study remained stable through the nine month research period. Residence patterns also emphasized the protracted dependency of children upon their parents for shelter as well as other kinds of resources. Requests to return to a parental home can arise from adult children in the middle years of their life. Other kin also participate in shared residence arrangements. The rule of thumb in such arrangements appeared to be that people contributed what they could afford to the household budget. The transactions were couched in terms of "helping out" the tenants rather than providing economic benefit from the extra cash income for the owners of the house, although clearly there may be some mutual benefits accorded by the sharing of housing.

The utilization of kinship ties is also apparent in various aspects of the substantial, class-based informal sector which extends beyond living arrangements.[4] Patterns of household occupancy and informal deals made between kin and neighbors are manifestations of culturally based structures which are not revealed by official statistics. In the informal sector in Glace Bay, men and women use skills learned in this historical context where necessity provoked a "do it yourself" and "help your own" (kith and kin) ethic. Skills were and are applied to produce, trade and/or purchase goods and services used for self-consumption. When possible, informally learned skills have also been carried into labour markets where confidence and good connections secured jobs without formal sector qualifications. (This has become increasingly difficult.)

For example, Linda MacDonald's husband Ted moved to Glace Bay as an adult. He had moved away with his father while still a young child but his father's ties to home had remained strong. Ted had been taught a variety of useful trade skills by his father, skills which he later applied to make a living at various jobs in several different localities. Linda tells the story which illustrates the viability of informal exchanges at the neighborhood level:

> My husband has got grade eight education. He went to school in Calgary where he lived with his father for eighteen years. The nuns told him they couldn't teach him anything he was that good with his hands. . . . Then he had this job out west taking samples for a mining company. He was that good with his hands they had him training people. When we came back here he had to get to know everybody all over again. He's still meeting people he didn't know before. . . .
> We get on well with the people here. Most of them are our relatives. People just love Ted, he's that type. He's invited everywhere. The old people, if they need anything done they'll call him. He put taps on for the old woman up the street. And

that woman who lives over there, she thinks he's a carpenter but he's not. If he has to move things, we'll hire a truck and they'll pay for the gas.

Present day processes of informal economy can best be described as two-tiered. When the available pool of skills can be matched with the work demands, many exchanges occur between kin, work-mates, and neighbors, preferably without cash having to change hands. For working class people in Glace Bay the noncash informal economy is the economy of choice. For middle class people in Glace Bay the informal economy is also an acceptable resource to tap for cash transactions priced at lower rates than those in the formal economy's marketplace. In the cash-based informal economy workers earn wages and gain a measure of flexibility over their work schedules which is not possible in the formal sector.

For work defined more often than not as men's responsibility, particularly in working class households, labour exchanges and/or below market value cash exchanges occur between households for otherwise major expenditures in construction trades, car, and home maintenance. While the ability to perform routine home maintenance and construction work represent important skills for men to hold and working class households to have access to for economic reasons, and for the culturally inspired satisfaction of "stretching the dollar," this order of informal work takes second place to working on cars.

For boys and men the ability to fix cars in highly regarded, an expression of the male gender's role in the culture of making do. Suspicious of my presence as a woman living apart from her husband and children yet still married, and about my seemingly unauthentic work, Michael, a young truck driver in his early twenties was ordinarily quite distant towards me although we shared a common entrance to our apartments. The social distance between us was bridged at his initiative when he discovered my family's car was badly in need of tuning and body work. His enthusiasm to set to work on the car when my husband visited Glace Bay, represented the carving out of some common male terrain which was taken by Michael to provide unquestionable intrinsic satisfaction as well as serving a practical purpose. On this occasion there appeared to be no expectation of any immediate return to Michael for his time and labor. Working on cars, usually with considerable success, is thus one pervasive element of male culture which falls within the province of informal economic activity but which is also well integrated into modes of re(-)cognition for working class male culture.

Construction and house repair work was less pervasive and more likely to include strict calculations of time with a view to the future reciprocal exchange of labor in kind or, quite possibly a cash payment. Several houses I visited had been completely renovated by members of the household with some assistance from friends and relatives holding appropriate skills. From these examples, it would appear that few working class households avail themselves of formal sector tradesmen.

As I have argued earlier, the gender division of labor requires that women's work is essential to livelihood practices and putting bread on the table. In addition to the domestically based work women perform on behalf of their households, women's skills are also applied to informal sector activities such as home decorating, sewing, cooking and catering, childcare, hairdressing, and the customary major annual house-cleaning project. All of these activities are so well integrated into everyday domestic routines that few women are forthcoming about the range of work activities they perform on behalf of others and about the benefits they derive from so applying their resources. Activities such as making new curtains and interior house painting were most likely to involve straight exchanges of labor, for example between mothers and daughters, or between sisters.

On the other hand, the example of catering is more likely to draw in labor resources from a wider pool of contributors. Catering for a large family gathering such as a christening, an engagement party, or a family reunion requires considerable management skills on the part of the hostess. After initial menu planning, female kin, neighbors, and some co-workers with longstanding ties to the hostess, will all be called upon to provide food for the party. It is expected that the women will contribute the food when requested and that contributions will be reciprocated in time. Through this system women earn reputations for their ability to prepare certain dishes which provide a measure of self-esteem for the cooks and some guarantee of quality control for the hostess. Infrequently, a cook's renown for skill in preparing a certain dish could result in a catering request from a relative stranger. On such occasions a cash exchange would take place between the cook and the hostess.

The case of hairdressing is different again. Hairdressing work almost always involves the exchange of modest amounts of cash above and beyond the basic costs for supplies, even between close female kin. Since many women and girls prefer hair styles involving permanent waving, short cuts and coloring, hairdressing exchanges occur more frequently than many other forms of exchange between women. However, because of the small amount of cash exchanged, no more than $10 in 1987 for several hours of work, hairdressing work does little more than supplement the service provider with the cash to become a service receiver. Because of the pervasiveness of the exchange of hairdressing services between women, girls who frequently accompany their mothers or are themselves recipients of the hairdressing, experience the occasions as part of learning their gender identity. Younger girls practice hairdressing on dolls and older girls (pre-teens) practice hairdressing on each other. Many girls aspire to a career as a hairdresser and I was told by one knowledgeable informant that there were many unemployed hairdressers in Glace Bay. Hairdressing, therefore, stands out as one example of the gendered integration of women into Glace Bay's informal economy and to the practices of making do.

Childcare is a further cash-based, female controlled nexus which is held to modest levels through cultural expectations about the nature of the work (seen as unskilled) and by the typically low level of wages earned by working class women who pay the child care costs as a deduction from their wages. Reliable child care proves as much of a challenge for working parents in Glace Bay as it does in other parts of the country (for example, Eichler 1983). Because of the strong familial ideology and a relatively strict gender division of labor in Glace Bay (elsewhere described as taking a patriarchal form, see Barber 1990) parents prefer to have their children cared for by female kin. Relatives are considered more trustworthy than strangers even when the relatives might have other responsibilities which provide distraction from the quality of care provided to younger children (for example, other children to care for or a corner grocery store to manage). Regardless of the familial status of the care givers and the ideologies of commitment and obligations entailed by ties of kinship, the regular provision of child care services always involves cash payments. As such, child care represents a modest cash supplement to unemployed or unemployable women tied to domestic responsibilities as well as a drain on women's wages.

Spencer (1988) argues that the informal economy in industrial Cape Breton takes a more structured form for middle class consumers of skilled trades labor. Spencer's study found viable informal economic practices operating on a cash payment basis which more closely resembled formal economy models and which might stem from formal sector enterprises. For example, mechanics from a car dealership might perform car repairs outside of working hours for cash payments. When this is done on their own time in their own space, the mechanics control the transaction. Where the company is involved, the company continues to achieve profit but can charge less for the provision of service through paying less than union wages. For the mechanic's part, there are benefits from non-taxable wages. The consumer also stands to gain from a lower price. Some tradesmen operate solely within the informal sector without the inconvenience of meeting the additional costs of complying with state regulations for the formal sector. Some less skilled workers seek to make their living solely in the informal economy by obtaining contracts through word of mouth and picking up unskilled labor jobs through a local pub which acts an informal sector "hiring hall." Other informal sector workers might work in the informal sector in order to supplement the cash income they receive from Unemployment Insurance benefits. Such practices are illegal if the additional earnings remained unreported to the Unemployment Commission. They are also illegal because, as with all informal sector work, the labor is unprotected by legislation and the income received by workers and employers remains untaxed.

Residents of Glace Bay have little difficulty with the concept of supplementing cash payments from unemployment insurance. This is because they view this program as an insurance scheme which they have contributed to and have earned the right to receive credit from. In their view, unemployment insurance is not an income support program stemming from the largesse of the state. Social assistance, or welfare falls into this latter category and there is social stigma attached to those households forced to rely upon welfare payments. A form of culturally inspired leveling mechanism thus comes into play for people who appear to have slipped out of the grooves of class and cultural conformity. Welfare recipients, along with economically successful Glace Bay residents who display some arrogance through the communication of their economic success, are shunned for their seeming betrayal of the core values of the localized culture of making do.

According to Spencer, who has close ties with the area, there is also a tacit acceptance by many members of the working class and the middle class in industrial Cape Breton communities that the informal economy provides legitimate alternatives to more expensive formal sector business. My research suggests that cultural processes underscore the success of the extensive, class-based commitment to the informal sector in Glace Bay; processes which have been exacerbated by persistent economic decline provoking widespread adaptation to unemployment and underemployment.

The literature on the informal economy suggests informal economic practices serve various "distinctive and contradictory functions" (Pahl 1985:24). This is certainly true in the case of Glace Bay. Aside from representing an adaptation to the vagaries of political economy, historically, the informal economy in Glace Bay facilitated the development of skills which could be transferred to the more regulated formal economy. Self-learned skills however, now appear to be less marketable in the formal economy as a result of processes of economic restructuring. Jobs in occupations typically filled by blue collar male workers have been eroded as a result of technological change, a decline in the manufacturing sector, and—more relevant to unskilled labour in Glace Bay—the requirement that all labor be better educated and trained regardless of the nature of the actual work requirement (Armstrong and Armstrong 1988).

In previous periods when informal economy activities proved more transferable, an informal sector such as Glace Bay's would have been beneficial to the formal economy in as much as self-learned skills represent cheap training. As Pahl points out, informal economy workers can function as a reserve army of labor in training. Without recourse to the legal forms of protection governing the conditions of their employment, informal workers learn to suffer long hours of work for low wages. This is the case in Glace Bay's informal sector today, which I am arguing is in the process of becoming more entrenched. Informal economy workers do not obtain unemployment insurance "stamps." They are without the possibility of union protection. Nor do they have access to other forms of benefits which might be provided in the formal economy, particularly for unionized labor. Instead, informal economy workers are inserted into the economy within an ideological nexus bound by community-based commitments and obligations with little hope of improving their circumstances in any large measure through a shift to formal economy labor markets. Both informal and formal labor markets remain vulnerable to further erosion from political and economic retrenchment. Those workers able to participate in income support programs such as unemployment insurance, still find themselves dependent upon and participating in informal sector practices which can:

... have the effect of driving down the wages in local milieux since shadow-work wage-rates typically undercut those in the recorded sector. Thus, whilst the work may get shared more widely, the spreading of resources between households may reduce the collective wealth overall (Pahl 1985:250).

Moreover, given that Glace Bay working class culture is accommodating to economic hardship as a way of life, household livelihood practices can serve to reinforce ideologies uncritical of the circumstances of political economy in spite of the earlier periods of community and union militancy. For example, kinship and neighbourhood based informal economic practices are built upon mutuality and social dependencies, while the actual labour processes of the work foster intimacy combined with a sense of control and shared satisfaction. One consequence of the pervasiveness and seeming success of informal economy practices in meeting peoples' needs might be to encourage disengagement from change-oriented social and political processes. This would explain the cultural dynamic of resignation apparent in many aspects of daily living in Glace Bay in 1987.[5]

Nonetheless, Pahl's interpretation of the political implications of informal economy appears rather too narrow to capture the complexities of a community like Glace Bay. Pahl suggests " ... if people are mending each others' cars they are not generally planning a revolution" (1985:250). In Glace Bay this would depend upon circumstances unrelated to the immediate work at hand. As I have argued, sociability and the mobilization of social networks is conventionally applied to processes of accommodation in making do and getting by, processes which serve as cultural confirmation. If sufficiently provoked however, these same activities might be just as readily supportive of collective action and resistance. Fixing cars and forms of militancy are not at all mutually exclusive.

Furthermore, regarding gender in informal work practices and related expressions of collective action, women's work presents quite different implications. Women's labor can sustain protracted industrial disputes but it may be more difficult for women performing certain types of work, particularly home-based work, to disentangle the objective conditions of their disadvantage in the labor contract. If while working the double day of domestic and wage labour women are also caring for each others' children and feeding other peoples' families, they are bound by emotional as well as economic commitments in their accommodation to local livelihood practices. Finally, I want to emphasize that both men and women create and build self esteem through the culturally defined contributions they make to their household economies. Pragmatism and loyalty are enduring and well proven values. Class-based mobilizations are less predictable.

CONCLUSION

In summary, the examples presented in this paper point to the need to reevaluate the boundaries which have been placed—sometimes arbitrarily and sometimes inadvertently—around significant institutions of social life in various debates, labor process theory being just one example. This research also demonstrates the political significance of local culture; a subject which achieved theoretical and methodological disfavor, particularly in anthropology sensitive to political economy, for reasons having to do with the primacy accorded structural forces and because of limitations inherent in conceptualizations of culture as symbolic life. Local culture in Glace Bay has been produced and reproduced for more than ninety years. For historical reasons, these processes provide us with a compelling case study of how potent are the culturally fused linkages between workplaces, households and the significant institutions of the community. Such linkages have both subjective and material dimensions. The workplace may provide the immediate set of social conditions which workers contend with—perhaps according to cultural blueprints (e.g., Burawoy 1985; Fantasia 1988)—but the circumstances which propel their collective responses forward into actions of organized resistance are drawn out of households and community-based resources. Furthermore, *the work* done in households is not only crucial to the survival capacities of household members in concert with waged work—particularly in the case of low wage jobs—but is essential in permitting forms of resistance in the workplace and forms of resiliency against economic crisis. Glace Bay culture is composed of a complex and dynamic engagement with these seemingly opposing conventions—accommodation and resistance—which originate in the town's specific historical conditions and, at key historical conjunctures and periods of crisis can be seen to mesh together. The complicity implicit in the paternalistic organization of local fish plants and the compliancy exhibited in Glace Bay community relations can thus become subversive to capital.

10

Work and *Gusto:*
Gender and Re-Creation
in a North Mexican Pueblo

"A Fistful of Dirt" is a Mexican song popular with the country-people of the *pueblo* of Namiquipa, located in Chihuahua's Western Sierra Madre, two hundred miles south of the border with the United States.[1] The chorus of this *corrido*[2] goes as follows:

> And on the day that I die,
> I won't take anything with me.
> One has to give *gusto* to *gusto*,
> Life is soon finished.
>
> Of what happened in this world,
> Only memories remain.
> Once I'm dead I'll take with me,
> Only a fistful of dirt.[3]

One of the meanings of *gusto,* which could be rendered as "gusto" in English, is pleasure and enjoyment. Its semantic range partially overlaps with that of the English "taste." Like taste, *gusto* denotes the flavor of food, as well as the sense of social decorum and aesthetics which is manifested in conduct and appearance. Pleasure and social taste are given a natural alibi in physical sensation. Savoring life is regarded as being as fundamental and natural a part of the human experience as savoring food. Similarly, the sense of social taste is seen as being as basic to personhood as the sense of physical taste. Indeed, to take *gusto* in things and experiences, to express *gusto,* or to do things with *gusto* is to realize the desires and choices of the self. Like food, pleasure and social taste are integral to personal re-creation and social reproduction.

One Sunday, I sang "A Fistful of Dirt" at a *convivio* or get-together in Namiquipa. When I finished, José[4] came over to where I was sitting. Like most of the men, José had been drinking all evening, and as they say in Namiquipa, "his tongue loosened itself" (*se le solto la lengua*). Waving a bottle of tequila with one hand and gesturing at the group of people talking and laughing with the other, José exclaimed:

> See Ana, we Mexicans know how to give *gusto* to *gusto,* we know how *convivir,* how to live together and enjoy life. On the other side, all people know how to do is work. The *gringos* have accomplished a lot with so much work: yes, in the United States one lives with many *comodidades* (comforts/commodities). In Mexico we don't have so many things. But as the song says, when you die you take nothing with you. I'm not saying we're lazy. No. We know how to work, but we also know how to enjoy life. Memories, yes, I have many—of the good times I've spent with my friends and family here in Namiquipa.[5]

What José's remarks stress is that work and *gusto* are forms of social activity and experience as well as capacities of social beings predicated on forms of knowledge (*saber*). From his point of view, Mexicans have the knowledge which enables them both to work and enjoy life, whereas Americans only know how to labor. Americans have *comodidades*—which signifies both comforts and commodities—but they have no *gusto.* For José, Mexicans are materially poorer but humanly richer. And as many Namiquipans commented in the course of our fieldwork, not only do Americans lack the knowledge necessary for enjoying life, they also do not know how to organize work so as to make it a source of pleasure, a form of personal and social re-creation.

The greater part of this paper explores how Namiquipans contrast their experiences of work and *gusto* on both sides of the border. I argue that for Namiquipans, work and *gusto* are forms of activity and experience through which social identities are negotiated and social value[6] is accorded to persons. For both men and women, these ideals of social identity, informed by gender, are difficult to realize in the United States. Indeed, when Namiquipans are in the United States, these notions of personhood are continually abrogated since in American society, work, and pleasure are differently organized and constructed. In relating their experiences in the United States, Namiquipans criticize the alienation, the polarization of the domains of work and pleasure, and the disciplinary forms of time which characterize mature capitalist society. But, at the same time, Namiquipans are uncritical of other aspects of capitalism and forms of oppression.

A consideration of Namiquipan accounts of work and other activities from which they derive *gusto* raises more general issues. How is gender negotiated through activities such as work and pleasure? How valid are either/or polarities such as work/entertainment, utility/pleasure, accommodation/resistance, and popular/dominant culture, as analytical categories? What are the complexities entailed in doing criticism from subaltern points of view? These and other questions will be addressed in the conclusions.

WORKING WITH AND WITHOUT *GUSTO:* TIME, MASTERY AND MASCULINITY

> The gradual extension of the wage-earning class brought with it a more detailed partitioning of time. But an attempt is also made to assure the quality of the time used: constant supervision, the pressure of supervisors, the elimination of anything that might disturb or distract; it is a question of constituting a totally useful time (Foucault 1979:150).

The majority of Namiquipan men were "agriculturalists" (*agricultores*) with effective control over the means of production. In Mexico, value is extracted from Namiquipan *agricultores* through market mechanisms. The prices paid for the corn and beans they sell to the government are barely sufficient to cover the costs of household reproduction. Consequently, many of these men have spent at least part of their lives engaged in wage-labor in the United States—largely in construction and commercial agriculture but also in services.

The goal of men's circular migration is to secure the resources which will allow them to "repeasantize,"[7] that is, to continue working as independent agricultural producers in Mexico. Even men who have spent years working on "the other side" (*el otro lado*, the most common way of referring to the United States), and who have taken their families with them, still aspire to return to life in Namiquipa. Carlos, for example, returns every year to plant his land, and he and his wife still own a house in the pueblo, despite years of living and working in the United States. For most Namiquipans, the true locus of their lives, status and identity lies in their natal community (*pueblo natal*). Migration to the United States is seen as a temporary expediency, a means to the end of continuing to live in the pueblo as *agricultores*. Yet this strategy is not without its drawbacks. Life and work in the United States are difficult; many men claim they can't stand to stay very long on the other side (*no aguantan mucho en el otro lado*).

Juan, a Namiquipan *agricultor*, once told us he would never work in the United States again. When asked why not, he answered:

> Here, I work for my family, because it is my obligation as a man to maintain my family, to give them food to eat, and maybe something more. I don't work to be rich, only so my family can have what is indispensable and maybe some comforts. And I work for myself not for a boss (*patrón*). . . . No one says, Juan, you must do this and that now. I work when I want to, when something needs to be done in the fields. And I work hard. But if I don't feel like working tomorrow, I don't. In the United States you work everyday or the boss fires you. . . . There is always someone telling you how to do things and when to do things. Americans are slaves to time. Here in Namiquipa we have more liberty. We sometimes don't even know what day of the week it is.

For Namiquipan men, the contrast between "liberty" (*libertad*) and "slavery" (*esclavitud*) is above all that between work on one's fields for oneself and one's family, and wage labor for a patron. The phrase *dedicarse a sus labores*, "to dedicate oneself to one's fields and/or tasks," embodies the ideal of productive activity held by men. The same term is used to designate the activity of work and its object: the noun *labores* means both fields and work on one's fields. Note that the verb *dedicar(se)* is reflexive: the self is both the subject and the object of the action. Moreover, the use of the possessive pronoun stresses personal control over the land and over the activity of work. Control of the means of production, of the labor process, and of its fruits configure the ideal of productive activity for Namiquipan men. Productive activity not only ensures the material reproduction of household and community but is also a process of re-creation of the social self.

Going to the *labor* is key to the production of a fully socialized masculine identity. The socialization of the "natural" self is mediated through the transformation of nature. A man who is hard-working (*muy trabajador*) fulfills the obligation to maintain his family (*mantener su familia*) enjoined by ideals of masculinity. Such a "good family chief" (*buen jefe de familia*) is also a "good community member" (*buen vecino*) and hence, a "man of respect" (*hombre de respeto*). "Respect" is the social esteem paid to those who are considered to be honorable (*honrados*). Honor is the basis for the legitimacy of men's status and authority in the domestic domain as well as in the public sphere of community life (see Alonso 1988a). Work produces not only economic but also social value; and this has concrete consequences in a face-to-face community where a good reputation (*buena fama*) is a prerequisite for almost all social activity, and where a bad reputation (*mala fama*) is tantamount to social death.

But to dedicate oneself to one's fields/tasks also affirms the self-mastery and the physical strength integral to what is conceived as the natural dimension of masculinity: working on one's own fields is seen as the only way to ensure control over one's own activity. From the Namiquipan point of view, a man only "works with *gusto*" (*trabaja a gusto*) when he controls the organization of his productive process. In such a case, work becomes not only a form of production but also of re-creation of the social self.

The struggle against "depeasantization" and for control over the means and the organization of production, was central to the decades of armed and everyday resistance waged by the Namiquipans in the second half of the nineteenth century, as well as to their mobilization in the Mexican Revolution of 1910–1920.[8] For Namiquipan men, wage labor, whether in the United States or in Mexico, is not a form of self-re-creation but instead, an emasculating form of personal alienation and subjection. To work for a patron is to be at his beck and call—is to be dominated and hence, emasculated. If a man has no control over his own activity, he becomes other to himself. Time is no longer his own, but the boss'.

E. P. Thompson has written that in peasant societies, time is reckoned in relation to tasks in the cycle of work and day-to-day life, as well as to "natural" rhythms, such as the alternation of light and darkness, seasonal changes, or alterations in the growing cycle of plants (1967). Work organized in relation to this "task-oriented" time is experienced as less alienated than that synchronized in relation to the disciplinary calculus of the clock:

> Three points may be proposed about task-orientation. First, there is a sense in which it is more humanly comprehensible than timed labour. The peasant or labourer appears to attend upon what is an observed necessity. Second, a community in which task-orientation is common appears to show the least demarcation between 'work' and 'life'. Social intercourse and labour are intermingled—the working day lengthens or contracts according to the task—and there is no great sense of conflict between labour and 'passing the time of day'. Third, to men accustomed to labour timed by the clock, this attitude to labour appears to be wasteful and lacking in urgency (Thompson 1967:60).

Though Namiquipans are familiar with clock-time, task-orientation is the predominant mode of constructing duration in everyday life. Though the organization of work in relation to tasks or to natural rhythms is as much a social product as are clock-based forms of labor regulation, it is experienced as more natural; whereas the signs of the clock are arbitrary symbols, the signs of task-oriented forms of time reckoning are indexes. Task-orientation is also perceived as allowing people more control over their own activity—tasks have to be accomplished, but they can be done today or tomorrow, earlier or later, and their performance can be interrupted. As Thompson points out, task-orientation is correlated with irregularity in the working day, week and year (1967:71–72). And Namiquipans perceive this irregularity as being not only a product of the fluctuations of seasonal and diurnal patterns, or of contingencies such as illness, but also of human choices. Hence, the irregularity of the work cycle is seen to be consonant with a sense of mastery over time and over the rhythms of activity. Liberty is also freedom from the clock that measures not one's own time, but the patron's.

Namiquipan men criticize the organization of production according to a calculus of clock time in the United States. For them, workers' loss of control over the rhythms of their own activity represents an unnatural and inhuman form of bondage. Time becomes objectified as a coercive force which stands outside workers and impinges upon their bodies and movements. People no longer work with *gusto*. As clock based forms of labor regulation are imposed, all nonutilitarian activities are banished from the work-place, and pleasure on the job is redefined as "distraction," a waste of (the boss') time (and money) (Foucault 1979:150; Thompson 1967:82–84). Work and life, utility and pleasure, become radically opposed. Indeed, from a Namiquipan point of view, as the calculus of the clock conquers more of the quotidian round, and extends its regulatory force into virtually every domain of activity, the knowledge of how to give *gusto* to *gusto* is lost.

When talking to Namiquipan men, I was frequently struck by the parallels between their critique of wage labor and that made by Marx. Writing of the relation of the laborer to the act of production in capitalist society, Marx commented:

This relation is the relation of the worker to his own activity as an alien activity not belonging to him; it is activity as suffering, strength as weakness, begetting as emasculating, the worker's own physical and mental energy, his personal life—[f]or what is life other than activity—as an activity which is turned against him, neither depends on nor belongs to him. Here we have self-estrangement (Marx [1844] in Tucker 1978:74–75).

Namiquipan men are aware that different work situations have differential implications for gender-identity: for them, independent agricultural production affirms masculinity whereas wage-labor is emasculating. From their point of view, the knowledge embodied in the organization of the labor process in the United States produces effects of power which enslave workers to time and to bosses. Though they admire American commodities, they are critical of the human costs of American forms of labor discipline.

Writing about the rationalization of production taking place in the United States after World War I, Gramsci commented that Fordist industry required the elaboration of a "new type of man suited to the new type of work" (1971:286). Ironically Gramsci was far less critical of the mechanization and automation of the worker than are the Namiquipans. Their practical experience of two divergent forms of productive activity, which are based on distinct knowledges and which articulate different forms of identity, has enabled them to develop a critical consciousness of wage labor. From the point of view of Namiquipan men, capitalist forms of work discipline are technologies of power which not only regulate production but also identities, which turn people into "slaves of time" and destroy their knowledge of how to enjoy both work and life.

As Thompson notes, task-oriented forms of work and time-reckoning are perceived by those accustomed to clock-timed labor as wasteful (1967:60). Indeed, the classic American stereotype of Mexicans portrays them as self-indulgent idlers. José, and other Namiquipans, are aware of this stereotype. Indeed, José's remarks contain an implicit refutation of this American evaluation of Mexicans, as well as of the dichotomization of work and pleasure that characterizes the labor regime of mature industrial capitalism: "I'm not saying we're lazy. No. We know how to work, but we also know how to enjoy life."

Significantly, "A Fistful of Dirt" conveys the opposite of the message articulated by the moral homilies on death and time advanced by proponents of industrial forms of labor-discipline. The message of these homilies is that life is too short to waste time in idleness and pleasure and those who so indulge themselves will be punished on judgment day (Thompson 1967:87–89). By contrast, according to "A Fistful of Dirt," the specter of death and the brevity of life makes it that much more urgent that we learn how to give *gusto* to *gusto*.

WORK, *GUSTO,* AND THE BORDERS OF FEMININITY

What do Namiquipan women say about work and life in Mexico and the United States? How are work and pleasure on both sides of the border implicated in the construction of their gender identities?

Namiquipan women tend to stay in the pueblo while men go to work "on the other side." Nevertheless, many women have visited husbands, adult offspring or other kin in the United States. Though male circular migration continues to be the predominant pattern, in recent years, some of the younger married women (born in the 1950s) have joined their husbands on the other side for at least part of the time.[9]

In Namiquipa, the household is the unit of both production and consumption; within the household, the division of labor is by gender and age. Male and female tasks are functionally and spatially distinguished. Agricultural production and cattle rearing, which take place outside the fully culturalized and domesticated space of home and community, are largely in the hands of men and their older sons, though some women help with the harvest and more rarely, with other agricultural tasks. By and large, women engage in "domestic work" (*trabajos domesticos*) within the house (*casa*), and the yard (*patio*)—an area which mediates between the inside of the *casa*, the intimate space of family life, and the outside world of community and public life. Like men, women have a task-orientation to time and work. Their tasks (*quehaceres*, literally things-to-do) include: caring for and "educating" children; cleaning the house, the yard, and the *banqueta* (that part of the sidewalk that borders the house); sewing and washing clothes; shopping in the local stores; turning the raw seeds which men produce into cooked food; and looking after domestic animals, such as chickens, pigs, and dogs, which range within the *patio* or the pueblo, in contrast to cattle which graze outside the town.

Though women's work is situated in the *casa*, it is not devalued in relation to men's labor in the fields (cf. Rosaldo 1974). Nor is women's work viewed as more closely linked to nature than men's, *pace* Ortner (1974). Rather, women's contributions to the reproduction of household, community, and society are accorded social recognition and value. This is *partly* because in agricultural communities, such as Namiquipa, the household is a key economic, social, and political unit; domestic work is not devalorized as it is in American industrial capitalist society (Rogers 1975).

Nevertheless, Namiquipan women are subordinated to patriarchal authority (and pace Rogers 1975, male dominance is not just a "myth," though women do wield informal power). But male domination and female subordination are not predicated on a dichotomous identification of women with nature, the domestic, and reproduction, and of men with culture, the public, and production (cf. Rosaldo 1974; Ortner 1974).[10] Instead, women's enclosure in the *casa* and subjection to men's authority is motivated by a contradictory construction of gender which has a long and complex history, one in which the Church and the state have played key roles (see Alonso 1988a).

Like masculinity, femininity is seen by the Namiquipans as having both natural and sociocultural dimensions. The natural qualities of femininity are contradictory. On the one hand, like the Virgin Mary, women are by "nature" pure and hence, spiritual: purity is embodied in the closure of the body, as indexed by the intact hymen. On the other hand, women by nature are capable of being opened by men: they are destined to have their bodily integrity ruptured and their sexual purity sullied by intercourse. As one Namiquipan man commented, sex, even with one's wife is always a "violation" (*violación*), a reinstantiation of the act by which the man affirmed his virility and the woman lost her sexual purity.

A high social value is accorded to women's reproductive capacities. One of the Namiquipan terms for the female role which in English is designated as "housewife" is *madre de familia*, family mother. Women are above all givers and reproducers of life. But the sacralization of a virginal maternity conflicts with what are thought to be the natural facts of conception—the sources of female pollution and shame. Simultaneously pure and polluted, closed and open, women, unlike men, are seen as having no natural control over the entrances and exits of their bodies.

The sociocultural dimension of femininity is configured by a public denial of these natural facts and by a concealment of this "naturally" based shame. Socialized femininity is above all *verguenza* and *pudor*, that is, sexual modesty, propriety, and chastity. In Namiquipa, a multiplicity of social practices mediate the contradictory nature of femininity by imposing a social closure on women. For example, women are forced to dress "decently" (*decentemente, recogidamente*), are restricted in their sexual activities, are subject to interdictions after giving birth, and are largely confined to the sphere of the *casa*. Women's limited participation in agriculture is justified not only by the claim that females lack the *huevos* or testicles—which are seen as the natural basis of the strength required for work in the fields—but also because work outside the house can jeopardize women's honor. Outside the protected sphere of domestic space, a woman can be violated by men other than her husband. In short, "feminine nature" is configured in such a way as to give a natural alibi to male control of female sexuality and reproductive capacities, and to the division of labor by gender.

When Namiquipan women talk about domestic work in the United States, they compare their experiences with work in the pueblo. They complain that with American technology, domestic tasks are accomplished so quickly that a woman has little to do apart from sleeping and watching television. María, one of the younger married women who joined her husband in the United States, told me that during her first few months on the other side she was sinking into a stupor:

> I put the little boy in the bed with me and sleep a lot of the day. I dream about Namiquipa. There I always had *quehaceres*

(things to do). I was always occupied. Here the houses don't get so dirty. There I worked with *gusto* because anytime I got bored or tired I could go have a cup of coffee at my friends' houses. Don't you remember? Pancha and I were in and out of each other's houses all day! Sometimes we'd make bread or biscuits together. Before I knew it the day had ended. Here I feel like night will never come. I have so much unoccupied time (*tiempo de oquis*[11]). Pedro works so hard. I'd like to do something to help him. But when he gave me permission to get a job house-cleaning, I left my two year old with my sister-in-law and he fell and broke his head. I got paid $25 for cleaning that house and had to spend $35 at the emergency room! After that Pedro told me I should stay at home. I often think I should go back to Namiquipa with the children. Here it is so much more expensive to live. With us here, Pedro can't save any money.

In contrast to Mexico, where they are "always occupied" (*siempre ocupadas*), some of the Namiquipan women who go to the United States feel that they do not have enough to do and their sense of making a visible and valued contribution to the reproduction of the household is diminished. Their work has lost the value and significance it had in Mexico: they feel that they are consuming more of the household income at the same time that they are contributing less of their work.

As a result, some of the younger women who have joined their husbands in the United States, engage off and on in wage labor, with their husband's permission. For example, one worked in a nursing home and subsequently, in a restaurant; another had a job in a laundry. But attitudes to female wage-labor are contradictory. On the one hand, female wage-labor is seen as a pragmatic exigency, a temporary way of supplementing household economic resources (and hence, speeding the return to Namiquipa) when the demands of *trabajos domesticos* have been attenuated. On the other hand, wage-labor is seen as interfering with women's natural role.

Husband's are often reluctant to let wives engage in wage-labor outside the home. Men (but also women) worry that the children will suffer for it and that other men may fail to respect women's sexual chastity and modesty (*faltar el respeto*). Women's wage-labor can jeopardize women's "decency" and men's exclusive rights over their wives' sexual and reproductive capacities. Significantly, compared to men, women talk much less of their experiences of wage-work in the United States; indeed, they told me very little about their work outside the *casa*. In part this is because their identity as *madres de familia* continues to be primary (and note that the jobs mentioned above are extensions of women's domestic roles). They worry that wage-labor may undermine their fulfillment of domestic duties. Their relative silence may be due to a fear that others will "criticize" them for neglecting their "real responsibilities."

Some women mediate the contradictions between constructions of gender and pragmatic desires to enhance household income through informal home production of commodities. María, for example, began to make *burritos* which her *compadre* would sell in the work-place.

On the whole, Namiquipan constructions of gender provide a natural alibi which tends to keep woman in "their place" (*su lugar*), the enclosed space of the home. This is one of the factors which produces the migration pattern whereby men work on the other side and women stay in the pueblo. Women themselves are reluctant to follow men to the other side: María is in the minority. And those women who do cross the border are caught in a contradictory situation. Their identity as *madres de familia* continues to be primary, but the rewards of their role are not so easily obtained on the other side. For the *casa* is a very different place in the United States.

Rogers points out that in mature industrial capitalist societies, the domestic sphere no longer has the social, economic and political importance it does in peasant societies (1975:751). Clearly, Mexico can no longer simply be characterized as a peasant society. Nevertheless, Rogers' observation applies to Mexican agricultural communities such as Namiquipa.

Namiquipan women in the United States feel that their domestic work has lost value. Moreover, they feel isolated in a society where the construction of the domestic sphere and the pervasiveness of alienation have attenuated the sense of female community. The networks of kin, neighbors, friends, and co-mothers which bind women in rural Mexican pueblos, which provide them with support, and which serve as circuits of knowledge, gossip (*la chirinola*) and criticism (*criticas*) through which women's speech becomes a powerful social and political force, one which can make or break both feminine and masculine reputations, are difficult to reproduce in the United States.

Like men, women talk about the different character of time and work in the United States. But whereas men criticize the automation of the worker—the coordination of the laborer's movements and activity to the clock—women lament the excess of time, and the slowness of its passing. In contrast to the men who work to the clock, Namiquipan women in the United States continue to have a task-orientation to time and work within the home. But whereas in the pueblo these women's tasks keep them "always occupied," in the United States they have much "unoccupied time." Time is no longer easily passed in productive activity and re-creative social interaction: the task-oriented time of the home has become a pre-social medium. For both men and women, work in the United States is not the re-creation of the social self but its estrangement and devaluation. Time becomes an alien force, one which is not in the worker's control. Like men, women do not work a *gusto* in the United States.

But what about other sources of *gusto* available to women? At the beginning of this paper, I pointed out that besides signifying enjoyment, *gusto* also signifies the sense of social decorum and aesthetics expressed in conduct and appearance. How do displays of social taste become sources of pleasure and value for Namiquipan women?

"THEY EVEN CALLED ME '*GUERA*' ": *GUSTO*, BEAUTY, AND VALUE

After two weeks in Namiquipa, Juana, the woman whose household we were living in, informed me that I had made myself respected in the community (*darse a respetar*)—I could go anywhere in the pueblo and nobody would act in a disrespectful way towards me (*faltar el respeto*). Not only was Juana telling me that I had complied with the norms and values of honor which apply to both sexes but more specifically, she was letting me know that I had behaved with *pudor*, with sexual modesty. Indeed, I had been careful to do so, never wearing shorts or skimpy shirts despite the heat, paying attention to the way I sat, stood or moved, lowering my eyes when walking past groups of men on the street, and limiting my interactions with men to socially appropriate contexts. Having been raised in a Cuban family in accordance with a code of honor which bears many similarities to that of the Namiquipans, I had a practical knowledge of what was entailed in being a "decent woman" and acting with the propriety enjoined by my married status. Had I behaved like a "whore" (*puta*), I would not have been accepted in the community. My husband's reputation would also have been compromised; in Namiquipan eyes, he would have become a (potential) cuckold, a figure of fun and pity.

Yet though I knew how to behave with *pudor*, I did not know how to embody local conventions of feminine beauty. Overly thin by local standards, dressed in baggy jeans and T shirts, wearing sneakers or sandals, my hair cut short, and my face devoid of makeup, I did not look like "a woman." My noncompliance with these norms and values of feminine *buen gusto* distanced me from the women in the community and made it difficult for me to participate in many conversations.

One night after three months in the field, my husband and I planned to attend a dance which was being held in the community's salon. We were living with another family. The teenaged daughter and her friend were preparing for the dance and I joined them, proferring advice and finally, curling my hair, putting on makeup, and donning a dress. When I was done, the older daughter proclaimed: "Now you finally look like a woman!" This was a turning point in how I presented and experienced myself as a gendered being and hence, in how I was viewed by Namiquipans. With increasing frequency, I began to conform to these conventions of feminine good taste. And it was this embodying of standards of beauty that made me realize how key this aspect of *gusto* is to women's lives.

For Namiquipan women, one of the key sources of *gusto* (in the sense of pleasure) is the opportunity to display their *gusto* (in the sense of social taste) in public festive contexts. Such public displays of "good taste" (*buen gusto*) and beauty are sources of social value for women, enhancing their prestige vis-à-vis both women and men.

One of the reasons María gave for not being *a gusto* in the United States is that she had no public opportunities to display her taste. María proudly showed me the American cosmetics, dresses, shoes, and earrings she had acquired. She called my attention to her new haircut and perm, and asked me if I had noticed that she had become "whiter" (*mas blanca*), and hence, from her point of view, more beautiful, in the United States. "But I can't display (*lucir*) any of this here," she lamented, "I haven't been to a dance since I left Namiquipa. What's the point of making myself beautiful (*ponerme guapa*): there is no one to see me!"

In Namiquipa, *ponerse guapa*, to make oneself beautiful, is to culturalize one's body, is to bring taste—those meanings and values which configure ideals of beauty and constructions of femininity—to bear on nature. Beauty and *gusto* are displayed, above all, at public festivities, particularly dances, for which women spend hours adorning their bodies with clothes, makeup, earrings, and

high-heeled shoes, curling their hair, and discussing whether this
or that dress, this or that shade of lipstick, make them look shape-
lier, taller, whiter, more womanly, and more fashionable. In recon-
stituting their "social skin" (see Turner 1980), women re-create
their social selves. But why should this be a source of pleasure?

There is another popular song which is frequently heard in
the pueblo and which is often sung by women—"The *Corrido* of
Namiquipa." In this community anthem, the pueblo is represented
as a woman, as a mother whose beauty is celebrated. She is "hum-
ble but not ugly," she is "the only queen of this region," she is a
delightful "paradise" created by God. Though women often forget
parts of this *corrido*, they always remember the third verse which
contains the following lines:

> I want to sing to this land
> Which God made with His power
> And in which He wished to put women
> Who are so graceful and beautiful
> That one can't choose among them (my trans.).

In Sunday *convivios*, it is common for women to sing this
song as a group while the men listen. When they sing these lines,
they do so with particular satisfaction, glancing and smiling at
each other and at the men with a certain shy triumph. Why?

As "The Corrido of Namiquipa" points out, the beauty of
Namiquipan women, like the beauty of the pueblo herself, is
pure—it is a divine creation. Beauty is a source of value for women
and the beauty of its women is a source of value for the community. As a result, women strive to embody ideals of beauty and
to re-create their social skin in accordance with such meanings
and symbols. This is one reason why beauty is a source of pleasure.
But in what do ideals of beauty and good taste consist? Here I can
only briefly deal with two of the key dimensions of beauty and
gusto—blancura or whiteness and *pudor*, that is, sexual modesty
and chastity.

The centrality of ethnicity to feminine beauty and taste is
made evident in Namiquipa on a quotidian basis as well as on extraordinary occasions such as dances. Whiteness and blondness are
key to ideals of beauty. Umbrellas are almost exclusively used by
women in Namiquipa—but to shelter themselves from the sun
which darkens the skin and not the rain which leaves its color un-
transformed. When I would dress for dances with my friend Elena,
she would constantly ask questions such as "Don't you think vio-

let makes me look whiter?" While she smeared her face with a mixture of honey and lemon juice, thought to whiten the skin, Elena would tell me that darker women (*morenas*) should wear bright or primary colors to make them look whiter. One day, after I'd known her for many months, Elena confessed to me that she was part Indian. "But hardly anyone has noticed," she said, "since my skin looks quite white. When I used to dye my hair blonde, they even called me *guera*, (blonde)!"

Elena's remarks demonstrate that women's transformation of their social skin is based on forms of knowledge and on technologies which permit the reinscription of bodily signs. Much of the knowledge and technology deployed to the end of whitening oneself (*blanquearse*), is acquired through the market and gleaned from the beauty magazines and television commercials which push its products. For example, knowledge and technology allow women in Namiquipa to cut, perm, curl and color their hair—and many do so since long, straight, black hair is a sign of Indianess. On television in Mexico, blondness is the privileged sign of beauty and *buen gusto*, and is used to sell everything from clothes and cosmetics to cars and beer. Indeed, an article in the *The Wall Street Journal* reports that cosmetic surgical procedures which Hispanicize the flat nose (*nariz chata*) which is a sign of Indianess are a booming business in Mexico (Moffett 1988). Those who cannot afford surgery can purchase an "orthopedic nose uplift," called *Nariz Bella* or "Beautiful Nose," which sells for the equivalent of eight American dollars (Moffett 1988).

The American market is a source of as many, if not more, commodities which are signs of whiteness than the Mexican one. Both Namiquipan men and women purchase American commodities whenever possible. On the one hand, they believe these to be "better made"; indeed, they continually contrast Mexican and American commodities and often comment, "Made in Mexico, badly made," (*Hecho en Mexico, mal hecho*). On the other hand, American commodities are signs of status, power and "whiteness." On the border, commodity fetishism acquires a specific ethnic character.

But the logic of the market place is not the only factor motivating the privileging of whiteness in Namiquipan ideals of beauty. A long and complex history informs an invented tradition of ethnic origins which constructs and affirms the "whiteness" of Northerners vis-à-vis the "brownness" of *Chilangos* (the contemptuous term used by Chihuahuans to refer to the Mexicans of the Center and South) and Indians. In Namiquipa, ethnicity is perhaps a more important aspect of identity than in other Northern pueblos. Established by the Colonial state, Namiquipa was one of several subaltern military colonies whose "civilized" peasant inhabitants were accorded social honor in return for fighting "barbaric indians" (*indios bárbaros*). In order to advance projects of territorial conquest and domination, the Colonial and Mexican states actively produced and enforced distinct forms of social identity. These forms of subjectivity made the reputations of men contingent upon their degree of "civilization" and their performance in warfare, and linked female reputations to ethnic and sexual purity. The social closure imposed on women guaranteed not only the ethnic honor of the civilized but also the gender honor of men: for one of the key ways men's reputations could be sullied was by violating their wives and daughters, mothers and sisters.

This complex history, which I have only been able to allude to here, (it is extensively discussed in Alonso 1988a), also informs the notions of *verguenza* and *pudor* which underwrite both beauty and *gusto*. *Verguenza* and *pudor*, that is, feminine sexual shame, chastity and modesty, are as central as whiteness in defining women's social skins. Above all, *verguenza* is the concealment of the ambiguous character of the pudenda, of a woman's "shameful" parts. The purity of beauty occludes what is considered to be the polluting and ugly character of a woman's genitals. Indeed, *arreglarse*, literally "to fix oneself up," one of the synonyms for the process of *ponerse guapa*, indexes the transformation of an ambiguous nature which is accomplished through the knowledge and technologies of taste. But beauty also makes women objects of men's desire. And eliciting desire can conflict with strictures of sexual modesty.

Negotiating this conflict is central to feminine strategies of embodying beauty. Women have to tread the narrow line which separates "decent" and "indecent" displays of beauty. Single women have a greater license to provoke masculine desire than do married women, who are held to more modest standards of bodily adornment. Married women have to be particularly careful not to appear to be consciously dressing to evoke the desire of men other than their husbands. Hence, even when they are implicitly dressing to gain the admiration of both men and women, they claim that they are only "fixing themselves up" for their husbands, or for members of their own sex. The following incident makes this clear.

One day when Elena was taking longer than usual to *ponerse guapa*, her husband asked her why she was "fixing herself up so much." "Don't you have a man already?" he inquired. Elena responded that she "fixed herself up" not for other men but instead, for other women. Didn't her husband know that if she did not "look well' at the dance, other women would "criticize" her?

Clearly, women do dress for other women; indeed, displays of beauty and taste are one of the ways in which women compete for social value against other women. The embodiment of gender ideals creates differences not only between men and women, but also, among them. Like men's, women's interrelations are simultaneously solidary and agonistic.

But women also dress for men. By configuring themselves as objects of generalized masculine desire (within the limits of *buen gusto*), women believe they gain informal power over their men. Men's reputations depend on the chastity of their women. But a man's patriarchal control over feminine sexual and reproductive capacities is always in danger of being challenged by other men. A man who has been cuckolded or whose daughter, sister or mother has been "dishonored" by another man, is himself dishonored. Hence, displays of beauty (and the covert elicitation of generalized masculine desire) are also displays of women's power to make or break their men's reputations. In constructing their own identities, women are also constructing those of men, and both are things they do with *gusto*.

CONCLUSIONS

Oppression needs to be understood not only in relation to its causes, but also, in terms of the ways it is experienced in everyday life and lived at the level of the body/self (Comaroff 1983; Brittan and Maynard 1984). My discussion of work and *gusto* indicates that the experience of oppression involves multiple aspects of identity including gender.

Namiquipan men and women's accounts of their experiences on both sides of the border point to the importance of gender for an anthropology of work. From a Namiquipan perspective, work and *gusto* are gendered practices through which social selves are re-created and endowed with value. Gender is a central dimension of social being, one which cannot be realized in the same way on both sides of the border.

For Namiquipan men, independent agricultural production generates both economic and social value; it is one of the key means through which men produce themselves as gendered beings and acquire social prestige. By contrast, they see wage labor as producing only economic value. Working for wages in the United

States is an alienating and emasculating experience; one which subordinates the worker to the *patrón* and which is only tolerated because it is a means to the end of consolidating and perpetuating men's "real" identities as *agricultores* in the pueblo. The notion that their real status lies on the Mexican side of the border helps men to reconcile themselves to the humiliations of wage labor on the other side.[12]

The New York Times reported that the chairman of the Xerox Corporation had stated that America's public schools had put the United States " 'at a terrible competitive disadvantage' . . . by turning out workers with 'a 50 percent defect rate.'"[13] Comments such as this, which reflect and promote the commodification of workers, are commonplace in the United States; so commonplace, indeed, that many Americans are no longer struck by the alienation they imply. By contrast, the remarks of Namiquipan men emphasize the extent to which workers have been dehumanized in the United States by forms of knowledge and technologies of power designed to commodify workers' very bodies and selves, and to tailor their subjectivities to the perceived requirements of capitalist production and class domination. Yet men's criticisms of the dehumanization of workers in American capitalist society are predicated on constructions of gender which underwrite the subordination of women.

The remarks of Namiquipan women allow us to understand some of the ways in which domestic work is devalued in American society. In addition, they help us to comprehend the diverse implications which different constructions of the public and the domestic spheres (and their interrelations) have for gender identities (see Collier and Yanagisako 1987). If Namiquipan women by and large choose to stay home in the pueblo rather than follow their husbands to the United Stataes, this is not only due to economic exigencies. Nor can we account for their choice by re-presenting them as passive victims of gender oppression. Being a *madre de familia* is a source of social esteem and personal satisfaction in Namiquipa where the domestic sphere is a key social, political, and economic unit. Moreover, while men are away on the other side, women become the de facto representatives of their households in the pueblo. Male circular migration has, if anything, enhanced women's status in the pueblo, and augmented the degree of influence and informal power they wield in both household and community affairs (see Rogers 1975:749–751).

Men's and women's criticisms of the organization of work in the United States take as their point of departure a notion of productive activity which is less estranged and more overtly aware of the social characater of work, than that which is hegemonic in mature industrial capitalist societies. However, as John Calagione pointed out (personal communication), such critical attitudes were present in early European (see Thompson 1967) and American industrialization and remain a key component of many work contexts in the First (see essays in this volume), Second (see Pahl 1988) and Third Worlds (see Nash 1979; Taussig 1980; Ong 1987). Nevertheless, it seems to me that it is easier for Namiquipans to understand the oppressive dimensions of work in American capitalist society because they can draw on their own experience of work under a different labor regime.

Notwithstanding, both Namiquipan men and women are surprisingly uncritical of other aspects of the capitalist market economy. For example, on the border, commodity fetishism takes a distinct form, one which is intimately linked to the construction of ethnicity. For men and women American commodities are signs of power and status. Women deploy these signs in their own politics of re-creation with much less overt awareness of the ways in which the knowledge and technologies which produced these signs have advanced a number of projects of domination. In fact, women appropriate the ethnic and gender inequalities inscribed in the knowledge and technologies of beauty. Yet they deploy them for their own ends. In doing so, they are competing for value and for the informal power which social esteem confers.

Is this accommodation or resistance? What I would argue is that it is simultaneously neither and both. Perhaps a more appropriate term is "negotiation."[14] By this I mean the quotidian struggle for value and power, for freedom and autonomy, that goes on all the time. Negotiation may reproduce hegemonic values. For example, women's struggle to embody conceptions of beauty inflected by constructions of gender which underwrite forms of their own oppression reproduces hegemonic meanings and symbols. But at the same time that they appropriate these hegemonic knowledges and technologies, women redeploy them for their own ends, to re-create their social selves so as to gain value and informal power.

What the foregoing suggests is that analytical dichotomies such as work and entertainment, utility and pleasure, popular and dominant culture, power and subjection, accommodation and resistance, are too sharply drawn. Moreover, these polarities are historical products and cannot be treated as static, universal contrasts. In order to account for the complex and contradictory texture of social practice and of peoples' constructions of their own action-in-the-world, we must stop thinking in either/or terms and adopt a processual perspective which locates social activity in its historical context (as suggested by Wilden 1980, among others).

Either/or thinking has resulted in a vision of popular culture as a homogeneous and static domain, one which is either wholly autonomous from or wholly determined by dominant discursive practices. But the concept of culture which such thinking presumes is no longer (if it ever was) tenable. As Rosaldo argues, we need a "renewed concept of culture," one which "refers less to a unified entity . . . than to the mundane practices of everyday life. . . . Ethnographers look less for homogeneous communities than for the border zones within and between them" (1989:217). By thinking in terms of verbs rather than nouns, processes instead of entities, we can achieve a view of the relationship between popular and dominant culture that comes closer to capturing the complexities and the contradictions inherent in the articulation of discursive practices that are produced in the context of multiple and shifting relations of power.

By way of conclusion, I would like to remark on the complexities entailed in doing cultural criticism from the point of view of subaltern groups. This topic has been raised recently by literary critics (e.g., Spivak 1987) as well as anthropologists (e.g., Marcus and Fisher 1986). The notion of "understanding the self through the other" has long been a part of the anthropological enterprise. What has been rarer is a politicized criticism, one overtly concerned with issues of power and meaning (e.g., Scholte 1974, 1986; Fabian 1983; and work by Feminist anthropologists).

Certainly, a perspective which takes as its point of departure subaltern criticisms of exploitation and domination should be integral to what Scholte called "a reflexive and critical anthropology" (1974). Such a perspective would provide a corrective to hegemonic metropolitan discourses on the Third World and subaltern First World groups. These metropolitan discourses, as Jean Franco points out, have generally adopted one of three devices in order to deny agency and critical consciousness to subordinated "others":

(1) *exclusion*—the Third World is irrelevant to theory; (2) *discrimination*—the Third World is irrational and thus its knowledge is subordinate to the rational knowledge produced by the metropolis; and (3) *recognition*—the Third World is only seen as the place of the instinctual (Franco 1988:504).

An anthropological perspective which endows subaltern groups with agency and critical consciousness would also provide a corrective to crude attributions of a whole-scale "false consciousness" to workers and peasants. Moreover, it would expose the socially constructed character of the differentiation between a dominant, First World and "masculine creativity" and a subaltern, Third World "feminine reproductive activity" which underpins and authorizes those hegemonic discourses which deny agency and consciousness to subordinate groups (Franco 1988:505).

However, there is a potential danger that criticism, if refracted through either/or thinking, will result in sort of heroic, uncritical romance which revalorizes distinctions between the West and the Rest, male and female, capitalist and peasants/workers, but ultimately reproduces them in an inverted form. I am not claiming that "speaking for" and "speaking with" should not be integral to a critical anthropology. Indeed, this paper is intended as just such an exercise. However, just as a critical reflexivity entails a knowledge of the limitations of our own consciousness, so too does it require an awareness of the limitations of the consciousness of the people we work with. In reflecting on Namiquipan reflections, I have tried to point out some of the ways in which they are critical of oppressive social forms and some of the ways in which they are not.

DANIEL NUGENT
DORIS FRANCIS
JOHN CALAGIONE

11

Conclusion

The chapters in this volume were written by anthropologists, folklorists, and social historians engaged in research in East Asia and South Asia, in Latin America, and North America, in the First World and the Third. Whether investigating growing old or growing up, women or men, factory workers in predominantly agrarian societies or craft specialists in industrial societies, playing music "on the job" or playing music *as* a job, the authors reveal new insights into the cultural impact of work in society. This they accomplish by orienting investigation toward the "analysis of actuality" (Shanin 1982:xi), the "analysis of the real practices subsumed by development" (Williams 1983:104) on the margins of capitalism.

These insights into the cultural impact of work are conveyed, and a recasting of the understanding of the labor process is accomplished, through the answers the authors suggest to the questions posed in the introduction. They derive from an interrogation of the relationship between action and knowledge. The authors demonstrate how "the labor process" differs radically from economistic accounts of it once workers' cultural representations of work are included in the analysis. They show how the boundaries between work and nonwork are not at all clearly fixed, that these boundaries shift in relation to both imposed demands of capitalist production and to quotidian practices.

The chapters present themes, topics, and interpretive perspectives that compare worker's expressions in relation to the labor process, sociocultural structure and historical context. While Chapter 1 sets the terms for a number of conceptual issues, each subsequent chapter picks up and develops an aspect of the argument from the previous one. Chapter 2, for example, mentions how music can be used to reorder the pace of work (and mediate interethnic relations) on a work site, while chapter 3 examines the work of musical performance and its reception in a particular cultural and political context. Chapter 4 carries on the study of popularly-produced folk-art (now sculpture instead of music), but to the end of advancing an argument about the articulation of identities, an issue also addressed in chapter 5, which is based on a study of the discourse of worker's while they are not working. Continuities of this sort are evident as the reader proceeds from one chapter to the next. The most important themes which reappear throughout the book are: understanding the relationship between individual and collective identity, conceptualizing the transformative consequences of accommodation and resistance when they are regarded as relational actions or processes rather than positional stances (Corrigan 1975), and determining the ways gender figures both as a cultural construction and as a social relation in work and production (chapters 6 and 8–10 are especially valuable in the latter respect). Finally, the collection as a whole sheds some light on the implications that engaged, reflexive work with subaltern groups and classes on the margins of capitalism bear for anthropological research and writing.

There are three discernable styles of argument linked to empirical material presented in this book. Following Chapter 1, the entire collection is framed by essays concerned with Jamaican workers in New York City, Mexican agriculturalists with practical experience as transnational wage-laborers in the United States and Mexico, and Cape Breton miners, fisherie, and informal sector workers. These studies by Calagione, Nugent, Barber, and Alonso explore how elements of popular culture are interpolated into the labor process and vice versa. A critical principle informing their analyses is that the polarized, static dichotomies of accommodation/resistance and work/leisure can no longer serve as devices for organizing and comprehending the complex texture of social experience. The chapters by Francis and McCarl, examine meanings of work, gender, age and self-representation on the fringes of urban North America, underscoring a perspective according to which conceptions of power, knowledge, gender, and the life-cycle are necessary components for comparison and analysis of the labor process. The chapters by Rofel, Friedlander and Hareven deal somewhat differently with industrialization, artisanal organization, and factory organization in South and East Asia. They analyze transformations in the political and symbolic realms of work, ritual, and public festival by paying attention to the discourses which are drawn into changing contexts of production.

John Calagione's "Working in Time" is based on research in the informal sector construction and rehab trades in New York City on crews composed primarily of Caribbean workers. The paper demonstrates how people arrive from the margins of the world capitalist system to one of its more potent centers and wind up transforming urban space for the benefit of others. But that feature is incidental to his related arguments about time and recorded music on the job. He shows how "everyday" struggles over the pace and character of productive action at the worksite are organized and framed by workers' drawing on knowledge and experience from outside the site of production. The organization of action in the workplace as well as worker's identities vis-á-vis those for whom they work and those who consume the products of their labor is achieved through imaginative reworkings of cultural codes. Calagione recounts how recorded music figures in the active linking of subjective and collective aspects of labor migration with urban work.

The chapter on "Popular Musical Culture in Rural Chihuahua" draws on ethnographic and historical research in a predominantly agropastoral region of northern Mexico, whose inhabitants have experienced laboring in the United States for the past century. Daniel Nugent's scientific research was both enhanced and subtly subverted by the time he spent playing with a local dance band. In this context, he is able to consider problems of an engaged historical consciousness from a unique and valuable perspective. Nugent is concerned in this chapter with how the work of performance and the performance of work may be situated relationally vis-á-vis supra-community organizations of domination and exploitation such as wage-labor, nationalism, and United States hegemony throughout most of Latin America. While presenting some original material on popular music, and outlining a critique of notions of authenticity in anthropological writing, at the heart of the essay is a discussion of the relationship between popular culture and the state.

Doris Francis provides a rich account of the subjective meanings of work and their relationship to the formation and consolidation of identity through her examination of "Artistic Creations From the Work Years." By carefully examining sculptures and paintings produced by retired workers she constructs a critical view of the sublimated relation between work and identity. Reflexive representations of work articulated after the work years are past, provide a unique, and heretofore largely unexplored, set of images through which it is also possible to explore the meaning of work and life when the former is a thing of the past and the latter is drawing to a close. Hence, the exposition can proceed at two levels, dealing both with how people "work to create" and see themselves as having accomplished that while on the job, and how they subvert or challenge readings of their own past experiences even as those are systematically devalued within the broader society as a function of the individual's imputed inutility.

In his tentative charting of the "Boundaries of Occupational Knowledge," Robert McCarl places the analysis of discourses about work by workers themselves firmly on the ground provided by the nexus of unequal relationships of class, gender, and ethnicity. However, McCarl's project is neither reductionist nor essentialist, and through his long conversations with firefighters in Washington, D.C., he was able to elucidate a profound understanding of the relationship between narrativity and productive action. Further, his work suggests that overlapping boundaries of knowledge and boundaries of self articulate and shape the formation of working identities.

In "Eating Out of One Big Pot," Lisa Rofel examines the contrast between current state programs of economic reform and the historical and cultural legacy of cultural revolution in the Peoples Republic of China. Her extensive and sensitively crafted descriptions of silkworkers in Hangzhou indicate that "productivity" is a critical arena for evaluating ordinary peoples' social agency in Chinese life. The problem of how ideologies of development are transformed in and by quotidian experience frames her discussion. Thus, she shows how *both* ideas of capitalism and socialism are generated in culturally constituted terms. She also shows how definitions of productivity lodged within hierarchical wage and bonus systems are changed by discourses between workers and managers about the new meanings of age and mastery. Finally, she demonstrates that the recent history of silkworkers' wages and the struggle to redefine them display a gendered incorporation of rural women into formerly male dominated industrial silk production.

Tamara Hareven's study of "The Festival's Work as Leisure" provides a behind the scenes account of the production of city parades, chronicling the interplay of meanings between craftsmanship and logics of social hierarchy in the annual Gion Festival of Kyoto, Japan. While the festival dates to the sixteenth century, it has changed dramatically in terms of its poltical and cultural implications for neighborhoods in the city. Hareven interrogates the ideological importance of "traditional" crafts in a society that values the appearance of stability while undergoing continuous economic transformation. By providing a detailed account of the preparation of towering floats, she shows how elder and younger craftsmen, and community leaders and sponsors voice very different concerns about the meanings of traditional craft production. Their incorporation into a televised display underlines the fact that these representations are entwined within the commercialization of identities and leisure.

Eva Friedlander demonstrates how shifts in both choice and representation of female deities express changes in gender relations and women's economic marginalization in Rajmath, West Bengal, a town created by villagers displaced by the construction of a steel plant. "Work and Worship: Changing Images and Changing Lives," shows the extent to which village women experience devaluation of productive agricultural roles in the face of successful factory based economies. Representations of female capacities are also transformed. By analyzing the establishment of a ritual cycle geared to a new class culture, Friedlander uncovers a changed interpretive framework for women's ambiguity as dependent daughters (requiring dowries) and managers of households who produce sons. However this ritual process articulates new possibilities for women to empower themselves vis-á-vis the collective power attached to male participation in the industrial order.

Pauline Barber's essay on "Working Through the Crisis" addresses the problems involved in making a radical distinction between what she calls "resignation" and resistance in the context of a fishing and mining town in Nova Scotia. She skillfully reframes her analysis to ask how do people develop strategies for survival in the face of a crisis of de-industrialization? Barber cogently documents the ways men and women cope with the crisis in Cape Breton's Glace Bay. But her unit of analysis is the community as a whole, grasped through an understanding of the linkages between household reproduction, informal sector work, and factory (or extractive industrial) production. One of her central points is to show the reciprocal imbrication of work in the household and in both the informal and formal sectors. A related point is to account for how "culture" is produced—and resituates social practice— through the ways bodies and selves are implicated in the processes of work and labor.

In "Work and *Gusto*" Ana Alonso draws together many of the issues considered throughout the volume. She provides a straightforward account of how men and women from a primarily agricultural and agropastoral region of Mexico regard work in their own community and in the United States. Her account explains how the nexus of wage labor and household production figures at a more general level in social reproduction. Her sensitive differentiation of men's and women's regard for work leads to a more exact analysis of the relationship between work and pleasure and how that distinction shapes the conceptualization of bodies and of selves. Finally, her chapter demonstrates how counter-hegemonic consciousness may provide a ground for refashioning sites and actions of production, even when it appears superficially to embody a kind of consent to domination. One of the sites of production which figures in her analysis is the very production of ethnographic accounts.

Together these papers make a strong case for analyzing the labor process in connection with everyday cultural practices. What is excluded from analysis by instrumentalist and structuralist approaches to work provides the very focus of these studies; namely, the recension by workers of both the pragmatic and the meaningful forms of oppression that confront them and the formation of critical consciousness among subaltern groups and classes. These papers demonstrate how the study of work builds on critical analyses of capitalism and accumulation on a world scale, by figuring the investigation through different units of analysis (many routinely ignored in the existing literature) and focusing on the cultural meanings of work, gender, and representation. Recognizing the multiple significations of work and labor, and their recension in popular consciousness, may be of some merit in undoing the distinction between action and knowledge. It is certainly of considerable value in attuning the anthropology of work to forces of rapid transformation and inequality.

Notes

CHAPTER 1

1. Among the people who have helped greatly in various stages of the production of the text, Stephen Nugent, Pamela Perry, Bryan Roberts and Greg Teal deserve our warm thanks. We would especially like to acknowledge Ana Alonso and Angela Zito for their tireless critical readings, contributions, and support.

2. "The developing world" and "development" appear under quotes for several reasons. Teodor Shanin has edited a series of books on "the sociology of 'developing societies'," in the preface to which he writes, "The very terminology that designates 'developing' or 'underdeveloping' or 'emerging' societies is impregnated with a teleology that identifies parts of Europe and the United States as 'developed'. Images of the world at large as rising unilinearly from barbarity to modernity (or vice versa, as a descent to hell) have often substituted for the analysis of actuality, as simplistic metaphors often are" (Shanin 1982:xi). Raymond Williams, discussing the concept of development in *Key Words* wrote: ". . . the pressure of what is often the unexamined idea of development can limit and confuse virtually any generalizing description of the current world economic order, and it is in analysis of the real practices subsumed by development that more specific recognitions are necessary and possible" (Williams 1983[1976]:104). See also Woost 1990, chapter 3, "The Ideological Apparatus of Development."

3. In this passage, the term "work" appears as both an act and an effect.

4. The proposition that the production process is, and thus means, only occupation leads analysts to violently abstract and privilege a limited aspect of human action, or into indefensible conundrums like Althusser's "lonely hour of the 'last instance' [which] never comes" (Althusser 1970:113). Althusser develops this point in the course of commenting on Engels' September 1890 letter to Joseph Bloch (Marx and Engels 1975:394–6). While acknowledging that Engels' (and Marx's) position was that "History 'asserts itself' through the multiform world of the superstructures,

from local tradition to international circumstance," Althusser goes on to argue for "leaving aside the *theoretical solution* Engels proposes for the problem of the relation between determination in *the last instance*—the economic—and those determinations imposed by the superstructures . . ." (Althusser 1970:112); all that is sufficient to retain is the expression "overdetermined contradiction" understood as "the accumulation of effective determinations . . . on the determination in the last instance by the economic" (1970:113). Thus Althusser can say Marx "understands *abstract economic reality* . . . as .the effect of a deeper, more concrete reality: the *mode of production* of a determinate social formation" (1970:110), but "from the first moment to the last, the lonely hour of the 'last instance' never comes" (1970:113). In our opinion, by discarding Engels' proposed theoretical "solution" (which is really a *problem* that needs to be addressed), Althusser throws out the baby with the bathwater.

5. Chavez's father and uncles were killed in 1892, during the Mexican state's final military attempt to suppress the uprising at Tomochi, Chihuahua, which ended with the physical destruction of the town and the death or forced emigration of most of the town's inhabitants (Almada 1938; Jordan 1981). Chavez uses the word "capital" to signify two very different things in the passage quoted: first as alienated, externalized "economic" capital or coalesced labor power, and second as a quality of persons who work.

6. Arendt's argument offers a critical exploration of how the Cartesian division of thought and action encodes the very problematic assumption that what are actually communal labor processes are seen as "achievements" of an essentialized individual self. She provides an early version of "post-modern" critiques of the Cartesian split between thought and action, action and effect. We agree that our post-Enlightenment worldview has tended to equate empowerment with the consumption and production of things and has discouraged an appreciation or examination of creativity in the labor process. That process is about more than just "labor," and as anthropologists we should try to open a space where problems of value and resistance to the dominant ideologies of capitalism can be reapprehended.

7. For a related point and further discussion of recent research on the labor process in the Third World which takes *Labor and Monopoly Capital* as it's point of departure, see Munck 1988:67ff.

CHAPTER 2

1. I would especially like to thank Angela Zito for patiently and critically reading every draft of this paper. Daniel Nugent discussed many ideas and long ago pointed out the cultural significance of Baldemar Huerta. Bonnie Urciuoli and Mindy Lazarus-Black helpfully commented

on earlier versions, and Ana Alonso also read and commented on the text. Many Jamaican construction workers have patiently discussed the meaning of work with me, and graciously invited me to share and document some of their experiences in exile.

2. See Berman, 1983, for an excellent account of this dilemma of modernity and the dilemmas forced upon residents of the Bronx in the 1950s. Zukin (1982) and Harvey (1989) provide excellent accounts of this process during the last decade.

3. The lower west side was also home to a huge population of artists and students, and closely identified with a gay and lesbian community. How many members of the latter now actually reside there is unclear, although my own casual observation is that working class gays and lesbians have been forced to relocate because of the higher rents which followed conversions of buildings into privately owned units.

4. I am thinking of the debate on assimilation/accommodation spurred by the work of Handlin (1951), but recently revived in debates about the nature of migration under capitalism. For an excellent review of recent work see Bukowczyk 1989.

5. This is the Jamaican term for getting a living by doing any number of temporary or dayjobs, in both formal and informal segments of the economy.

6. Freddy Fender is the stage name of Baldemar Huerta, the "great Texan singer and song writer" (Nugent, this volume) whose music is released in both Spanish and English versions, and was played frequently enough on both English and Spanish language stations in New York City to be familiar to virtually all of the workers.

7. "Dub" is a Jamaican recording form in which lyrics are suppressed and rhythm sections are electronically enhanced. [This track] is then played as background to a spoken narrations or "toast."

8. I use the term "West Indian" here because it was used by workers on the job to distinguish English from non-English speaking Caribbean immigrants.

CHAPTER 3

1. Much of this research was financed by a generous grant from the Henry and Grace Doherty Fellowship Committee, Program in Latin American Studies. Additional support was secured through travel grants from the Center for Latin American Studies, University of Chicago. I acknowledge my gratitude to both these organizations. Versions of this paper have been presented to the AAA Annual Meetings in Chicago in 1987, at

Occidental College, and to the Anthropology Departments in the Universities of Arizona and California, Riverside, where the audiences were always stimulating. John Calagione earned my special thanks for encouraging me to write this paper and Ana Alonso, as always, has reviewed and corrected drafts repeatedly. I'd also like to thank Amy Burce, Noel Samaroo, Pablo Vila and Michael Woost for help with this text to which the standard disclaimers apply. Finally, none of this would have made any sense to me were it not for the members of *Fase Cinco* (Chalía, Carlos, Salomón, and Francsico) and the people of western Chihuahua.

2. Nugent 1985, Nugent 1988a:155ff.; CNA.RP 6 Ago 1926; AGCCA e.23/432(721.1).

3. The incantation appearing under quotes is not an expression derived from some esoteric, alien ritual, but the opening to the Little Richard song, "Tutti Frutti."

4. Cf. Cornelius 1986, NACLA 1987 for national level discussions of "The Crisis" in Mexico; *Proceso* nrs. 486, 508–512 [1985–6]; Alonso 1986, 1988b; Lau 1989; Nugent 1988b, for analyses of the crisis in Chihuahua.

5. During 1984 and 1985 the IRCA was usually referred to as the "Simpson-Mazolli Bill," a version of which was eventually passed under the sponsorship of Congressmen Simpson and Rodino in 1986. This "immigration act which is really a labor-control act" (Cockcroft, pers. comm.) was sedimented in popular consciousness in rural Mexico, indexed as "Simpson-Mazolli." A Chihuahuan in his twenties, who had worked for several years in Colorado, had an excellent command of English, followed events in the United States through the newspapers and TV news, and who understood the basic impact the "Simpson-Mazolli" Bill would have on his future possibilities working illegally in the United States, told me in conversation he understood the implications of the law. What he wanted to know was, "What is a Simpson-Mazolli?"

6. One compelling example of this awareness—which simultaneously illustrates a fetishistic attitude towards United States-produced goods—is the Tarahumara couple from the sierra near Tomochi who named their son "John Deere" because that is the name of a powerful tractor. The priest—who as it turns out was a Spaniard—to whom they brought the child for baptism was horrified and upset, and told us he would have preferred to baptise the child with an authentic Mexican, or better still, a "Tarahumara" name (like what? Juan Venado?).

7. As a rule, until the 1980s it was men who went to work in the United States—sometimes alone, more frequently with neighbors or relatives, but only infrequently taking along their families. If men took their wives and children to the United States it was usually with the thought of permanent settlement north in mind.

8. Cf. Kay 1975, Roseberry 1983, and S. Nugent 1988 on the effects of merchant's capital in the "periphery" of the capitalist system.

9. Indeed, the break up of the group that occurred in early 1985 came about as a result of band members going north in search of steady work.

10. The rythym guitarist eventually secured a permanent job as a *Transito* or highway patrolman. This became a source of collective embarrassment to the rest of us. But we did toy with the idea of outfitting ourselves in the blue shirts worn by *Transitos* and billing ourselves as *"Paco Y sus Mordelones"* (Paco and his 'Biters'; *mordelones* from the verb *morder* [to bite], but in Mexico *morder* also means "to bribe,"and hence the colloquialism *la mordida* [the bribe]).

11. Despite the fact that Freddy Fender recorded a very good Spanish language version of the song which is on the juke box in a cantina in Namiquipa, people prefered to hear the song sung in English, as the men had doubtless heard it many times on jukeboxes in the United States. An interesting point relevant to the current argument is that the great Texan singer and song-writer Baldemar Huerta is best known through his stage and recording name Freddy Fender; Fender is the brand name of an immensely popular United States-made guitar.

12. During the moratorium on dances, the Sunday meetings of an evangelical sect, which until then had made little in-roads in the community, were suddenly crowded with new participants who joined their meetings (sometimes after attending the Catholic Mass) because they enjoyed the music, since the evangelicals sang all afternoon.

CHAPTER 4

1. An earlier version of this paper was delivered at the 1987 annual meeting of the American Anthropological Association, Chicago, at an invited session "Workers Expressions: Accommodation and Resistance" organized by Doris Francis and John Calagione for the Society for Humanistic Anthropology. I would like to thank Mark Luborsky, Maria Vesperi, Sharon Kaufman, and Daniel Nugent for their helpful comments on this essay. Portions of the data for this chapter are derived from an earlier analysis, "Images from the Occupational Years: The Reminiscences of Retirees and Their Implications for Social Work Practice."*Journal of Gerontological Social Work* 1988, 12(3–4):111–125. New York: Haworth Press. (Special Double Issue, "Twenty-Five Years of the Life Review: Theoretical and Practical Considerations," R. Disch, ed.)

2. "The World of Work: An Exhibition of Occupational Folk Art by Retirees," co-sponsored by Municipal Employees Union, Local 237 and the

Elder Craftsmen, Inc., co-curated by Doris Francis and Geri Wasserman. "The World of Work" was exhibited at the NCOA Gallery Patina, Washington, D.C.; the Local 237 Gallery; and the Robert F. Wagner Labor Archives, New York University, 1986.

3. Taylor's time-management studies greatly affected the reorganization of labor processes (Taylor, Frederick Winslow, 1911, *The Principles of Scientific Management*. New York: Harper and Row.) See Braverman 1974.

4. The writings of Sennett, Cobb, and Terkel extend this discussion to issues of self-worth confronting the worker through his/her life. (Sennett and Cobb 1972, Terkel 1974). Searle-Chatterjee describes a strikingly parallel example of Benares sweepers' efforts to establish a positive sense of identity and self-esteem, despite the socially-debased nature of their work, through claims to physical strength and toughness (Searle-Chatterjee 1979).

5. There were only two women in the exhibition. Three other women artists were contacted, but declined the invitation to exhibit their work.

6. I would like to express appreciation to Steve Zeitland for suggesting that I interview Mr. Bergomi.

7. My appreciation to Joseph Sciorra for introducing me to Mr. Bernstein.

8. Quotation from an interview with Louis Bernstein by Joseph Sciorra (Sciorra, J., Louis Bernstein. IN Made by Hand, Played by Heart: A Guide to Folk and Ethnic Culture in Queens. C. Condon, ed. Queens, New York: Queens Council on the Arts. Forthcoming).

CHAPTER 5

1. Recorded on May 1, 1979, District of Columbia Fire Fighters Project. Tape 1, page 5. Field notes.

2. Recorded on September 20, 1979, District of Columbia Fire Fighters Project, Tape 1, page 1. Field notes.

CHAPTER 6

Acknowledgements: I would like to thank the workers, managers, and state bureaucrats of the Hangzhou silk industry who patiently taught me about their world; the CSCPRC for research funds without which I would never have been able to enter that world; and the following people who read and commented on earlier drafts of this essay: John Calagione, Arif

Dirlik, Akhil Gupta, Emily Honig, Susan Mann, G. William Skinner, Sylvia Yanagisako.

This essay is based on an article that was originally published in Arif Dirlik and Maurice Meisner, eds., *Marxism and the Chinese Experience* (Armonk, New York: M. E. Sharpe), under the title "Hegemony and Productivity: Workers in Post-Mao China." It has been revised in the present version. It is printed here with permission from M. E. Sharpe, which holds the copyright.

1. Penelope B. Prime, in "Socialism and Economic Development: The Politics of Accumulation in China," in Arif Dirlik and Maurice Meisner, eds., *Marxism and the Chinese Experience* (1989), questions the predominant view that the Cultural Revolution was an utter economic disaster. She argues that substantial economic growth occurred during the Cultural Revolution, although attendant problems followed upon this Maoist model of growth.

2. Margery Wolf, *Women and the Family in Rural Taiwan* (1972). In *The House of Lim* (1968), Wolf writes, "If the guest hall can be considered the symbol of the larger family, the stove is the symbol of the living family. Members of a family are defined as those who share a cooking stove; the colloquial term for the act of family division is literally 'the dividing of the stove'. This identification of stove and family is so important that those who cannot afford to add a room to house the stove of a newly created family unit build a second stove in the same kitchen" (p. 28).

3. The wage system during the Cultural Revolution was actually much more complex. Those who entered the factory during those years received the same wages regardless of job task, but those who were already in the factory had their wages frozen at the then current hierarchical levels.

4. I use the term "discipline" here in both its Weberian and Foucauldian senses. I take it to mean both that work, or production activity, becomes the goal of human efforts instead of the reverse through self-conscious norms and rules, and that workers imperceptibly internalize and habituate themselves to routines of work through micro-techniques directed at the movements of the body (e.g., spatial relations) and through hierarchical rankings (e.g., by "skill" or production quotas fulfilled). See Max Weber, *The Protestant Ethic and the Spirit of Capitalism* (1958 [1905]), and Michel Foucault, *Discipline and Punish* 1979 [1975].

5. Factory cadres have discussed other measures for ridding factories of the "unproductive" burdens of family-like obligations. For example, they are pressuring the state to take over the pension payments for retired workers.

6. For a recent elegant argument about how the "economic" base needs the superstructure of cultural meaning to institute and uphold it,

see Donald L. Donham, *History, Power, Ideology: Central Issues in Marxism and Anthropology* (1990).

7. The phrase is Donham's. See note 6 above.

8. Elsewhere I have discussed the meanings and practices of work in the 1950s as well. See Lisa Rofel, *'Eating Out of One Big Pot': Hegemony and Resistance in a Chinese Factory.* Ph.D. Dissertation, Stanford University, 1989.

9. Even the appearance of the term "productivity" signals a rejection of the Maoist political order.

10. One might think of this fixation in terms of the Marxist notion of fetishism. See Karl Marx, *Capital, Vol. 1* (1967 [1867]): 71–84). See also Michael T. Taussig, *The Devil and Commodity Fetishism in South America* (1980) for a slightly different usage of the concept.

11. Raymond Williams, *Marxism and Literature,* (1977). Williams' and my own treatment of hegemony are based on Antonio Gramsci, *Selections from the Prison Notebooks,* (1971). There is now a growing literature on the concept of hegemony. See Perry Anderson, "The Antinomies of Antonio Gramsci," *New Left Review* 100 (1977):5–78; James Brow, "In Pursuit of Hegemony: Representations of Authority and Justice in a Sri Lankan Village" *American Ethnologist* 15, 2 (1988):311–27; Chantal Mouffe, ed., *Gramsci and Marxist Theory* (London: Routledge and Kegan Paul, 1979); and Kathleen Weiler, *Women Teaching for Change: Gender Class and Power* (South Hadley, Mass.: Bergin and Garvey, 1988).

12. My approach differs therefore from James Scott. Scott's work was exemplary in calling attention to the need to understand the ordinary and nonspectacular ways that peasants question dominant class authority. However, his theoretical approach does not examine, for example, how these male peasants also reproduce the dominance of men as heads of households. See Scott, *Weapons of the Weak: Everyday Forms of Resistance* (New Haven: Yale University Press, 1985).

13. E. P. Thompson, "Outside the Whale," in his *The Poverty of Theory and Other Essays* (New York: Monthly Review Press, 1978 [1963]); Perry Anderson, *Arguments within English Marxism* (London: Verso, 1980).

14. Rudolf Bahro, *The Alternative in Eastern Europe* (London: Verso, 1978); Michael Burawoy, *The Politics of Production* (London: Verso, 1985).

15. An elaboration of this point can be found in Ernesto Laclau and Chantal Mouffe, *Hegemony and Socialist Strategy* (London: Verso, 1985).

16. For a more detailed discussion of the position-wage system, see my dissertation, entitled, *'Eating out of One Big Pot': Hegemony and Resistance in a Chinese Factory* (Stanford University, 1988).

17. See Rofel, in the work cited, for a more detailed explanation of the position-wage system.

18. I have given pseudonyms to all my informants for obvious reasons of protection. *Zhuren* means the head of an office. These hierarchical titles of address, in the telling reflection of current concerns, have replaced the ubiquitous 'comrade' *(tongzhi)*.

19. This preoccupation with the positive qualities of youth recalls the May Fourth Movement—a period, not coincidentally, that inspired many of the older Party leaders. Chow Tse-tsung, *The May Fourth Movement* (1967).

20. As Aihwa Ong has recently noted about women workers in Malaysian factories, "These ideologies operate to fix women workers in subordinate positions in systems of domination . . . " (Ong 1988:35)

21. I would like to just briefly note here that this approach to housework as a strategy of resistance has implications for leading us out of the impasse in feminist arguments about whether housework is socially necessary labor and provides a "material" basis of women's oppression; whether the family is the locus of women's oppression or provides support for working class families; and in what ways the "reproductive" sphere of the family is related to the productive sphere of work from the point of view of female actors.

22. I have not taken up the relations between factory managers and state bureaucrats in this article, but they, too, accuse one another of improper interpretations of capitalist practices and socialist goals as they vie for control over factory resources.

23. I am suggesting that we consider 'needs' as historical products tied to changing social divisions of labor. For a more thorough discussion of this issue, see Agnes Heller, *The Theory of Need in Marx* (London: Allison and Busby, 1976).

CHAPTER 7

1. I am grateful to Professor Toshinao Yoneyama and to his students, who first introduced me to the Gion Festival, to the community leaders of the *Yamahako Cho* and to the craftsmen, who generously shared their time and knowledge with me; to Doshisha University's Sociology Department and Institute for the Humanities and Social Sciences, where my research project was based, especially to Professor Masato Tanaka, and to Richie Sakakibara one of my key interpretors in the Festival. Part of this research was carried out while I was a Senior Fulbright Scholar in Japan in 1986–87; I am grateful to the U.S. Japan Educational Commission for partial support of my research. My special gratitude goes to the editors of this

volume, especially to John Calagione and Doris Frances, for their painstaking editorial help and guidance, and to Kathleen Adams for her valuable comments.

2. I observed the construction process of the *hoko* and followed the parade (this was made possible by a special arm band which I had obtained from the festival's committee). I also participated in the various activities following the conclusion of the festival, which involved the dismantling of the hoko, the cleaning and polishing of the various parts, and the packing up of the treasures and tapestries for storage. These were the only activities a woman was allowed to help in. All others I watched closely.

3. Since the construction and decoration of the *yama* requires only a minimal involvement of the part of the craftsmen during the initial construction, this paper will focus primarily on the work surrounding the *hoko*, because of the elaborate skills required both in constructing and moving them.

CHAPTER 8

1. Field research for this article was conducted with generous support in 1966–67 from a Fulbright Grant, in 1971–72 with support from the America Institute of Indian Studies and in 1979–81 with support from the American Institute of Indian Studies and the Indian Council of Social Science Research.

CHAPTER 9

1. This paper is based on field research undertaken for a doctoral degree in social anthropology from the University of Toronto. During nine months of community residence, life and work histories were collected from approximately forty fish processing plant workers in a semi-structured, extended interview context. Numerous additional interviews took place with plant managers and with members of the workers' households, and with other knowledgeable members of the community. Interview data was confirmed through participant observation strategies.

2. All names used to refer to informants are pseudonyms.

3. For example, Harris and Young (1981) document the tendency to prejudge the substance of relations of reproduction. With criticism of widespread recourse to biological explanations for women's subordination, these authors seek to clarify the concept of reproduction. The range of biological explanations noted by these authors includes the more simple form of direct reference to an imputed physiological basis for gender inequities. Also, Harris and Young identify a more subtle evolutionary ap-

proach wherein the subordination of women is seen as an essential historical process. Meillassoux's work is used in illustration of the second approach. In his exposition of the necessity of male domination over women's labor in household units of production, it is argued, Meillassoux collapses together two different uses of the concept of reproduction; namely the process of daily reproduction of labor power and that of human (biological) reproduction. In so doing, Meillassoux raises interesting questions about whether certain groups of men must exert control over women for the reproduction of the social formation. Nonetheless, Meillassoux fails to capture the complexity of the intersections between productive and various reproductive relations. The Harris and Young critique is polemical and at times obfuscating, but the overall impact has been useful in encouraging more careful approaches to the complex relations of production and reproduction (e.g., Bouquet 1982; Redclift 1985).

4. The concept of the informal sector is used here advisedly. Recent commentary on the informal sector, often a provisional title, is increasingly appreciative of the complexity of the wide-ranging activities relegated to the informal realm by virtue of the fact that these activities occur outside the accounting systems of the formal economy. Well aware that the restructuring of capital has unique implications in localized political economies, authors such as Pahl (1985) have attempted to conceptualize informal economic exchange in a manner which is sensitive to the gender, class, and cultural particularities of any given context. Moreover, Pahl insists that no purpose is served by postulating a separate economic framework to cover forms of unrecorded work and remuneration since the so-called informal sector activities occur within a formal economic framework containing one banking system and one official currency. Hoping to side-step the question of linkages which is posed by dualistic models, discussed earlier with regards to debates surrounding domestic labor, Pahl reaffirms the concept of household work strategies as a most useful approach to draw out "how the whole assemblage of work in distinctive milieux relates to the restructuring of capital." (p. 246) Nonetheless, I suggest the convention for referring to patterns of 'informal' work and exchange occurring beyond the reaches of formal systems of reckoning, continues to serve a useful purpose in comparative political economy. This is particularly so when it is appreciated that informal exchanges are not tied to specific spheres of activity. Rather such exchanges can generate from the social encounters in the workplace, the neighborhood, and of course, as is most relevant in Glace Bay, through kinship links. None of these domains are mutually exclusive.

5. The informal economy of Glace Bay contrasts with Pahl and Wallace's discussion of the Isle of Sheppey in Kent. In Sheppey forms of privatization and dependent domesticity accompany deindustrialization (1985). Unemployment on Sheppey generates unemployment. It is the employed who are more likely to be active in informal exchanges and self-provisioning. Life in Sheppey is grim. The authors suggest two ways of

dealing with the despair. People can maintain a modest degree of security through domestic self-sufficiency. Or they can drink themselves silly. Alcohol consumption in Sheppey is high. In Glace Bay, I am suggesting there is a tendency towards the former although the latter manifestation of despair is not absent either. One might look to historical-cultural and perhaps methodological aspects of Pahl and Wallace's work to further elaborate on these differences.

CHAPTER 10

1. This paper is dedicated to the memory of Bob Scholte.
The ethnographic and historical observations presented in this paper were made during the course of research carried out during 1983–1985 and July–August 1986, in collaboration with Daniel Nugent. My research was supported by grants from the Inter-American Foundation, the Social Science Research Council, the American Council of Learned Societies, and the Center for Latin American Studies, University of Chicago. An earlier version of this paper was delivered at the 1987 annual meeting of the American Anthropological Association, Chicago, in the session "Workers's Expressions: Accommodation and Resistance" organized by John Calagione and Doris Francis.

In revising this paper for publication, I have benefited greatly from comments provided by John Calagione, Doris Francis, and Daniel Nugent. I would also like to thank John Calagione for the letters he wrote to us while in Mexico; the importance of the material on beauty presented here was in part made evident to me through correspondence with John.

2. The *corrido* is a Mexican "folk" genre of narrative verse sung to music (Mendoza 1954; Simmons 1957). The ideal metric structure of the *corrido* consists of octosyllabic quarters but in practice, many *corridos* depart from this "norm." "A Fistful of Dirt" consists of two verses, both octosyllabic sextets, followed by a chorus of two octosyllabic quartets. The second verse and the chorus are then repeated.

3. Since I have opted for a literal translation, I have not been able to render either the octosyllabic metric structure or the rhyme scheme in English. The rhyme scheme is loosely abab.

4. José is a fictitious name; following anthropological convention, real names will not be used in this paper.

5. This and all subsequent quotes from conversations with Namiquipans are my translations.

6. I am using "social value" in the sense of evaluative sociocultural ideals whose embodiment confers social esteem and whose transgression entails social opprobrium, contempt, or other negative sanctions.

7. On "repeasantization" see Roseberry 1983:201–208, and Mintz 1973; for Namiquipa, see Nugent 1988a.

8. See Alonso 1988a & 1989d; the immediately preceding paragraphs closely follow the discussion in Alonso 1988a & 1988d.

9. Our fieldwork was conducted during what may be a transition period in patterns of migration both to the United States and to urban centers in Chihuahua. The economic crisis of the 1980s and the increasingly limited availability of land for agriculture are contributing to more permanent out-migration by men who either take their families with them or marry outside the community. Moreover, when in Namiquipa during the summer of 1989, I noticed that more single women had left the community in order to find jobs in Chihuahua, Juárez, or the United States—a relatively rare occurrence in the past—but more research is needed on this question and on the changing demographics of migration generally.

10. For criticisms of Rosaldo and Ortner's early universalist explanations of male dominance and female subordination see, among others, essays in MacCormack and Strathern 1980 and Collier and Yanagisako 1987; also Leacock 1978. Rosaldo 1980 provides a critique of her own earlier position.

11. The dictionary spelling is *de oque;* I use *de oquis* because it follows the Namiquipan pronunciation more closely.

12. Michael Piore in his study of Puerto Rican immigrants (1979) makes a related point. He argues that these immigrants are better able to tolerate low status jobs in the United States because their primary source of status lies in their sending communities. I thank Jessica Chapin for pointing this out to me.

13. *The New York Times,* Tuesday, October 27, 1987. The interconnections between pedagogic practices and disciplinary forms of power imposed in the work-place under capitalism are made evident in Foucault 1979.

14. "Negotiation" is not a term I am entirely happy with since it has connotations which link it to corporate contexts and it seems to evoke shades of transactionalism. The etymology of the term, however, provokes other associations. The use of negotiate "in the sense of 'tackle successfully' (a fence or other obstacle or difficulty) originated in the hunting field," and was first quoted in 1862 (Fowler 1965:386). Apparently, this novel usage of the term was felt "to need the apology of inverted commas" (ibid). In Fowler's opinion, "it might be pleaded in defense of this invasion of the domain of words such as clear, get past or round or over, dispose of, surmount, overcome, etc., that *n.* implies a special need for skill and care" (ibid).

References

AGCCA *Archivo General del Cuerpo Consultativo Agrario,* Gomez Palacio, Durango, Mexico.

Abrahams, Roger D. 1982. "The Language of Festivals: Celebrating the Economy" in Victor Turner ed., *Celebration: Studies in Festivity and Ritual,* Washington, D.C.: Smithsonian Institution Press.

Abu-Lughod, Lila. 1990. "The Romance of Resistance: Tracing Transformations of Power Through Bedouin Women." *American Ethnologist* 17(1):41–55.

Alleyne, Mervyn. 1989. *Roots of Jamaican Culture.* London: Pluto Press.

Almada, Francisco. 1938. *La Rebelion de Tomochi.* Chihuahua: n.p.

Alonso, Ana María. 1986. "Chihuahuan Peasants and the Contemporary Political and Economic Crisis in Mexico: The Meaning of Democracy." Paper presented to the Research Seminar on Mexico and U.S.-Mexican Relations. Center for U.S.-Mexican Studies, University of California at San Diego, La Jolla, October 1986.

————. 1988a. *Gender, Ethnicity and the Constitution of Subjects: Accomodation, Resistance and Revolution on the Chihuahuan Frontier.* Ph.D. thesis (anthropology), University of Chicago.

————. 1988b. "The Effects of Truth: Representations of the Past and the Imagining of Community." *The Journal of Historical Sociology* 1(1):33–57.

————. 1988c. "U.S. Military Intervention, Revolutionary Mobilization, and Popular Ideology in the Chihuahuan Sierra" in Daniel Nugent, ed., *Rural Revolt in Mexico and U.S. Intervention,* San Diego: Center for U.S.-Mexican Studies.

————. 1988d. " 'Progress' as Disorder and Dishonor: Discourses of *Serrano* Resistance." *Critique of Anthropology* 8(1):13–33.

Althusser, Louis. 1970. *For Marx* (B. Brewster, trans.). New York: Vintage.

Anderson, Benedict. 1983. *Imagined Communities.* London: Verso.

Anderson, Perry. 1977. "The Antinomies of Antonio Gramsci," *New Left Review,* 100:5–78.

————. 1980. *Arguments Within English Marxism,* London: Verso.

Applebaum, Herbert 1984. *Work in Market and Industrial Societies.* Albany: SUNY Press.

Arendt, Hannah. 1958. *The Human Condition.* Chicago and London: University of Chicago Press.

Armstrong, Pat and Hugh Armstrong. 1988. "Taking Women into Account: Redefining and Intensifying Employment in Canada" in Jane Jenson, E. Hagen, and C. Reddy, eds., *Feminization of the Labour Force: Paradoxes and Promises.* Cambridge: Polity Press.

Asad, Talal. 1987. "Are There Histories of People without Europe?" *Comparative Studies in Society and History* 29(3):594–607.

Bahro, Rudolf. 1978. *The Alternative in Eastern Europe,* London: Verso.

Barber, Pauline T. 1989. "Culture, Capital, and Class Conflicts in the Political Economy of Cape Breton." *Journal of Historical Sociology* 3(4)

Bateson, Gregory. 1972. *Steps to An Ecology of Mind.* New York: Chandler Publishing Company.

Bender, Thomas. 1988. "Metropolitan Life and the Making of Public Culture" in John Hull Mollenkopf, ed., *Power, Culture, and Place.* New York: Russel Sage Foundation.

Bennholdt-Thomsen, V. 1981. "Subsistence Production and Extended Reproduction" in K. Young, C. Wolkowitz and R. McCullagh, eds., *Of Marriage and the Market.* London: CSE Books.

———. 1984. "Towards a Theory of the Sexual Division of Labor" in Joan Smith, I. Wallerstein, and H. D. Evers, eds., *Households and the World Economy.* Beverly Hills: Sage.

Berman, Marshall. 1988. *All That is Solid Melts into Air: The Experience of Modernity.* New York: Penguin Books.

Bestor, Theodore C. 1989. *Neighborhood Tokyo.* Stanford: Stanford University Press.

Bilby, Kenneth M. 1985. "The Caribbean as a Musical Region" in Sidney W. Mintz and Sally Price, eds., *Caribbean Contours.* Baltimore: Johns Hopkins University Press.

Blauner, R. 1964. *Alienation and Freedom.* Chicago: University of Chicago Press.

Bourdieu, Pierre. 1985. "The Social Space and the Genesis of Groups," *Theory and Society* 14 (6):723–744.

Bradley, Harriet. 1989. *Men's Work, Women's Work: A Sociological History of the Sexual Division of Labour in Employment.* Cambridge: Polity Press.

Branford, Sue and Bernardo Kucinski. 1988. *The Debt Squads.* London: Zed Books.

Braverman, Harry. 1974. *Labor and Monopoly Capital.* New York: Monthly Review Press.

Breytspraak. L. M. 1984. *The Development of Self in Later Life.* Boston: Little Brown and Co.

Brittan, Arthur and Mary Maynard. 1984. *Sexism, Racism, and Oppression.* Oxford: Basil Blackwell.

Brow, James. 1988. "In Pursuit of Hegemony: Representations of Autority and Justice in a Sri Lankan Village," *American Ethnologist* 15(2):311–327.

Brown, Bruce. 1972. *Marx, Freud, and the Critique of Everyday Life.* New York: Monthly Review Press.

Bukowczyk, John. 1989. "Migration and Capitalism." *International Labor and Working Class History.* No. 36 (Fall):61–75.

Burawoy, Michael.

———. 1979. *Manufacturing Consent: Changes in the Labor Process under Monopoly Capitalism.* Chicago: University of Chicago Press.

———. 1985. *The Politics of Production: Factory Regimes Under Capitalism.* London: Verso.

Butler, R. N. 1963. "The Life Review: An Interpretation of Reminiscence in the Aged." *Psychiatry, Journal for the Study of Interpersonal Processes* 26(1):65–76.

———. 1967 "Studies of Creative People and the Creative Process After Middle Life" in *Psychodynamic Studies on Aging: Creativity, Reminiscing and Dying,* S. Levin and R. J. Kahana, eds. New York: International Universities Press.

———. 1975. *Why survive? Being Old in America.* New York: Harper and Row.

Calzadiaz, Alberto. 1979. *Hechos Reales de la Revolución, sexto tomo. Proque Villa atacó Columbus. Intriga internacional.* Mexico: Editorial Patria.

Carr, Barry. 1973. "Las peculiaridades del norte Mexicano: Ensayo de interpretación." *Historia Mexicana* 22(3):320–46.

Castoriadis, Cornelius. 1976. "The Hungarian Source" in *Telos* 9(3):4–22.

Chamberlain, Greg. 1987."Up by the Roots." *NACLA Report on the Americas.* May/June 1987 21(3):15–24.

Chaterjee, Partha. 1983. "More on Modes of Power and the Peasantry" in Ranajit Guha, ed. *Subaltern Studies–II.* Delhi: Oxford University Press.

Chavez Calderón, Placido. 1964. *La Defensa de Tomochi.* Mexico: Editorial Jus.

Chow Tse-tung. 1967. *The May Fourth Movement.* Stanford: Stanford University Press.

CNA.RP. *Comisión Nacional Agraria: Resoluciones Presidenciales.* Located in the Archivo General de la Nación, México D. F.

Cohen, Abner. 1974. *Two Dimensional Man: An Essay on the Anthropology of Power and Symbolism in Complex Society.* Berkeley: University of California Press.

———. 1981. *The Politics of Elite Culture.* Berkeley: University of California Press.

Cohen, Sheila. 1987. "A Labor Process to Nowhere." *New Left Review #165.* September–October 1987, pp. 34–50.

Coleman, P. G. 1974. "Measuring Reminiscence Characteristics from Conversation as Adaptive Features of Old Age." *International Journal of Aging and Human Development* 5:281–94.

Collier, Jane F. and Silvia J. Yanagisako, eds. 1987. *Gender and Kinship: Essays Toward a Unified Analysis.* Stanford: Stanford University Press.

Comaroff, Jean. 1983. "Bodily Reform as Historical Practice: The Seman-
tics of Resistance in Modern South Africa." Manuscript prepared for
International Journal of Psychology 18(2).

Comaroff, Jean and John L. Comaroff. 1987. "The Madman and the Migrant: Work and Labor in the Historical Consciousness of a South
African People." *American Ethnologist* 14(2):191–209.

Cornelius, Wayne. 1986. "The Political Economy of Mexico under de la
Madrid: the Crisis Deepens." *Research Report Series, no. 43*. San Di-
ego: Center for U.S.-Mexican Studies, University of California at San
Diego.

Corrigan, Philip. 1975. "On the Politics of Production: A Comment on
'Peasants and Politics' by Eric Hobsbawm." *The Journal of Peasant
Studies* 2(3):341–49.

Dirlik, Arif and Maurice Meisner, eds. 1989. *Marxism and the Chinese
Experience*, Armonk, New York: M. E. Sharpe.

Donham, Donald L. 1990. *History, Power, Ideology: Central Issues in
Marxism and Anthropology*. Cambridge: Cambridge University
Press.

Edholm, F., O. Harris, and K. Young. 1977. "Conceptualizing Women." *Critique of Anthropology, vol. 3, nos. 9 and 10:101–30*.

Edwards, B. 1986. *Drawing on the Artist Within*. New York: Simon &
Schuster.

Edwards, Richard. 1979. *Contested Terrain*. New York: Basic Books.

Eichler, Margrit. 1983. *Families In Canada Today: Recent Changes and
Their Policy Consequences*. Toronto: Gage.

Elder, G. 1978. "Family History and the Life Course" in *Transitions*, T. K.
Hareven, ed. New York: Academic Press.

———. 1982. "Historical Experiences in the Later Years" in *Aging and
Life Course Transitions: An Interdisciplinary Perspective*. T. K.
Hareven and K. J. Adams, eds. New York: Guilford.

Fabian, Johannes. 1983. *Time and the Other: How Anthropology Makes Its
Object*. New York: Columbia University Press.

Fantasia, Rick. 1988. *Cultures of Solidarity: Consciousness, Action and
Contemporary American Workers*. Berkeley: University of California
Press.

Fernandez, James. 1979. "Persuasions and Performances: Of the Beast in
Everybody . . . And the Metaphors in Everyman" in Clifford Geertz,
ed., *Myth, Symbol and Culture*. New York: W. W. Norton.

Foucault, Michel. 1979. *Discipline and Punish: The Birth of the Prison*.
New York: Vintage Books.

———. 1980. *The History of Sexuality*, vol. 1, New York: Random House
[1976].

Fowler, H. W. 1965. *A Dictionary of Modern English Usage*. New York:
Oxford University Press.

Francis, Doris. 1988. "Images from the Occupational Years: The Reminiscences of Retirees and Their Implications for Social Work Practice."
Journal of Gerontological Social Work 12(3–4):111–25.

Franco, Jean. 1988. "Beyond Ethnocentrism: Gender, Power, and the Third-World Intelligentsia" in Gary Nelson and Lawrence Grossberg, eds., *Marxism and the Interpretation of Culture.* London: Macmillan Education.

Frank, David. 1979. *The Cape Breton Coal Miners, 1917–1929.* Ph.D. dissertation. Halifax: Dalhousie University.

———. 1981. "Company Town/Labour Town: Local Government in the Cape Breton Coal Towns 1917–1926," *Histoire Sociale/Social History* 14 [May]:177–96.

———. 1988. "J. B. McLachlan. The Trial; The Image; The Legacy." Commemorative Issue, *New Maritimes,* vol. 6:4–5.

García Canclini, Nestor. 1987. *Políticas culturales en América Latina.* México: Grijalbo.

———. 1988. "Culture and Power: The State of Research." *Media, Culture and Society* 10:467–97.

Geertz, Clifford. 1973. *The Interpretation of Cultures.* New York: Basic Books.

Giddens, Anthony. 1979. *Central Problems in Social Theory.* Berkeley: University of California Press.

———. 1982. "Power, the Dialectic of Control and Class Structuration" in Anthony Giddens and Gavin Mackenzie, eds. *Social Class and the Division of Labour.* Cambridge: Cambridge University Press, pp. 29–45.

Gluckman, Max. 1963. *Order and Rebellion in Tribal Africa.* London: Cohen & West.

Gramsci, Antonio. 1971. *Selections From the Prison Notebooks.* Q. Hoare and G. Nowell-Smith, eds. and trans. New York: International Publishers.

Guha, Ranajit, ed. 1982a. *Subaltern Studies I. Writings on South Asian History and Society.* Delhi: Oxford University Press.

———. 1982b. "On Some Aspects of the Historiography of Colonial India" in *Subaltern Studies I.* Delhi: Oxford University Press.

Guillemard, A. M. 1982. "Old Age, Retirement and the Social Class Structure: Toward an Analysis of the Structural Dynamics of the Latter Stage of Life" in *Aging and Life Course Transitions: An Interdisciplinary Perspective.* T. K. Hareven and K. J. Adams eds. New York: Guilford.

Gutman, Herbert G. 1976. *Work, Culture, and Society in Industrializing America.* New York: Vintage Books.

Hall, Stuart. 1981. "Notes on Deconstructing 'The Popular' " in Raphael Samuels, ed. *People's History and Socialist Theory.* London: Routledge and Kegan Paul.

Hand, Wayland D. 1942. "California Miners' Folklore: Below Ground." *California Folklore Quarterly [Western Folklore]* 1(2):127–155.

Handlin, Oscar. 1951. *The Uprooted.* Boston: Little Brown and Company.

Hareven, Tamara K. 1978. "Introduction: The Historical Study of the Life Course" in *Transitions: The Family and the Life Course in Historical Perspective.* T. K. Hareven, ed. New York: Academic Press.

———. 1982a. "Preface" in *Aging and Life Course Transitions: An Inter-disciplinary Perspective*, T. K. Hareven and K. J. Adams, eds. New York: Guilford.

———. 1982b. "The Life Course and Aging in Historical Perspective" in *Aging and Life Course Transitions: An Interdisciplinary Perspective*, T. K. Hareven and K. J. Adams, eds. New York: Guilford.

———. 1982c. *Family Time and Industrial Time: The Relationship Between Family and Work in a Planned Industrial Community.* New York: Cambridge University Press.

Harper, D. 1987. *Working Knowledge: Skill and Community in a Small Shop.* Chicago: University of Chicago Press.

Harris, Olivia. 1981. "Households as Natural Units" in K. Young et al. eds., *Of Marriage and the Market.* London: CSE Books.

Harris, Olivia and Kate Young. 1981. "Engendered Structures: Some Problems in the Analysis of Reproduction" in Joel Kahn and Josep Llobera, eds. *The Anthropology of Pre-Capitalist Societies.* London: Macmillan.

Harvey, David. 1989. *The Condition of Postmodernity.* Oxford: Basil Blackwell.

Hebdige, Dick. 1987. *Cut 'n' Mix, Culture, Identity, and Caribbean Music.* London: Methuen and Co.

Heilbroner, Robert. 1975. "Men at Work." *New York Review of Books* 21(21–22):6–7.

———. 1980. *Marxism: For and Against.* New York: W. W. Norton.

Heller, Agnes. 1976. *The Theory of Need in Marx,* London: Allison and Busby.

Huizinga, Johan. 1949. *Homo Ludens.* London: Routledge & Kegan Paul.

Jansen, William Hugh. 1965. "The Esoteric-Exoteric Factor in Folklore" in Alan Dundes, ed., *The Study of Folklore.* Englewood Cliffs: Prentice-Hall.

Jones, M. O., ed. 1984a. "Introduction" in Special Section, "Works of Art, Art as Work, and the Arts of Working: Implications for Improving Organizational Life." *Western Folklore* 43(3):172–8.

———. 1984b. Special Section, "Works of Art, Art as Work, and the Arts of Working: Implications for Improving Organizational Life." *Western Folklore* 43(3):172–221.

Jordan, Fernando. 1981. *Crónica de us País Bárbaro.* Chihuahua: Centro Librero La Prensa [1956].

Kaminsky, M. 1978. "Pictures From the Past: The Use of Reminiscence in Casework with the Elderly." *Journal of Gerontological Social Work* 1(1):19–32.

Kanter, R. M. 1977. *Work and Family in the United States: A Critical Review and Agenda for Research and Policy.* New York: Russell Sage Foundation.

Katz, Friedrich. 1978. "Pancho Villa and the Attack on Columbus, New Mexico." *American Historical Review* 83(1)101–30.

Kaufman, S. R. 1986. *The Ageless Self: Sources of Meaning in Late Life.* Madison: University of Wisconsin Press.

Kay, Geoffrey. 1975. *Development and Underdevelopment*. London: Macmillan.

Kleinberg, J. 1983. "Where Work and Family Are Almost One: The Lives of Folkcraft Potters" in *Work and the Life-Course in Japan*. D. W. Plath, ed. Albany: State University of New York Press.

Laclau, Ernesto, and Chantal Mouffe. 1985. *Hegemony and Socialist Strategy*. London: Verso.

Laite, Julian. 1981. *Industrial Development and Migrant Labor.* Austin: University of Texas Press.

Langness, L. L. and G. Frank. 1981. *Lives*. Novato, California: Chandler & Sharp.

Lau Rojo, Rubén. 1989. "Las Elecciones en Chihuahua (1983–1988)." Special issue of *Cuadernos del Norte: Sociedad*Politica*Cultura*. January 1989, Chihuahua.

Leacock, Eleanor. 1978. "Women's Status in Egalitarian Society: Implications for Social Evolution." *Current Anthropology* 19(2):247–75.

Leys, Colin. 1971. "Politics in Kenya: The Development of Peasant Society." *British Journal of Political Science* 1:301–37.

Limon, José. 1983. "Western Marxism and Folklore: A Critical Introduction." *Journal of American Folklore* 96:34–52.

Lockwood, Y. R. 1984. "The Joy of Labor" in Special Section, "Works of Art, Art as Work, and the Arts of Working: Implications for Improving Organizational Life," M. O. Jones, ed. *Western Folklore* 43(3):202–11.

Luborsky, M. B. 1987. "Analysis of Multiple Life History Narratives." *Ethos* 15(4):366–81.

MacCormack, Carol P. and Marilyn Strathern, eds. 1980. *Nature, Culture, and Gender.* Cambridge: Cambridge University Press.

Macgillivray, Don. 1980. "Military Aid to the Civil Power: The Cape Breton Experience in the 1920s" in Don Macgillicray and Brian Tennyson, eds., *Cape Breton Historical Essays*. Sydney: University College of Cape Breton Press.

Mackintosh, Maureen M. 1988. "Domestic Labour and the Household" in R. E. Pahl, ed., *On Work: Historical, Comparative and Theoretical Approaches*. Oxford: Basil Blackwell.

Marcus, George E. and Michael J. Fisher. 1986. *Anthropology as Cultural Critique: An Experimental Moment in the Human Sciences.* Chicago: University of Chicago Press.

Marx, Karl. 1964. *The Economic and Philosophic Manuscripts of 1844.* New York: International Publishers [1844].

———. 1963. *The Eighteenth Brumaire of Louis Bonaparte.* New York: International Publishers [1852].

———. 1967. *Capital, Vol.1,* New York: International Publishers [1867].

———. 1972. *A Contribution to the Critique of Political Economy in Karl Marx: The Essential Writings*. Frederick L. Benden, ed. New York: Harper and Row [1859].

———. 1973. *Grundrisse*. M. Nicolaus, trans. New York: Vintage [1857–1858].

Marx, Karl and Frederick Engels. 1975. *Selected Correspondence*, 3rd ed. Moscow: Progress Publishers.

Mayer, P. 1961. *Townsmen and Tribesmen: Conservatism and the Process of Urbanization in a South African City.* Cape Town: Oxford University Press.

———. 1962. "Migrancy and the Study of Towns in Africa." *American Anthropologist* 64:576–92.

McCarl, Robert S. 1974. "The Production Welder: Product, Process and the Industrial Craftsman." *New York Folklore Quarterly* 30 (1/0):-243–54.

———. 1978. "Occupational Folklife: A Theoretical Hypothesis" in Robert H. Byington, ed., *Working Americans: Contemporary Approaches to Occupational Folklife.* Washington, D.C.: Smithsonian Institution Press. Monograph. Folklife Studies, no. 3.

———. 1985. *The District of Columbia Fire Fighters' Project: A Case Study in Occupational Folklife.* Washington, D.C.: Smithsonian Institution Press. Monograph. Folklife Studies, no. 4.

———. 1988. "Occupational Folklife and the Public Sector: A Case Study" in Burt Feintuch, ed., *The Conservation of Culture: Folklorists and the Public Sector.* Lexington: University of Kentucky Press.

———. 1991. "Public Folklore: A Glimpse of the Pattern That Connects" in Robert Baron and Nick Spitzer, eds., *Practicing Folklore.* Washington, D.C.: Smithsonian Institution Press.

McKay, Ian. 1983. "Strikes in the Maritimes, 1901–1914." *Acadiensis* 13(1):3–46.

Mendoza, Vicente. 1954. *El Corrido Mexicano.* Mexico: Fondo de Cultura Económica.

Myerhoff, B. 1978. *Number Our Days.* New York: E. P. Dutton.

———. 1984. "Rites and Signs of Ripening: The Intertwining of Ritual, Time and Growing Older" in D. I. Kertzer and J. Keith, eds., *Age and Anthropological Theory.* Ithaca: Cornell University Press.

Meyerhoff, Barbara and Jay Ruby. 1982. "Introduction" in Jay Ruby, ed., *A Crack in the Mirror. Reflexive Perspectives in Anthropology.* Philadelphia: University of Pennsylvania Press.

Mies, Maria. 1986. *Patriarchy and Accumulation on a World Scale: Women in the International Division of Labor.* London: Zed Books.

Mintz, Sidney. 1974. *Worker in the Cane, A Puerto Rican Life History.* New York: Norton [1960].

———. 1973. "A Note on the Definition of Peasantries." *Journal of Peasant Studies* 1(1):91–106.

Mitchell, J. C. 1969. *Social Networks in Urban Situations: Analyses of Personal Relationships in Central African Towns.* Manchester: Manchester University Press.

Moffett, Matt. 1988. "In Mexico, the Rich Hasten to Turn up Noses—Surgically." *The Wall Street Journal*, Thursday, October 27.

Morris, Lydia. 1990. *The Workings of the Household: A U.S. U.K. Comparison.* Cambridge: Polity Press.

Mouffe, Chantal. ed. 1979. *Gramsci and Marxist Theory*, London: Routledge and Kegan Paul.

Munck, Ronaldo. 1988. *The New International Labour Studies*, London: Zed Books.

Nash, June. 1979. *We Eat the Mines and the Mines Eat Us: Dependency and Exploitation in Bolivian Tin Mines*. New York: Columbia University Press.

Noble, D. F. 1979. "Social Choice in Machine Design: The Case of Automatically Controlled Machine Tools" in A. Zimbalist, ed., *Case Studies in the Labor Process*. New York: Monthly Review Press.

North American Congress on Latin America (NACLA) *Report on the Americas*. 21(5–6), September-December 1987.

Nugent, Daniel. 1985. "Anthropology, Handmaiden of History?" *Critique of Anthropology* 5(2):71–86.

———. 1988a. *Land, Labor and Politics in a Serrano Society: The Articulation of State and Popular Ideology in Mexico*. Ph.D. thesis (anthropology). University of Chicago.

———. 1988b. "Mexico's Rural Populations and 'La Crisis': Economic Crisis or Legitimation Crisis?" *Critique of Anthropology* 7(3):93–112.

———. 1989. "Contrasting Ideological Views of the Ejido in Northern Mexico." *Texas Papers on Mexico*, no. 88–03. Austin: The Mexican Center.

Nugent, Stephen. 1988. "The 'Peripheral Situation' " in *The Annual Review of Anthropology*, no. 17:79–98.

Ong, Aihwa. 1987. *Spirits of Resistance and Capitalist Discipline: Factory Women in Malaysia*. New York: State University of New York Press.

———. 1988. "The Production of Possession: Spirits and the Multinational Corporation in Malaysia," *American Ethnologist* 15(1): 28–42.

Ortner, Sherry B. 1974. "Is Female to Male as Nature Is to Culture?" in Michelle Z. Rosaldo and Louise Lamphere, eds., *Woman, Culture, and Society*. Stanford: Stanford University Press.

Oster, A. 1984. "Chronology, Category and Ritual" in *Age and Anthropological Theory*. D. I. Kertzer and J. Keith, eds. Ithaca: Cornell University Press.

Pahl, R. E. 1984. *Divisions of Labour*, Oxford: Basil Blackwell.

———. 1985. "The Restructuring of Capital, the Local Political Economy, and Household Work Strategies" in Derek Gregory and John Urry, eds., *Social Relations and Spatial Structures*. London: Macmillan.

———. 1988. ed. *On Work: Historical, Comparative, and Theoretical Approaches*. Oxford: Basil Blackwell.

Pahl, R. E. and C. D. Wallace. 1985. "Forms of Work and Privatisation on the Isle of Sheppey" in Bryan Roberts, Ruth Finnegan, and Duncan Gallie, eds., *New Approaches to Economic Life: Economic Restructuring, Unemployment, and the Social Division of Labour.* Manchester: Manchester University Press.

Palmer, Bryan D. 1990. *Descent into Discourse: The Reification of Language and the Writing of Social History.* Philadelphia: Temple University Press.

Phillipson, C. 1982. *Capitalism and the Construction of Old Age.* London: Macmillan.

Piore, Michael. 1979. *Birds of Passage: Migrant Labor and Industrial Societies.* Cambridge: Cambridge University Press.

Prime, Penelope B. 1989. "Socialism and Economic Development: The Politics of Accumulation in China, in Dirlik, Arif and Maurice Meisner, eds. 1989. *Marxism and the Chinese Experience,* Armonk, New York: M. E. Sharpe.

Proceso nos. 486. 508–12 [1985–6].

Pryce, Ken. 1979. *Endless Pressure,* Harmondsworth: Penguin Books.

Redclift, Nanneke and Enzo Mingione, eds. 1985. *Beyond Employment: Household, Gender, and Subsistence.* Oxford: Basil Blackwell.

Rofel, Lisa. 1989. 'Eating Out of One Big Pot': Hegemony and Resistance in a Chinese Factory, Ph.D. Dissertation (anthropology), Stanford University.

Rogers, Susan C. 1975. "Female Forms of Power and the Myth of Male Dominance: A Model of Female/Male Interaction in Peasant Society." *American Ethnologist* 2(4):727–56.

Rosaldo, Michelle Z. 1974. "Woman, Culture and Society: A Theoretical Overview" in Michelle Z. Rosaldo and Sherry B. Ortner, eds., *Woman, Culture, and Society.* Stanford: Stanford University Press.

———. 1980. "The Use and Abuse of Anthropology: Reflections on Feminism and Cross-Cultural Understanding." *Signs* 5(3):389–417.

Rosaldo, Renato. 1989. *Culture and Truth: The Remaking of Social Anthropology.* Boston: Beacon Press.

Roseberry, William. 1983. *Coffee and Capitalism in the Venezuelan Andes.* Austin: University of Texas Press.

———. 1988. "Political Economy." *Annual Review of Anthropology* 17:161–85.

Ross, Robert and Kent Trachte. 1983. "Global Cities and Global Classes: The Peripheralization of Labor in New York City." *Review* 6(3) [Winter]:393–431.

Sahlins, Marshall. 1972. *Stone Age Economics.* Chicago: Aldine.

———. 1976. *Culture and Practical Reason.* Chicago: University of Chicago Press.

Schneider, David M. 1980. *American Kinship.* [2nd ed.] Chicago: University of Chicago Press [1968].

Scholte, Bob. 1974. "Toward a Reflexive and Critical Anthropology" in Dell Hymes, ed., *Reinventing Anthropology.* New York: Vintage Books.

———. 1986. "The Charmed Circle of Geertz's Hermeneutics; a Neo-Marxist Critique." *Critique of Anthropology* 6(1):5–15.

Sciorra, J. n.d. "Louis Bernstein" in *Made by Hand, Played by Heart: A Guide to Folk and Ethnic Culture in Queens,* C. Condon, ed. Queens: Queens Council on the Arts. Forthcoming.

Scott, James C. 1985. *Weapons of the Weak.* New Haven: Yale University Press.

Searle-Chaterjee, M. 1979. "The Polluted Identity of Work: A Study of Benares Sweepers" in *The Social Anthropology of Work*, Sandra Wallman, ed. London: Academic Press.

Sennett. R. and J. Cobb. 1972. *The Hidden Injuries of Class.* New York: Knopf.

Shanin, Teodor. 1982. "Preface" in Hamza Alavi and Teodor Shanin, eds., *Introduction to the Sociology of "Developing Societies."* New York: Monthly Review Press.

Sharma, Ursula. 1986. *Women's Work, Class, and the Urban Household: A Study of Shimla North India.* London: Tavistock.

Shaw, Arnold. 1978. *Honkers and Shouters.* New York: Collier Books.

Sider, Gerald. 1986. *Culture and Class in Anthropology and History: A Newfoundland Illustration.* Cambridge: Cambridge University Press.

Simmons, Merle. 1957. *The Mexican Corrido as a Source for Interpretive Study of Modern Mexico (1870–1950).* Bloomington: Indiana University Press.

Singer, Milton. 1972. "Industrial Leadership, the Hindu Ethic and the Spirit of Socialism" in *When a Great Tradition Modernizes.* New York: Praeger.

Sirianni, Carmen. 1981. "Production and Power in a Classless Society." *Socialist Review 2(5) [no. 59]:33–82.*

Smith, Gavin. 1989. *Livelihood and Resistance: Peasants and the Politics of Land In Peru.* Berkeley: University of California Press.

Smith, M. G. 1956. "Patterns of Rural Labor" in Lambros Comitas and David Lowenthal, eds., *Work and Family Life: West Indian Perspectives.* Garden City, New York: Anchor Books.

Smith, R. T. 1956. *The Negro Family in British Guiana.* London: Routledge and Kegan Paul.

———. 1982. "Race and Class in the Post Emancipation Carribbean" in Robert Ross, ed., *Racism and Colonialism.* The Hague, Boston, London: Martinius Nijhoff.

Soeda, Hiroshi. 1973. "Festivity and City: Mobile Stages of Gion Festival." *Concerned Theatre Japan.* 2(3–4): 190–207.

Spencer, Gerald. 1988. "Informal Economic Practice as Workers' Self Activity: A Case Study in an Underdeveloped Community." Paper presented to the Atlantic Association of Sociologists and Anthropologists. Halifax: Saint Mary's University.

Spivak, Gayatri Chakravorty. 1987. *In Other Worlds: Essays in Cultural Politics.* New York: Methuen.

Stack, Carol. 1974. *All Our Kin.* New York: Harper Colophon.

Susser, Ida. 1982. *Norman Street.* New York: Oxford University Press.

Swingewood, Alan. 1979. *The Myth of Mass Culture.* Atlantic Highlands: Humanities Press.

Taussig, Michael. 1980. *The Devil and Commodity Fetishism.* Chapel Hill: University of North Carolina Press.

Taylor, F. W. 1911. *The Principles of Scientific Management.* New York: Harper & Row.

Terkel, Studs. 1974. *Working.* New York: Pantheon.

Thompson, E. P. 1966. *The Making of the English Working Class,* New York: Vintage.

———. 1967. "Time, Work-Discipline, and Industrial Capitalism." *Past and Present* 38:56–97.

———. 1978. "Outside the Whale" [1963], in E. P. Thompson, *The Poverty of Theory,* New York: Monthly Review Press.

Timpanaro, Sebastiano. 1975. *On Materialism.* L. Garner, trans. London: New Left Books.

Tucker, R. C. ed. 1978. *The Marx-Engels Reader.* New York: W. W. Norton & Co. Inc.

Turner, Terence. 1980 "the Social Skin" in J. Cherfas and R. Lewin eds. in *Not Work Alone* London: Temple Smith.

Turner, Terence. 1986. "Production, Exploitation, and Social Consciousness in the 'Peripheral Situation'." *Social Analysis no. 19,* August 1986, pp. 91–115.

Turner, Victor. 1967. *The Ritual Process.* Chicago: Aldine.

Walker, A. 1986. "The Politics of Aging in Britain" in C. Phillipson, M. Bernard, and P. Strang, eds., *Dependency and Interdependency in Old Age: Theoretical Perspectives and Policy Alternatives.* London: Croom Helm.

Wallman, Sandra, ed. 1979. *The Social Anthropology of Work,* New York: Academic Press.

———. 1984. *Eight London Households.* London: Tavistock.

Weber, Max. 1958. *The Protestant Ethic and the Spirit of Capitalism,* New York: Charles Scribner's Sons [1905].

Weiler, Kathleen. 1988. *Women Teaching for Change: Gender Class and Power,* South Hadley: Bergin and Garvey.

White, William J. 1978. *Left Wing Politics and Community: A Study of Glace Bay, 1930–1940.* M. A. thesis. Halifax: Dalhousie University.

Wilden, Anthony. 1980. *System and Structure: Essays in Communication and Exchange.* London: Tavistock Publications.

Williams, Raymond. 1961. *The Long Revolution.* New York: Columbia University Press.

———. 1977. *Marxism and Literature.* Oxford: Oxford University Press.

———. 1983. *Key Words.* New York: Oxford University Press [1976].

Williamson, Bill. 1982. *Class, Culture, and Community.* London: Routeldge and Kegan Paul.

Willis, Paul. 1981. *Learning to Labor: How Working Class Kids Get Working Class Jobs.* New York: Columbia University Press.

Wolf, Eric. 1982. *Europe and the People Without History.* Berkeley: University of California Press.

Wolf, Margery. 1968. *The House of Lim.* Englewood Cliffs: Prentice Hall.

———. 1972. *Women and the Family in Rural Taiwan.* Stanford: Stanford University Press.

Woost, Michael. 1990. *Developing a Nation of Villages: Development and the Formation of Community on Sri Lanka's Frontier.* Ph.D. thesis (anthropology). University of Texas.

Yanagisako, Sylvia J. 1979. "Family and Household: The Analysis of Domestic Groups." *Annual Review of Anthropology,* no. 8:161–205.

Yoneyama, Toshinao. 1974. *Gion Matsuri: Toshi Jiniurur Gaku Kyothajime.* (Gion Matsuri: Urban Anthropology in its Beginnings) Tokyo: Chuo Koronsha.

Yoneyama, Toshinao, et.al. 1986. *Documento Gion Matsuri (Documenting Gion Matsuri)* Tokyo: NHK Books (Nihon Hoso Shuppaqn Kyokai).

Zimbalist, Andrew. 1979. *Case Studies on the Labor Process* New York: Monthly Review Press.

Zukin, Sharon. 1989. *Loft Living. Culture and Capital in Urban Change.* New Burnswick: Rutgers University Press [1982].

Contributors

ANA MARIA ALONSO is Assistant Professor of Anthropology at the University of Arizona, where she teaches courses on theories of gender and historical anthropology. Recently a Rockefeller Humanist-in-Residence at the Southwest Institute for for Research on Women, University of Arizona, she is completing work on *En/Gendering Subjects: Domination and Resistance on Mexico's Northern Frontier*. Formerly a postdoctoral Fellow at the Pembroke Center for Teaching and Research on Women at Brown University, and Assistant Professor of Anthropology at the University of Texas at Austin, she has published articles on revolutionary mobilization, social memory, gender, and the role of the state in the formation of social subjectivity in Mexico.

PAULINE BARBER received a doctorate in Social Anthropology from the University of Toronto. She has extensive teaching experience in the fields of gender and work, gender and development, and in women's studies. Recent publications appear in *The Journal of Historical Sociology* and in J. Jermier and D. Knights, eds., *Studies in the Labour Process. Theories and Empirical Studies of Resistance* (Macmillan Press), and R. Apostle and G. Barrett, eds., *Small Capital and Rural Industrialization: A Study of the Fishing Industry in Nova Scotia* (Toronto). Currently holding a postdoctoral fellowship at Dalhousie University, her research examines the historical, cultural, and class underpinnings of contemporary responses to threatened livelihoods in the Nova Scotia fishery.

JOHN CALAGIONE teaches anthropology and history at the City College Center for Worker Education, CUNY. Trained in anthropology at the University of Massachusetts-Amherst, Princeton University, and the University of Chicago, he has extensive experience working in the building trades in New York City.

DORIS FRANCIS, an anthropologist, is on the faculty of The Graduate School of Management and Urban Policy at the New School for Social Research and is a Research Associate at the National Center for Women and Retirement Research, Long Island University. She is the author of the prize-winning book *Will You Still Need Me, Will You Still Feed Me, When I'm 84?* She is the Assistant Director of Retirees for Public Employees Union

Local 237 where her research focuses on women and retirement. During 1992–93, she has been affiliated with the Polytechnic of North London, doing comparative research on work friendships in later life.

EVA FRIEDLANDER is associated with the Southern Asian Institute at Columbia University and with Hunter College. She received her MA from the University of Chicago and Ph.D. from Brown University in Anthropology. She has conducted fieldwork with Native Americans and spent over five years in India researching kinship, family structure, and industrialization, as well as questions of aging and disabilities. She is currently Director of Education for the National Center For Vision and Aging.

TAMARA K. HAREVEN, is Unidel Professor of Family Studies and History at the University of Delaware. She is also Adjunct Professor of Population Studies at Harvard University. She is author of numerous books and articles in the history of the family and social history, notably *Amoskeag: Life and Work in an American Factory City* (Pantheon 1978), and *Family Time and Industrial Time* (Cambridge University Press 1982). She is currently completing the book *The Silk Weavers of Kyoto: Family and Work in a Changing Traditional Industry*. Hareven is also the editor of *The Journal of Family History*.

ROBERT MCCARL has been conducting research in and with occupational groups since 1974. He received his Ph.D. in Folklore from Memorial University of Newfoundland and he currently lives and works in Boise, Idaho. He is completing an ethnographic film on urban firefighters in Washington, D.C., and planning a series of research projects with miners in north Idaho.

DANIEL NUGENT is Assistant Professor of Anthropology at the University of Arizona. Prior to this he taught at the University of California, Riverside, and the University of Texas at Austin, where he also helped direct The Mexican Center of the Institute of Latin American Studies. He is the editor of *Rural Revolt in Mexico and U.S. Intervention* (San Diego 1988) and articles of his have appeared in *Critique of Anthropology* and *The Journal of Historical Sociology*. Ongoing projects include writing popular histories of Namiquipa, Chihuahua, a study of the agrarian question in northern Mexico, and work on the relationship between popular culture and state formation.

LISA ROFEL is Assistant Professor in the Programs of Anthropology/Archeology and Science, Technology, and Society at the Massachusetts Institute of Technology. Her interest is in how people actively create cultural forms in societies where the state has well developed mechanisms for social control. Her forthcoming book is *Work, Gender and Identity in Contemporary China*, and her current research examines political economy as a cultural process and the popularization of science in China.

Index

A

Abrahams, Roger D., 99
Abu-Lughod, Lila, 2, 9
Affirmative action, 76
Agrarian reform: and Mexican
  state formation, 30
Alleyne, Mervyn, 18, 19, 22, 23
Almada, Francisco, 194
Alonso, Ana Maria, 17, 30, 34,
  35, 36, 38, 168, 172, 180,
  196, 205
Althusser, Louis, 32, 193, 194
Americanism, 9. *See also* Ameri-
  canness
Americanness, 34. *See also* Ameri-
  canism
Anderson, Benedict, 34
Anderson, Perry, 200
Anthropology, feminist, 184; of
  work, 1, 2, 4, 10, 98, 181, 191
Apache Indians, 29, 34
Applebaum, Herbert, 2, 3
Apprenticeship: and work culture,
  76, 125, 126
Arendt, Hannah, 7, 8, 194
Armstrong, Hugh, 161
Armstrong, Pat, 161
Asad, Talal, 10
Authenticity: as historical pro-
  duct, 43, 46, 47; and its cri-
  tique, 189
Authority, patriarchal, 172
Autobiography: as self-creation, 48,
  66, 67

B

Bahro, Rudolf, 200
Barber, Pauline, 147, 159
Bateson, Gregory, 73
Beauty, 177; feminine, 178, 181;
  decent versus indecent displays
  of feminine, 180; knowledge
  and technologies of feminine,
  183. *See also* Femininity,
  dimensions of
Bender, Thomas, 18, 19
Bennholt-Thomsen, V., 131
Benoit, Victor, 37
Berman, Marshall, 195
Bestor, Theodore C., 99
Bilby, Kenneth M., 19
Biswakarma, creator of the uni-
  verse, 132, 134, 135
Black Uhuru, 12, 17
Blauner, R., 66
Bloch, Joseph, 193
Botswana, 6
Bouquet, J., 203
Bourdieu, Pierre, 9, 97
Bradley, Harriet, 152
Branford, Sue, 45
Braverman, Harry, 8, 9, 66, 198
Breytspraak, L. M., 60
Brittan, Arthur, 181
Brow, James, 200
Brown, Bruce, 5
Bukowczyk, John, 195
Burawoy, Michael, 8, 66, 70, 73,
  75, 163, 200

D

Dance, 41, 155; "illegal", 42, 197;
public, 40, 45, 177, 179, 181;
public, dimensions of, 41–2
Davis, William, 149
Deindustrialization, 146, 147, 190;
and domesticity, 203
Depeasantization, 168
Dependency theory, 3
Desire, 175
Development: ideology of, 3, 131,
146, 189, 193; industrial, 130;
urban, 14
Dirlik, Arif, 199
Discipline, 199; labor, 81, 166,
170; and regulation of identity,
171; ordering of subjectivity
through, 9
Division of labor: by age, 171; gendered, 92–93, 94, 95, 97, 151,
158, 159, 171, 172, 173; hierarchical, 84, 90
Domestic production. *See* House-
hold, economic practices of, as
unit of production; Labor, domestic; Work, domestic
Dominican Republic, 16, 22
Donham, Donald L., 200
Dowry, and indebtedness, 133, 140
Durga, goddess of creation, 136,
138, 139

E

Eastern Europe, 15
Economic reform. *See* China, Peo-
ple's Republic of: economic re-
form in
Edwards, B., 50
Edwards, Richard, 8
Eichler, G., 159
Ejido, 39, 40
Elder, G., 58, 60
Elizabeth, Queen of England, 64

Employment, 3
Engels, Frederick, 193, 194
England, 153
Ethnicity: and commodity fetish-
ism, 183; and feminine beauty,
178. *See also* Identity, ethnic

F

Fabian, Johannes, 184
Factory, as family, 81, 199
Fantasia, Rick, 148, 163
Femininity, dimensions of, 172,
173, 177
Fender, Freddy. *See* Huerta,
Baldemar
Fernandez, James, 73
Fernandez-Kelly, Maria Patricia, 10
Fire fighters, 69–78
Fischer, Michael J., 69, 184
Folk art, 40, 50, 70, 187
Fordism, 9, 170
Foucault, Michel, 94, 166, 170,
199, 205
Fowler, H. W., 205
Franco, Jean, 11, 184, 185
Frank, David, 149
Frank, G., 48
Free markets, 90
Freud, Sigmund, 5
Functionalism, sociological, 8

G

Garcia Canclini, Nestor, 33
Geertz, Clifford, 18, 32, 42
Geishas, 121
Gender, 166, 181; constructions of,
172, 175, 178, 182, 183, 187;
and the labor process, 148, 188;
and power relations, 145; as
social relation, 187. *See also*
Identity, gender
Gender roles: female, 133; male,
157

Y

Z